THE
ARAB BUREAU

Bruce Westrate

THE
ARAB BUREAU

British Policy
in the
Middle East, 1916–1920

The Pennsylvania State University Press
University Park, Pennsylvania

Library of Congress Cataloging-in-Publication Data

Westrate, Bruce.
   The Arab Bureau : British policy in the Middle East, 1916–1920 /
Bruce Westrate.
       p.   cm.
   Includes bibliographical references (p.   ) and index.
   ISBN 0-271-00794-X (alk. paper)
   1. .Arab Bureau (Cairo, Egypt) 2. Middle East—Foreign relations—
Great Britain. 3. Great Britain—Foreign relations—Middle East.
I. Title.
DS63.2.G7W47   1992
327.41056'09'041—dc20   91-12353
                                               CIP

It is the policy of The Pennsylvania State University Press to use acid-free paper for the first
printing of all clothbound books. Publications on uncoated stock satisfy the minimum
requirements of American National Standard for Information Sciences—Permanence of
Paper for Printed Library Materials, ANSI Z39.48–1984.

For my loving mother,
Joan Koster Westrate

They that dig foundations deep,
* Fit for realms to rise upon,*
Little honour do they reap
* Of their generation,*
Any more than mountains gain
Stature till we reach the plain.

> —*Rudyard Kipling*
> *"The Pro-Consuls"*

CONTENTS

PREFACE

The historical rhythms of the Middle East seem timeless. At this writing, nearly one-half million Americans stand at the ready in Saudi Arabia and the Persian Gulf, poised to spring against Iraq's occupation of Kuwait and the hegemonic dreams of its new dictator, Saddam Hussein. And while the Middle East assumes, yet again, its place at center stage in world affairs, the recurring image is stark. The actors in this venerable drama change with time, but its plot seems hauntingly familiar. Perhaps this is why Middle East crises, above all others, appear to fit so nicely into the apocalyptic fantasies of biblical literalists.

For all the economic promise afforded by the region's vast petroleum reserves, the transition from the old world to the new remains fitful and despairingly incomplete. Confronted by the eternal hobgoblins of sect, clan, and class, the Middle East lies trapped in a treacherous political mire between tradition and modernity, orthodoxy and secularism, East and West. This entrapment has left the dreams of pan-Arabists stillborn and regional politics chronically debilitated.

Notwithstanding this, the area's geopolitical prominence seems more striking than ever, given its geographic predicament as the flash point of three continents and the Western world's persistent craving for oil. And this unfortunate combination of (to paraphrase Ronald Robinson and John Gallagher) strategic vitality and political unreliability has proved compelling enough during this century to ensure a discomfiting preoccupation among Western powers regarding developments there.

The outbreak of World War I in 1914 would provide those powers with an irresistible opportunity to direct the course of events in the Middle East and to erect the political framework within which subsequent crises would be played out. Ultimately, Great Britain stood to gain the most from the collapse of Turkish power in Asia (exclusive of Anatolia) and the "liberation" of its subject peoples. Many of the region's most nettlesome political problems stem directly from the policies pursued by Britain during this era.

In 1991 as in 1916, Western armies, bolstered by Arab allies, oppose a regionally dominant power. Britain and France, although participants once more, stand reduced in stature beside the military colossus of the United States. Again, a fragile allied coalition, including many "friendly" Arab contingents, is threatened by dissension over the future of Israel/Palestine; Muslims worldwide fret for the sanctity of Arabia's holy cities and shrines; possession of vital oil fields looms as a pressing concern; and numerous rivals within the Arab world maneuver for position—and a chance at becoming the next Nasser—while the region continues to grope for a highly coveted but elusive political consensus.

Whatever the ultimate outcome, the United States faces a dilemma not far removed from that faced by British imperialists seventy-odd years ago: how to strike the delicate and seemingly unattainable balance in the Arab world between obliging stability and unnerving political unity, so as to safeguard long-term strategic interests in the area on Western terms without resorting to costly, unpredictable military adventures. Unfortunately for the world, those Britons who had a hand in the conception and implementation of complex remedial formulas succeeded only in sowing the seeds of future conflict.

That they did so is not surprising. For in an age well before the advent of instantaneous global communication, such endeavors were not always the sole purview of the king's ministers, field marshals, and MPs. Amid the confusion of world war and the enormous constraints of time and distance, even Gordian knots were often left for lesser lights to cleave. This inescapable fact must never be overlooked in examining this subject.

My interest in the Middle East derives originally from study of the British Empire and the obsession of its protectors with the Indian subcontinent. My curiosity was piqued particularly by the saga of the Arab Revolt against the Turks during World War I and the part played in that drama by British advisers. One small group of officers in particular, I felt, had not only been neglected by historians, but essentially eclipsed by the mythic proportions of one of their number—T. E. Lawrence.

The Arab Bureau was a small collection of British intelligence officers gathered in Cairo during 1916 for the purpose of centralizing the collection and dissemination of intelligence about the Arab world. Because policy-makers in Cairo, Delhi, and London had persisted in an unseemly competition, operating along different (and often divergent) lines respecting Arab policy, there was no single, impartial, expert source of information and advice available to British leaders grappling with the intricacies of Middle Eastern questions. It was this void that the Arab Bureau was created to fill.

Deprived of the necessary authority to resist, however, the new agency was quickly subsumed by another political power center, Khartoum. Thereafter, its members evolved into advocates of policies that would, at once, advance the war effort against the Turks by shepherding an Arab revolt and lay the groundwork for indirect postwar control by the British of a region long deemed vital to the strategic well-being of the empire, lying as it did athwart the lifeline to India. Bureau officers hoped thereby to accomplish three critical objectives: (1) protect the imperial trunk routes to India, (2) mollify the anticipated upsurge in Arab demands for self-government through the medium of British-sponsored client states, and (3) obviate the burden of direct postwar annexation and/or occupation.

For its efforts, the bureau was vilified, especially in Indian circles, as a group of amateurish, incompetent Arabophiles laboring to appease liberal notions of self-determination best left undisturbed. Such hostility, combined with transcendent British commitments to the French regarding Syria and the Zionists regarding Palestine, would have fatally undermined bureau objectives at any event. Yet it is odd that the agency has subsequently borne much of the blame for Britain's terrible mishandling of Middle Eastern policy during and shortly after World War I.

My objective with this book is twofold: (1) to write a history of this intriguing group as an executive participant in unfolding events, and (2) to assess those impressions that persist in light of available documentary evidence so as to determine the nature of the bureau's role and the extent to which the calumny levied against it both by its contemporary and current detractors is justified.

I should also make plain what this book is not. It is not presented as either a comprehensive history of British policy in the Middle East during this period or a history of the Arab Revolt. Nor have I set out to diminish the historical stature of T. E. Lawrence (which, in any case, would probably be a futile exercise) but rather to expand the spotlight to illuminate those colleagues and superiors with whom that remarkable man worked and from whom he took direction. To do less merely contributes to the apotheosis of Lawrence as legendary eccentric, somehow above the machinations of imperialist guile.

Scores of books have been written over the years about British policy in the wartime Middle East. Many of these, while undeniably valuable, are inevitably polemical—wrangling over the actual motives and meanings behind secret treaties and policies that gave rise to a French Syria, a Jewish Palestine, and a Palestinian diaspora. The Sykes-Picot Agreement, the Hussein-McMahon Correspondence, the Declaration to the Seven, the Anglo-French Declaration, and the Balfour Declaration have all become mileposts along the road to misunderstanding, recrimination, and impasse.

I have tried to avoid this distracting thicket in order to focus on events from ground level, from the vantage point of bureau officers and their informed perspectives on Syria, Arabia, and Palestine rather than from the rarefied state rooms of Whitehall or the Quai d'Orsay. To the extent that my views challenge old stereotypes of the Arab Bureau, they are revisionist. Rather than a lot of bumbling romantic Arabophiles, I see its officers as a remarkably prescient group of sober-minded tacticians seeking to exploit opportunities proffered by the war, the Arab Revolt, and the Turkish decline in order to secure the region against imperial and commercial competitors. I am confident, moreover, that the research contained herein amply buttresses my view.

This book, therefore, is intended both to chart the bureau's growth and development and to liberate Lawrence's comrades from the obscurity to which the strictures of legend have for so long consigned them, thereby gaining a clearer understanding of their perspectives on the formative forces of modern Middle Eastern history: imperialism, Zionism, and Arab nationalism.

The officers of the Arab Bureau schemed, studied, suffered, and fought for common ideals, not the least of which was the integrity of the imperial idea. And the fortunes of the British Empire, they generally agreed, could not be left to the caprice of imperial rivals or the temperament of unreliable aborigines. In the decades of their obscurity since World War I, ironically enough, the self-effacing members of the Arab Bureau may have effected their greatest deception.

My work has taken me to numerous archival sources. The Public Record Office in Kew houses the Arab Bureau files along with related documents from the Foreign Office, War Office, Admiralty, and Jeddah Agency. The personal papers of F. Reginald Wingate, Gilbert Clayton, and Valentine Chirol reside in the Sudan Archive at Durham and were of particular value. The papers of David Hogarth, Harry Philby, and Wyndham Deedes as well as the Sledmere Papers of Mark Sykes were made available to me at St. Antony's College, Oxford University, and I wish to thank archivist Gilian Grant in this connection. The *Times* opened its files on Philip Graves to me, for which I am very grateful. *Times* librarian Gordon Philips was especially generous with his time and patience. I gained access to the *Arab Bulletin* through Houghton Library, Harvard University. My deepest appreciation also to Mrs. Anne Edgerley of Saxmundham, England, for allowing me to examine the personal papers of Alfred Parker. Her hospitality and numerous cups of tea on a particularly brutal autumn day are not forgotten.

During the final stages of preparation of this manuscript, I enlisted the services of several noted scholars in the field, both to read the work and to offer criticism. The latter was forthcoming in abundance and was indispensable to fashioning a better book. Albert Hourani was kind enough to tolerate my intrusion on his retirement and lent invaluable advice. My thanks as well to John Broomfield, author of *Elite Conflict in a Plural Society,* for similar contributions. Most of all, perhaps, I am beholden to Ernie Dawn of the University of Illinois for allowing me to tap his vast expertise on the Middle East. His contributions, both to the work and to my morale during the ordeal of revision, are impossible to overstate. I also wish to express my heartfelt gratitude to and affection for the late Richard P. Mitchell of the University of Michigan, whose enthusiasm for my project and expansive knowledge of the subject were critically important. Moreover, I would like to thank Peter Potter for his assistance and gentle criticism. One could not ask for a more supportive editor. And without the skill and tenacity of typists Nancy Brown and Patti Dyche this project might well have remained eternally hypothetical.

Lastly, I want to thank my wife Sally for the innumerable sacrifices she has made and the inexhaustible forbearance she has exhibited throughout. Thank you, Sally.

THE
ARAB BUREAU

INTRODUCTION

Images of the Arab Bureau

Much has been written in the last seventy years on the subject of Britain's role in the Middle East during World War I. Scholarly debate still rages over ambiguous diplomatic commitments and alleged prevarications, which stand as glaring examples of failed British diplomacy: the Hussein-McMahon Correspondence, the Sykes-Picot Agreement, and the Balfour Declaration. More often than not, the continuing controversy has turned on an axis of documentary evidence, interpreted so as to indict or acquit British policymakers. In the rush to assign or deflect responsibility for the Middle East muddle, the temptation to focus on key figures such as Lawrence, Kitchener, Sykes, McMahon, or even Winston Churchill in an effort to identify a culprit or discern a clear diplomatic pattern often has proved irresistible to historians. Consequently, scholars have overlooked sources of potential illumination in the chase for larger game. The Arab Bureau is a case in point.

Established early in 1916 in an effort to lend some measure of consistency and coordination to a badly disjointed imperial bureaucracy in the region, the Arab Bureau, a collection of presumed experts, proved signally effective (despite good intentions) in inciting the very divisiveness and departmental rivalry it had been created to suppress. Even so, the bureau was uniquely placed not only to influence the conduct of operations and policy, but also to observe the shifting sands of British policy implementation from the perspective of the intermediary in matters of both military and political importance to the success of the Arab Revolt.

Its muster included some rising stars as well as the nondescript—antiquarian scholars, career diplomats and soldiers, professional journalists, barristers, and former M.P.s—pooling their efforts to execute a policy that has drawn little but opprobrium ever since.

Assessments of the Arab Bureau's performance, as gleaned from contemporaries, are mixed. One member of the Hejaz military mission, who served for a time in Jeddah, described the bureau as "a queer mixture of brilliant men . . . handicapped by too close a view of the revolt. Too greatly influenced by the ebb and flow of its events, they mostly forgot the rest of Arabia."[1] That the bureau proved quite useful in orchestrating and sustaining Arab resistance to the Turks in the Hejaz is seldom left unappreciated. Neither is the agency's apparent aptitude for alienating certain departments in the imperial bureaucracy. Members of the India Office and the government of India were often strident in their opposition to bureau objectives, and the agency was widely perceived in such circles as an encroaching organism in the demesne of viceroys. The military establishment in Egypt, at least in the war's early stages, was also suspicious of bureau motives and zealously protective of its own jurisdiction in intelligence matters. In Mesopotamia, these hostile bureaucratic currents reached a confluence, widening the already considerable Cairo-Delhi gulf and diverting the war effort rather than stimulating a positive interchange of ideas and the cooperation of fractious bureaucracies. Sir Arnold Talbot Wilson, who served in the Mesopotamian command throughout the war and later rose to the post of acting civil commissioner there, offered a typical postwar appraisal of the Arab Bureau.

> Its function was to coordinate Arab policy; it was however captured at a very early date by partisans of a policy which sought to impose

King Hussein and his family upon the whole of Arabia, and at no time did its directors show any desire to look at the problems of Iraq from any other angle. From our point of view in Iraq the existence of the Arab Bureau was an embarrassment rather than an advantage: the relative proximity of Cairo to Paris and London gave the exponents of the Hashemite policy, themselves for the most part untrammeled by office or by administrative responsibilities, an advantage over the accredited representatives of the British Government in Iraq and in the Persian Gulf. Some of these Arab enthusiasts became more fervent believers in the Arabs than the Arabs themselves. In their view, if our engagements to France were incompatible with Arab ambitions, so much the worse for France.[2]

Once the Sharif of Mecca raised the standard of revolt in June 1916, the new agency's stature in Indian and Mesopotamian circles declined. While the bureau was outraged by Delhi's conspicuous lack of cooperation, hostile authorities grew resentful at "the free rein given to nationalism by Arabophiles in Cairo."[3]

It is not surprising then that historians have not been generous with the Arab Bureau, employing the barbs of "romanticism," "amateurism," and injudicious "enthusiasm" in critiques of its performance. Nor has the suspicion of messianic fervor been overlooked. "The so-called Arab Bureau in Cairo," writes the author of one compendium on the period, "which began as an intelligence-gathering agency, believed in the importance of Husayn, and one suspects in their own importance for promoting the idea of an Arab revolt."[4] More often than not, scholars have tended to queue up behind a particular perspective, whether from Delhi, Baghdad, Cairo, or London. Another noted scholar of Arabia contrasts the attributes of the Arab Bureau—"dynamic, amateurish, self-confident, persuasive, and admirable even when they were wrong"—to those of Indian and Mesopotamian officials—"cautious, sympathetic, professional, and a little lacking in imagination."[5] Hints of Indian resentment evident during the bureau's existence also have surfaced in subsequent secondary literature dealing with Mesopotamia. One author has observed, "The mixed success of the Mesopotamian Campaign had begun to load the dice in favour of the Arab Bureau in Cairo, which had got largely into the control of dilettantes and scholars in whose hands the molding of policy seemed increasingly to lie."[6]

What remains curious, however, is the absence of direct scholarly inquiry into the bureau's life as a distinct organic participant in the formulation and implementation of British policy in the Middle East. This is not to suggest that the bureau has been purposely ignored. On the contrary, the activities and views of bureau members often have been resurrected to assist historical polemic. No one has conducted a comprehensive examination of this agency's activities, to gain insight into the evolution of the Arab Bureau as a political entity. Its story has been left to languish beneath mountains of misinformation, or simply relegated to insignificance beside the dashing figure of T. E. Lawrence.

It is difficult to elude the suspicion that this inadequate treatment of the bureau owes a great deal to the larger-than-life shadow of Lawrence, which continues to influence the scholarly work on this period. Elizabeth Monroe recognized this in her seminal work *Britain's Moment in the Middle East, 1914–1956,* in which she describes the Arab Bureau as "a versatile group of men whose virtues included Hogarth's scholarship, Storr's [*sic*] wit and brilliance, Cornwallis's steady head and Clayton's equable leadership, but of whom T. E. Lawrence is the only remembered name."[7] The romantic legend of Lawrence of Arabia, as Sari Nasir emphasizes, was largely attributable to Lowell Thomas's journalistic embellishments and Valentino's coincidental appearance as *The Sheikh,* possessing the myriad desert virtues of "nobility, dignity, manliness, gracefulness and virility."[8]

Against Lawrence's magnified exploits, the Arab Bureau itself has often been consigned to a footnote or depicted as a devoted corps of disciples swept up in the romance of the Arab Revolt "à la Lawrence," engaged in a clandestine effort to champion the territorial pretensions of Hussein and Feisal at the expense of the French. Illustratively, one biographer seizes on Lawrence's Francophobic missives to mentor David Hogarth, which were "received without protest from him, and Hogarth became Director of the Arab Bureau with all its avowed and concealed influences on British policy."[9] This inference is both misleading and simplistic. But it is in this way that the Arab Bureau has, posthumously, transcended its administrative reality. Lawrence himself contributed to this impression. He fancied himself a rebel in the ranks and was somewhat prone to exaggerate his own role in the early days of Cairo intelligence. He wrote of his attempts and those of his colleagues "to break into the accepted halls of English foreign policy, and build up a new people in the East, despite the rails laid down for us by our ancestors. Therefore, from our hybrid Intelligence office in Cairo . . . we began to work upon our chiefs, far and near."[10] This is heady stuff and did much to promote an image of the "intrusives" (as Lawrence dubbed this group), and of the Arab Bureau that evolved from it, as an

Arabophile coterie of idealistic amateurs working autonomously and, all too often, at variance with the diplomatic master plan.

Usually, this impression conforms to a standard pattern in its depiction of the bureau's role: sympathy toward the aspirations of Arab nationalists, along with a keen appreciation of the military value of the Hejaz revolt; remorse over the disingenuous pledges made by Egyptian High Commissioner Sir Henry McMahon to Sharif Hussein; outright and ill-concealed hostility toward the Sykes-Picot partition of the Middle East; disenchantment with Balfour's Zionist proclamation; and acute suspicion toward the French with respect to Syria. According to one historian, "Long before the firing ceased in the Middle East Lawrence and his colleagues in the Arab Bureau had clearly fixed the image of the adversary, and that enemy was not the Turk."[11]

A comprehensive examination of the Arab Bureau's files, along with those of the principals involved, reveals a far more wide-ranging and sophisticated view of wartime events. And the policies that the bureau ultimately chose to pursue extended far beyond the fate of the Arab Revolt or even of Syria. They mirrored its members' collective determination to exploit Arab disaffection to Britain's long-term advantage in order to both win the war and manage the peace. Such strategies derived less from some giddy sense of protonationalism or reflexive Fashodist Francophobia than from concern for the fortunes of the British Empire. One recent work seems to verify the author's prior conclusion that the Arab Bureau was guided by an imperial star, but with an Egyptian perspective that suggests the agency sought "to expand British Egypt's control of the Arab World." Notwithstanding the popular image of bureau officers, the record reveals more artifice than naïveté, more cynicism than idealism, and more guile than the label "enthusiast" suggests.[12]

The putative influence wielded by the bureau has also been much exaggerated. Edouard Bremond, commander of the French military mission to the Hejaz, suggested that Whitehall conformed itself to that agency's directives.[13] With the conclusion of hostilities, asserts one writer, the specter of Lawrence and the Arab Bureau hovered over the machinery of the Paris peace conference itself. He suggests that even the formidable Lord Curzon "remained under the spell of the Arab Bureau in Cairo whose officials insisted that the spoils of victory should go to those Arabs who had fought successfully on the side of the allies."[14] Thus have the Arab Bureau's officers been branded zealots, possessed of "amateur enthusiasm, fired by the exigency of war and intrigued by the allure of Arabness, from across the Arabian Sea."[15] In this same vein, Sudan scholar Robert O. Collins rather drastically describes the Arab Bureau as "more Arab than the Arabs" and as a group of men who "succeeded in stimulating the nationalism of the Arabs far beyond their wildest daydreams. In other ways they were a boyish group, immature and irresponsible, but imaginative, appealing, and above all successful."[16] The perspective of Arab scholars, who view the bureau largely through the prism of Lawrence's career, is likewise consistent. The legacy of the Hussein-McMahon Correspondence, Zeine N. Zeine has alleged, was due in part to the "confusion and muddle of the 'experts' on Arab affairs at the Arab Bureau in Cairo," whom he goes on to label "archeologists and travellers, romanticists and idealists, all inexperienced in the art of politics."[17] Renowned Middle East scholar Elie Kedourie also hints that officials such as those staffing the Arab Bureau "had put so much of themselves into [the Sharifian cause] that it veritably became their cause."[18] "Their cause," as Kedourie explained in an important work, was that sort of doctrinaire liberalism that allegedly lay behind the bureau's distaste for secret treaties like the Sykes-Picot Agreement. Some of those liberals were opposed because they "thought that the world should be composed of small sovereign nations living side by side in amity; others again because they feared a French foothold in the Levant; still others because of a personal involvement in the cause of Arab nationalism. All these tendencies may be seen in the words and deeds of members of the Arab Bureau."[19] Actual members at the agency scarcely would have recognized themselves from this description.

So the Arab Bureau has become lost in scholarly literature within a larger Cairene context, strained in an enervating tug-of-war with Baghdad and Delhi over the direction of British policy in the Middle East. As a result, it has borne the brunt of criticism for the complex involvement from which Whitehall was so long extricating itself. Perhaps the most scathing indictment of the bureau's performance has come from H.V.F. Winstone, a biographer of Harry Philby and Gertrude Bell, who castigates the "junior officers in the Bureau's service [who] were able to wander freely around the Middle East with inexhaustible supplies of money, in defiance of generals and in open contempt of official policies and campaign strategies, at a time when the allied cause and the lives of millions of men hung in the balance."[20]

What then were the goals of the Arab Bureau? Did it arrogate to itself more initiative in the political realm than had been intended for it, or were these officers victimized by the policy contradictions and paralytic indecision of Whitehall in this theater? What were the attitudes of its members toward negotiations with Sharif Hussein, the French, and the Zionists, and to what extent did the bureau blaze its own trail, as is so frequently charged?

By examining the bureau's wartime activities, I intend to probe for the answers to these questions and so attempt to settle the dust raised over the bureau three generations ago. I also hope to explore the extent to which the bureau itself achieved consensus regarding policy. Moreover, I will analyze whether the Arab Bureau initiated policy compatible with its members' views or simply yielded to irresistible pressures, thereby lapsing into redundancy as yet another advisory group.

Finally, I shall address the perception of the Arab Bureau as a cabal of boat-rocking, dreamy-eyed intellectuals bent on scuttling established policy at the expense of stability and coherence. While the existence of "official" policy with regard to the Arabs has been thrown open to question,[21] the Arab Bureau more often worked in pursuit of policy directives from London (albeit with occasional reluctance) than in contradiction of them.[22] The truth is more prosaic and certainly less alluring than the image of Lawrentian misfits tilting at Arabian windmills.

Uneven historical treatment of the Arab Bureau in the past has obscured a wealth of documentary evidence behind a tantalizing veil of accusation and controversy. Again, while references to the bureau's activities abound, comprehensive inquiry into its history has been slighted beyond examination of the careers of Clayton, Lawrence, and a few other principal actors. Exhaustive if somewhat tedious dissection of complex diplomacy has occupied center stage for so long that illuminating perspectives from inside the Arab Bureau have been consigned to the wings. And those, while occasionally blinkered and unfailingly political, are the products of imperialistic, not idealistic, minds. Yet the bureau's own perspective was not monolithic. Differences with London and Delhi were fundamental, and as a result members of the Arab Bureau had perforce to respond flexibly to changing signals and events in an attempt to seize political consistency from the jaws of bureaucratic parochialism. The final irony is that the Arab Bureau, by virtue of its singleness of purpose, stood out among all the various interests to lobby for well-defined imperial objectives rather than for vague manifestations of liberal instinct or ideological crusade.

1

FLAWED FOUNDATIONS

For the British Empire, the onset of hostilities with Turkey in November 1914 made real the daunting prospect of a military confrontation with the Ottoman Empire and its subject peoples. For officials in both Egypt and India, the building tension was disquieting. Along the Suez Canal the threat of an Ottoman offensive loomed, exacerbated by the indignation of Egyptians opposed to the protracted British occupation. In India, government administrators grew increasingly nervous that an opportunistic call to jihad by the Turkish sultan/Islamic caliph might provoke India's volatile and enormous Muslim community. For the Royal Navy, the threat of a disruption in the flow of petroleum, which propelled an increasing proportion of the fleet, was yet another cause of concern, especially with respect to the safety of the large Persian Gulf refinery complex at Abadan. Winston

Churchill underlined these strategic considerations before the House of Commons a short time before, making it clear that it would be the policy of his government to become the owners, or, failing that, the controllers of at least a portion of the oil required by the navy.[1] This vital priority led to the occupation of Basra in late 1914, the first step in the Indian Army's torturous conquest of Mesopotamia.

For Egypt, the question of how best to defend the Suez Canal was more complicated. The imperial garrison there was engaged in stiff competition for proper troops in the face of the profligate expenditure of men along the western front. Britain's military leaders were sharply divided on how to hasten the collapse of the Young Turk regime in Constantinople. Egyptian officials such as Lord Kitchener (Egyptian consul general cum field marshal), Sir F. Reginald Wingate (governor-general of the Sudan), and Sir John Maxwell (General Officer Commanding in Egypt) had earlier favored the dispatch of a sizable expedition to Alexandretta, in Syria, to divert attention from the Suez Canal and possibly precipitate an uprising among its native population. But the combined effect of the Gallipoli debacle and French objections to a British invasion of a region of special French interest helped erase this scheme from War Office drawing boards. British operations in Egypt were limited to passive defense by its swollen garrison, easily able to parry Turkish jabs but conspicuously underutilized.

Faced with devastating Allied setbacks on the western front and in the Dardanelles, policymakers at Whitehall began to consider a more forward policy toward the Arabs inhabiting vast portions of the Ottoman domain. As a result, the British increased contact with Arab representatives from Arabia and Syria, from tentative communication at first to serious negotiation by 1915; this necessitated further accommodation of France. Great Britain's attempt to lure the Arabs into the war on the side of the Allies, while retaining the diplomatic latitude necessary to avoid a breach with the Quai d'Orsay (the French Foreign Office), has caused seemingly endless controversy ever since. However, the opportunity presented to Britain by Arabian discontent was unmistakable.

By 1912, according to many writers, resentment was smoldering in Arabia against the Young Turk regime that had displaced the Ottoman sultan. This mood stemmed less from a sense of injured national identity than from popular distress over the state of the empire and of Islam. Ethnic sensibilities of Arabs throughout the Middle East, according to this view, had been buffeted by the policies of the usurpers. Arab advisers at court had been dismissed by Turanian xenophobes, and Arab numbers were underrepresented in the Ottoman parliament. Yet to many bedouin in the more remote areas, these complaints were trifles alongside the rankling Turkish inability to defend Islam against Western intrusion. The legitimacy of Constantinople as the seat of Islam's destiny had long been eroding. Steady encroachment by European interlopers (Germans included) simply became intolerable to the many Muslims incensed by the Turks' failure to fend off territorial incursions by the Christian West. Such wells of discontent provided outsiders with the means to incite disaffection against the Turks. A number of Arab nationalist or autonomy parties had already emerged in Mesopotamia and Syria. Yet it was in Arabia that the most promising opportunity for Anglo-Arab cooperation arose, around the figure of Sharif Hussein of Mecca.

The sharif, who was the most prominent member of the Arabian nobility, claimed direct lineal descent from the Prophet and held authority from the Ottoman regime to supervise the holy city of Mecca and the Hejaz district along the north-central coast of the Red Sea. Hussein was an ambitious man who had spent many years in Constantinople by the command of the sultan, being held as a hostage to prevent revolt in the Hejaz. His subjects, approximately six hundred thousand tribesmen of the Harb confederation, saw the sharif restore a semblance of order from the anarchy he found upon his return from exile. He was also instrumental in the subjugation of recalcitrant clans on the district's periphery. Naturally, other chieftains of note on the peninsula—Emir Abdul Aziz Ibn Saud of Nejd, Mohammad ibn al-Idrisi of Asir, Imam Yahya of Yemen, and Ibn Rashid of the Jebel Shammar region—had hegemonic dreams of their own and so tendered only perfunctory courtesies to the sharif's. Even so, Hussein's position was commanding if not invulnerable. Mecca, in addition to its stature as a holy city, was the center for communications on the peninsula, a valuable asset. More significantly, by virtue of his titles the sharif commanded enormous prestige both within and without Arabia. A letter written by the renowned Captain W. H. Shakespear, the officer who pioneered British relations with Ibn Saud of Nejd early in the war, is particularly telling. "A Jihad," he warned, "especially if proclaimed at Mecca by one of the Sherif's standing in Islam, is a contingency of which the consequences are unforeseeable and incalculable. Such a proclamation would, at least, raise the whole Arab World, . . . This contingency—a 'Jihad,' proclaimed by the acknowledged and accepted descendant of the Prophet at Mecca—I venture to submit needs the most serious consideration, and to be constantly kept in mind at the present critical time in all our dealings with Arab Chiefs in general."[2]

Yet the sharif had problems despite his local preeminence. Although the old sultan had detained him under house arrest, Hussein was a dynastic loyalist and an opponent of the Young Turks, not an aspiring Arab nationalist. Moreover, because the Young Turks were busily consolidating Turkey's hold on the Hejaz prior to the outbreak of World War I, desert isolation was not what it once was. Deposed sultan Abdul Hamid's Hejaz railway now snaked southward from Damascus through Aqaba to its terminus at Medina. This served as the major artery for the resupply and reinforcement of the four divisions of the Turkish Army in western Arabia (including one and a half divisions in the Hejaz itself). Given the hostility of many local bedouin whose monopoly on control of the pilgrim traffic was now threatened, this was a tenuous link with the rest of the empire, but a link nonetheless. Of course, Hussein was alarmed by the railroad, which greatly increased the potential for Turkish interference. And even though he was successful in opposing its extension past Medina and managed to extract an agreement from the Young Turks recognizing his titles as hereditary and confirming them in perpetuity, Hashemite unease remained high.

As consul general in Egypt, Lord Kitchener made the first overtures to the sharif through Hussein's second son in 1912 or 1913. He met Emir Abdullah, who was the khedive's guest in Cairo, on the pretext of improving the traveling conditions of pilgrims to the holy cities. Abdullah renewed the acquaintance in 1914 while on a journey to Cairo seeking British support in the event of a Turkish attempt to depose his father. Officially, since Britain was not yet at war with Turkey, Kitchener could only sympathize. Privately, however, he felt that the destruction of Turkish power was imminent, that Britain was powerless to prevent it, that Arabs within Turkey's empire would strike for independence, and that Arab lands were absolutely critical to the British position in Egypt and India. Prior to his departure for Europe, therefore, Kitchener established a channel of communication with Hussein's family (and his appointed representative in Cairo, Mohammad al-Faruqi) via Oriental Secretary Ronald Storrs. Because of his critical position in the subsequent negotiations, it is difficult to overstate Storrs's influence over coming events. Before the arrival of a new high commissioner (an office created under the new status of "protectorate"), Sir Henry McMahon, in January 1915, these exchanges were little more than effusive but vague and noncommittal statements from Kitchener pledging British support in the event of an uprising and promising an independent Arabia after the war, yet declining to expand on the exact nature and extent of that support. It seems this was a calculated effort to keep the sharif "in play" with ambiguous transmissions while the Foreign Office deliberated over what precise commitments, if any, it should make.

By early 1915, developments began to overtake the sharif. Syrian representatives of the nationalist society al-Ahd had also met with the British in Cairo but grew disillusioned by McMahon's refusal to guarantee independence outside of the Arabian peninsula. This impasse with the British set the stage for a proposal to Sharif Hussein. Emissaries from both al-Ahd and al-Fatat arrived in the Hejaz to request assistance in fomenting a revolt among Arab troops in Syria. The sharif was asked to lead it and was requested either to receive a deputation in Mecca or to send a delegation of trusted advisers to Damascus to coordinate measures.[3] On the face of it, this seems an unlikely proposal. Hussein, as mentioned, had long been known as an ardent Ottomanist, despite the forced exile in Constantinople. Yet he did seem to hanker for the wider popularity that a new "nationalist" image might confer. At any rate, his options had narrowed significantly by January, once his son Ali discovered documents detailing a Turkish plan to depose him.[4] Feisal, his third son, then traveled to Syria where, as the guest of Ottoman Fourth Army commander Mehmed Jemal Pasha, he was compelled to witness the brutal destruction of the nationalists' scheme. Tipped off that a plot was afoot to seize Alexandretta, the Turks struck quickly. Retribution was swift as scores of actual and fancied traitors were marched to the gibbet.

But before leaving Damascus on 23 May, Feisal was secretly presented with a plan from the nationalists for a future Arab state. This document, called the Damascus Protocol, set an acceptable price for collaboration with Britain against the Ottoman Empire. Since the Turks had preemptively thwarted an uprising, the document amounted to an offer regarding postwar desiderata in the event of a revolt by the sharif. The protocol specified the need for "recognition by Great Britain of the Independence of Arab countries" within precisely defined frontiers comprising all of Arabic-speaking Ottoman Asia north and east of the Sinai, including Mesopotamia, Syria, and Palestine.[5] Since the political nature of the envisioned state was left undefined, the prospect of rule over a vast Arab empire was, in effect, dangled before Sharif Hussein. The initiative for revolt, however, would have to be his own.

The exact nature of Hussein's philosophical relationship to the Arab nationalists still provokes spirited debate. While conceding that his son Abdullah may have been a convert to Arabism, Professor Dawn has concluded that the sharif was merely an alienated Ottomanist who united with Arab nationalists (particularly in Syria) to reach a common goal, adopting and pursuing their aims and territorial aspirations. Moreover, notions about modern nationalism were unfamiliar to the sharif's traditional sense of Muslim community. Alongside the incentive to preserve and, possibly, enhance his standing in the Islamic world there was his desire to maintain the fundamental integrity of Islam and its institutions. The benefits of Hussein's union with the forces of Arab nationalism would prove rather one-sided, however, as the coming Arab Revolt "made a far greater contribution to the advancement of the Arab movement than the latter did to the Arab revolt."[6]

The Hussein-McMahon Correspondence was a milestone in the diplomatic history of the Middle East. It was composed of a series of letters exchanged between High Commissioner McMahon and Sharif Hussein. In effect, this correspondence constituted the last stage in a process of communication and negotiation set in motion by Lord Kitchener, supposedly outlining the political price to be paid by Great Britain (and a vanquished Turkey) for the sharif's revolt against his suzerains in Constantinople.

Diplomatic understandings between the British Empire and Arab chieftains within the Ottoman realm were not new. Long before, Whitehall had entered into treaties on behalf of the Indian government with various sheikhdoms along the Persian Gulf and South Arabian rim. London maintained a long-standing tradition of close contact with local potentates in these areas in order to safeguard communications with the Raj, protect Indian trading interests in the area, and, as war approached, to secure British influence in an increasingly vital oil-producing region. After the outbreak of hostilities with Turkey, the Indian government extended its diplomatic feelers inland to such rulers as Imam Yahya of Yemen, the Idrisi of Asir, and Ibn Saud of Nejd. In 1915 Indian officials concluded what were essentially mutual defense treaties with the latter two, despite the presence of Ottoman garrisons in Asir. Yet these British commitments would be overshadowed by those undertaken toward Hussein.

While a policy designed to draw the sharif into the war effort against the Turks had such powerful champions as Kitchener and Wingate (governor-general of the Sudan), it also drew fire from prominent skeptics such as Lord Hardinge, Viceroy of India; Lord Chelmsford at the India Office; and

Lord Curzon, Lord Privy Seal. Foreign Secretary Sir Edward Grey straddled the middle ground, favoring a more forward policy but unsure about how best to secure the sharif's cooperation without compromising British good faith with France.

On 22 August 1915 McMahon communicated the text of a message received from Hussein shortly before. After the initial felicitations and expressions of good will, the sharif set forth a list of demands calling upon the British government to support the independence of the "Arab countries" within an area bounded on the north by the Mersina-Adana line and the 37th parallel, on the east by the Persian frontier and the Persian Gulf, on the south by the Indian Ocean (excepting Aden), and on the west by the Red and Mediterranean seas. Hussein also requested the establishment of an Arab caliphate to supplant the Turkish sultan, along with an end to the capitulations long enjoyed by European powers in the Ottoman territories. In exchange for these concessions, the sharif offered economic preference to Great Britain and a defensive alliance renewable after fifteen years.[7] McMahon's reply, over which he had been granted wide discretion by the Foreign Office, mirrored prior statements. It reaffirmed Kitchener's earlier pledges, including the hope that an Arab of the "true race" would eventually succeed to the caliphate. But again it carefully avoided specific commitments on either that score or the territorial demands. Kitchener had never alluded to an independent Arab region beyond the Hejaz and the Arabian peninsula, and officials in Cairo were somewhat taken aback by the breadth of Hussein's demands, which were now complicated by French sensibilities. The sharif remained undaunted, however, dispatching a message on 9 September that chastised the British for their dilatory response.[8]

McMahon proposed to the Foreign Office a reply that would guarantee British paramountcy in the region, with the Arabs operating under London's guidance. Grey preferred to alter this provision (in deference to French sensitivity) to a simple guarantee of Arab independence, with boundaries to be determined in consultation with properly designated representatives of the sharif. Ominously, the foreign secretary conceded that McMahon would have to use his discretion—and "if something more precise is required, you can give it."[9] This prompted what was probably the most substantive letter in the correspondence, dispatched on 24 October, which more precisely outlined the territorial parameters within which the British were prepared to recognize Arab independence. These boundaries corresponded roughly with those asked for by the sharif earlier, with several

important differences. In view of Britain's "established position and interests" in the vilayets of Basra and Baghdad, these were excluded. Also
excised were those areas of Syria west of the districts of Damascus, Homs,
Hama, and Aleppo that, McMahon concluded, "cannot be said to be purely
Arab," as well as the districts of Mersina and Alexandretta. Hussein's
response of 5 November accepted the exclusion of the latter two districts
but objected to the exception of what was essentially the Lebanon and the
Latakia coastal area. The sharif was willing to accept the British claim to
the two Mesopotamian vilayets in exchange for monetary compensation,
pending the region's eventual return to Arab rule. But in his return letter
of 14 December McMahon held firm, emphasizing that "prior French
interests" in the Syrian littoral precluded the inclusion of that area within
the Arab sphere and reaffirming Britain's willingness to abide by its

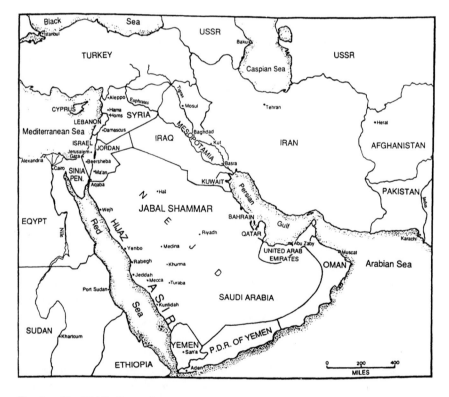

FIG. 1.   The Middle East today.

commitments in the letter of the twenty-fourth where it was "free to act without detriment to the interests of her ally, France."[10] In a later letter the sharif was conciliatory but indecisive, expressing a willingness to leave the question of western Syria in abeyance until the war's end but "at the first opportunity after this war is finished, we shall ask you (what we avert our eyes from today) for what we now leave to France in Beyrout and its coasts."[11] Here the specific territorial discussions were laid to rest while emphasis shifted to effecting the revolt itself.

These negotiations rank as some of the most controversial ever conducted and in many ways the most difficult to chronicle precisely. Largely, this was due to the unorthodox manner in which communications were received and transmitted. Mohammad al-Faruqi, the intermediary through whom the sharif's correspondence was channeled, held a position of authority in the Arab movement that was, and still is, rather unclear. It is uncertain just how accurate or effective he and Storrs were in communicating the true feelings of, or translating and interpreting messages for, their superiors. Storrs himself acknowledged that he was "often under high pressure," and that his assistant Ruhi was "a fair though not profound Arabist." Regrettably, during Storrs's absences the work was carried on by others, and "the continuity was lost."[12] Moreover, both parties often sent verbal communications through these two men, messages that were never recorded and are therefore impossible for later historians to reckon with.

However, the written record does point to two salient qualifications by which McMahon may be said to have technically shielded British policymakers from charges of perfidy. The first is that Hussein was never promised personal rule of the territory in question, and an Arab caliphate was only obliquely "approved" in the written correspondence. Secondly, the qualifications included in McMahon's letters of 24 October and 14 December, which pledged Britain to the fulfillment of the terms as far as it was "free to act without detriment to the interests of her ally, France," seems, at least technically, to absolve London of responsibility for outrage aroused by subsequent and allegedly contravening accords with France. The high commissioner had, after all, considerable experience with borders, extensive enough perhaps to preclude simple inattention as an adequate explanation for the alleged imprecision of the correspondence. He served for years on the Punjab Commission and in the Indian Political Department, demarcating the boundary between Baluchistan and Afghanistan. McMahon also served as Britain's plenipotentiary in negotiations with China over India's border with Tibet. The subsequent border was appropriately dubbed the "McMahon Line." While this may be true, it remains difficult to acquit McMahon and his superiors of the charge that Hussein was misled as to British intent both toward himself and the French. Indeed, many officials directly involved seem to have been aware that the sharif would be disappointed by the fruit of the correspondence. This was partially attributable to the nature of the communication itself. Never set down with the specificity of a formal treaty (as Britain had always used before in its dealings with Arab chiefs), the wording was more permissively ambiguous and sometimes self-negating. Whether purposely or not, such procedures constituted a blueprint for misunderstanding—and such was their unfortunate result.

Apportionment of blame for the consequences of this accord has been generous. Dawn suggests that the negotiations were inconclusive, "an agreement to disagree" regarding their conflicting demands, and were knowingly put into effect on that basis by both sides.[13] Zeine N. Zeine attributes the ostensible pledges to the sharif to "the confusion and muddle of the 'experts' on Arab affairs at the Arab Bureau in Cairo," which is curious given that the bureau was created in 1916, some time after the pivotal correspondence between McMahon and the sharif took place.[14] Suleiman Mousa, on the other hand, argues that Hussein later felt himself ill-used, "duped by British prevarication over promises."[15] Elie Kedourie suggests that there were no contradictions at all in the British pledges, even alongside the subsequent Sykes-Picot Agreement. This compatibility between the two agreements, he maintains, was because "what they had said was so vague and ambiguous that it was compatible with almost anything."[16] Kedourie's contention that such ambiguity and vagueness were deliberately contrived is perhaps closest to the mark and is lent credence by a note from Wingate to Gilbert Clayton from May 1916: "Thanks also for wiring up the text of the High Commissioner's letter to the Sharif; in view of the restrictions placed on him by H.B.M.'s Government, I think he has got round the difficulties in a very diplomatic manner, but of course we cannot expect that the addressee will not see through some of the sentences."[17]

An astounding misimpression has persisted among certain writers over the years that attaches blame to the Arab Bureau for pledges made during the Hussein-McMahon Correspondence. Such notions are manifestly untrue. Those negotiations were conceived and largely completed by the end of 1915, while the decision to create an Arab Bureau was not even officially approved until January 1916, and the agency did not begin to function effectively until some months after that. The critical letters of the Hussein-McMahon Correspondence were written and relayed the preceding autumn. While it is true that members of the so-called "intrusives" in the British intelligence community in Cairo may have been involved in the negotiations (e.g., Storrs), a bureau that had yet to be constituted cannot be held responsible for the outcome. Despite these facts, erroneous conclusions such as the following linger in the general literature: "Each of the Allies was on tiptoe to gratify century-old ambitions and acutely sensitive to any pretensions by a fellow eagle to grab more than its share of the carcass. But how to deal out the spoils without at the same time upsetting the applecart of the Arab Bureau, which was just then slowly drawing Hussein nearer to revolt against Turkey by promises of hegemony as future King of the Arabs. Both sets of negotiations were running concurrently."[18] The Arab Bureau did not promise, nor was it in a position to negotiate, matters of "hegemony" or "kingship" on behalf of the British crown.

British negotiations with France regarding the postwar Middle East also proceeded apace. Whitehall had not initiated these discussions. In 1915, diplomatic activity intensified, aimed at resolving the long-standing competition over the anticipated division of Turkish territory. The Dardanelles expedition coincided with British agreement to concede control of Constantinople and the straits to the Tsar. This prompted France to insist on a formal recognition of its own claims to Syria. Such discussions bespoke a reluctant shift by the Foreign Office away from the traditional policy of maintaining the territorial integrity of the Ottoman Empire as a bulwark against Russian territorial expansion in the Near East and the Mediterranean. An interdepartmental committee of the cabinet was created in mid-1915 to formulate Britain's requirements and priorities with respect to postwar desiderata in the Ottoman Empire. This body, chaired by Foreign Office expert Sir Maurice de Bunsen, submitted a report to the cabinet that favored talks with the French but also expressed a preference for decentralization of Turkish control in the region. This preference reflected the time-honored British attitude that Ottoman authority be preserved, at least nominally. As a result, a French emissary was dispatched in November to negotiate a settlement. His name was Francois Georges-Picot. His counterpart was the flamboyant Mark Sykes, an experienced traveler in the East who had practiced at the South African bar, served in Constantinople as honorary attaché for the British government, and held office as Conservative M.P. from Hull in 1911. By 1915, Sykes had achieved prominence as foremost adviser on the Middle East to the War Cabinet.[19] By April, the two men had successfully concluded an arrangement.

The Sykes-Picot Agreement, as the accord became known, has become something of a pariah in the history of British diplomacy, synonymous with duplicitous double-dealing. What it established (at least on paper) were spheres of direct and indirect control for both Britain and France. The French were to be allowed direct control over the Syrian littoral west of the Damascus, Homs, Hama, and Aleppo line and northward to include Cicilia and the coast between Alexandretta and Acre. This was the so-called Blue Zone. An Arab state under French "protection" would be established in the Syrian hinterland, including the Mosul vilayet of upper Mesopotamia and most of the Syrian interior south to the Yarmuk River. Direct British control (the Red Zone) would extend over the vilayets of Baghdad and Basra, with informal control embracing the Persian Gulf and Transjordan eastward to the Kirkuk district of Mesopotamia. Most of Palestine was to be administered under an Allied condominium, and the Arabian peninsula left independent (excepting Aden). Where McMahon's correspondence with Hussein fit in the scheme of things was anybody's guess. But surely the spirit of their understanding seemed, at the least, undermined.

The Arab Bureau had little to do with the content of either the Hussein-McMahon Correspondence or the Sykes-Picot Agreement. Both were concluded before the unit had begun its work in Cairo. Indeed, Storrs would later write, "Until Mark Sykes appeared in Cairo in 1916 we [the intelligence community and Clayton] had but the slightest and vaguest information about the Sykes-Picot negotiations."[20] However, the two agreements constituted the framework within which official British policy would be conceived and implemented. This is not to suggest that either accord enjoyed the unqualified support of the men who would be charged with executive authority over political affairs in this theater. As the war progressed, officials in Cairo became increasingly critical of the French and of Sykes's accord with them. The Anglo-Indian authorities, on the other hand, had from the beginning regarded McMahon's pledges to Hussein as reckless and unnecessary. The result was that these accords further polarized centers of regional political influence, thereby rendering the new Arab Bureau's raison d'être less tenable.

In retrospect, it is difficult to discount the need for this new agency. For the British, the Middle East was an administrative morass that saddled officials with enormous but nebulously defined spheres of authority. Worse, political and military control within those spheres was so subdivided as to

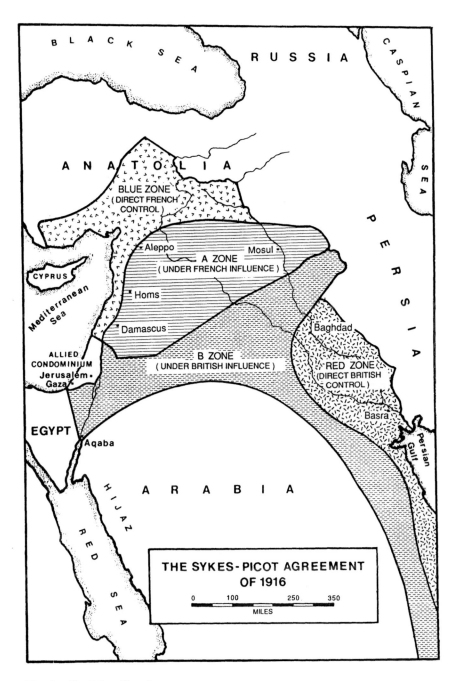

FIG. 2. The Sykes-Picot Agreement.

create much departmental duplication, inefficiency, and internecine rivalry. The resulting confusion bred ignorance, intrigue, and practical paralysis. "The telegrams," moaned Sykes, "are a perfect babel of conflicting suggestions and views, which interweave and intertwine from man to man and place to place in an almost inexplicable tangle."[21]

This "tangle" seemed more like a Gordian knot. Eighteen individuals were empowered to advise on the content and direction of British policy in the Middle East, exclusive of Persia. Worse, these officials were scattered among numerous and often rival agencies, departments, and bureaus. On the military side were several Egyptian centers of authority: General Archibald Murray, commanding British Expeditionary Forces along the Suez front (based at Ismailia); the Mediterranean Expeditionary Force under Sir Ian Hamilton (based at Alexandria); and the British Army in Egypt under Maxwell (based at Cairo). In the Sudan, Wingate was sirdar of the Egyptian Army; in the Red Sea, Vice Admiral Rosslyn Wemyss commanded the East India Squadron, which included the Red Sea Patrol. In Cairo, Colonel Gilbert Clayton headed Murray's intelligence network until early 1916, when Thomas Holdich, Director of Military Intelligence for General Murray, succeeded him. Clayton then devoted himself to political intelligence and the operation of the Arab Bureau and the Sudan Agency in Cairo. In Mesopotamia, the responsibility for military command, along with political supervision of eastern and southern Arabia, rested with the government of India. But military control lay with the British commander along the Tigris, Sir Percy Lake, while the political aspects remained under Lake's chief political officer, Sir Percy Cox. Adding to the confusion, relations with southwestern Arabia, including Asir, the Yemen, and the Hadhramaut, were handled by the British Resident in Aden, who answered directly to his superiors in Bombay. Political affairs in Cairo were overseen by the high commissioner, who was assisted by the residency staff for Egypt and responsible directly to the Foreign Office.

Under ideal conditions, the efficient and harmonious operation of such a system would have been a great challenge. Under the political conditions prevailing at the time, however, it was a pipe dream. Indian and Mesopotamian officials differed fundamentally in their Arab policies from officials in Cairo. In the absence of sustained and resolute Foreign Office direction, inconsistency and conflict prevailed. Further, the uncertainty that shrouded their respective spheres of authority ensured persistent friction, while the unwillingness of Egyptian and Indian officials to cooperate with one another accelerated the development of rival political camps. "I have no doubt whatever," Storrs would write, "that if the officers behind the Arab campaign in the Hejaz had been allowed to exchange awhile with or even to meet their colleagues from the Persian Gulf, well before instead of long after the Arab Revolution, they could have achieved an intense concentration of purpose and a sure economy of many thousands of pounds."[22]

Fissures often opened up between military and political authorities in both Mesopotamia and Egypt. Cox did not get on well with Lake, nor Clayton and Wingate with Murray. McMahon distrusted both Wingate and Murray—and they all were suspicious of Lake and the Indian viceroy, Lord Hardinge. Predictably, McMahon, Wingate, and Murray all had their own ideas as to whether and how the Arabs should be incorporated into the war effort against the Turks. Truly, as Sykes admitted, this was a system fated to stumble "from crisis to inertia, and from coma to panic, watching assets frittered away and opportunities missed."[23]

In London the situation was much the same. The Admiralty, the War Office, the India Office, and the Foreign Office all sparred for influence over the conduct of affairs in the Middle East. Each department held its own views on how best to incorporate Arab policy into various military and political contexts. Before such pervasive confusion, the War Cabinet and the Committee on Imperial Defence flopped about in irresolution, unable to subdue competition or rechannel competitive energies into more constructive outlets. Middle East policy was reactive rather than anticipatory, creating an environment in which indecision and disagreement flourished and leaving a vacuum into which officials on the spot in Cairo, Jeddah, or Basra were forced to step. Gertrude Bell complained bitterly of this shortly after her arrival in Basra in early 1916: "Politically too, we rushed with the business with our usual disregard for a comprehensive political scheme. . . . The coordinating of Arabian politics and the creation of our Arabian policy should have been done at home—it could only have been done successfully at home. There was no one to do it, no one who had ever thought of it, and it was left to our people in Egypt to thrash out, in the face of strenuous opposition, from India and London, some sort of wide scheme, which will, I am persuaded, ultimately form the basis of our relations with the Arabs."[24]

This diffusion of authority was made worse by the vague and often curious definition of administrative boundaries. This was especially true in Arabia, where the Indian view of the extent of its political supervision differed radically from the one prevailing at Whitehall. The embarrassing incident at Kunfidah in late 1916 (see page 94 below) was one unfortunate consequence. The setup in Mesopotamia was similarly confused; militarily it was under Delhi's authority, yet it remained in Cairo's sphere of political intelligence. Sadly, Iraq was "the foster child of both Simla and Whitehall and the acknowledged child of neither."[25] These mechanical anomalies did not go unnoticed by a major figure in the impending drama. "You speak to me continually of the British Government and British Policy," Sharif Hussein later complained to British agent Lt. Col. C. E. Wilson. "But I see five governments where you see one, and the same number of policies. There is a policy, first of your Foreign Office; second of your Army; third of your Navy; fourth of your protectorate in Egypt; fifth of your Government in India. Each of these British Governments seems to me to act upon an Arab policy of its own."[26]

This contest between Cairo and Delhi for influence in London was only one factor of the equation. Add to it the convoluted relationships maintained by the British government with its allies and the Zionists, and the muddle is complete. The familiar malaise of British diplomacy, that of attempting to please all parties to the satisfaction of none, infected the body of internal administration as well. The result was functional paralysis. Once again, it was the story of the British government resorting to policy by committee. "It may be safely said," Sykes lamented, "that with the exception of the ancient constitution of Poland it would be difficult to find a precedent for so complex or unworkable a political arrangement as the British system which has evolved itself in Arabia since the war broke out in August 1914. Attention is drawn to this mess because instead of getting better it gets worse, more and more people get a right of deprecation, and suggestions are fired from all quarters of the earth—Simla, London, Paris, and Rome."[27]

Determined to assess the situation firsthand, Sykes set off on an inspection tour of the Near East in late 1915. Inspired, he returned with a remedy for Britain's Middle East logjam. He would create yet another agency—an "Islamic" Bureau—to manage the unmanageable and suppress the cacophonous squabbling. By the onset of the autumn of 1915, Sykes had begun his campaign to establish a coordinating bureau. The administrative confusion and conflict that he had so eloquently condemned had to be subdued for the British war effort in the Middle East to be salvaged.

From the very beginning, proponents of the new agency lobbied vigorously against centering its activities anywhere other than Cairo. At the forefront of such efforts was Colonel Clayton, chief of Egyptian intelligence

under Generals Maxwell and Murray and the Sudan government's representative in Cairo. "I am of [the] very strong opinion," he wrote to the War
Office, "that this section should be formed here, and attached to the
Intelligence Department." Continuing, Clayton reiterated familiar arguments used by the Arab Bureau's supporters in their battle for a Cairene
nexus of Middle East intelligence: "It is only by working on the spot, where
they would have the full benefit of all the detailed information which we
get, and have the opportunity of seeing all the various people who gravitate
to Cairo, and they could be able to get a really clear grasp of the whole
situation."[28]

Unfortunately, other opinions blocked the proposed unit's smooth assimilation into Clayton's command. In the frenetic atmosphere of wartime
London, Sykes was preoccupied with fending off several departments that
were arguing over control of the fledging agency even before it had been
officially sanctioned. The political influence that the new bureau might
command was not lost on anyone. Indeed, from its inception, the Arab
Bureau was regarded as a high priority item in London, championed at the
highest levels; military authorities were advised that temporary ranks
assigned its members were in no way indicative of their political status or
duties.[29] As contenders jockeyed for position, the Foreign Office vacillated
over where supervisory control should rest. M.P. Aubrey Herbert warned
Clayton from the War Office that, despite an appreciation of the advantages
that location in Cairo might afford, Whitehall had "pretty cold feet" in the
wake of the Gallipoli debacle, and "I don't think they understand the
importance of time."[30]

One of the earliest contestants for control over the new bureau was the
Admiralty, with which Clayton was in early touch. Since 1914, the Red
Sea Patrol had been involved in intelligence activities along the Hejaz
coast. British patrols were also assigned to prevent Turkish mine-laying and
enemy infiltration into Egypt and the Sudan. In addition to these defensive
functions, each patrol was accompanied by an officer with some experience
in the area, assigned to explain British government policy to the Arab
chiefs. From the early autumn of 1915, Clayton conducted a regular
correspondence with the Admiralty. In late December, Naval Intelligence
even dispatched a set of its own guidelines to him explaining primary
functions for the proposed bureau. This scheme was ambitious, envisioning
an agency that would closely coordinate Cairo's propaganda and intelligence activities with those of the government, refine and homogenize

British political activity in the Near East, and harmonize Allied propaganda with India's special concerns.

Delhi wasted little time in attacking Sykes's project, fearing that creation of the new bureau would mean surrender of control over relations between its forces in Mesopotamia and the local Arab population. Indian officials were also fearful of the reaction that anti-Turkish propaganda might provoke among Indian Muslims. An exasperated Sykes frequently inveighed to Clayton against "those idiot Sahib-landers who are jealous and provincial."[31]

The Admiralty scheme (for which Sykes was largely responsible) was based upon a tripartite secretariat to aid Sykes as director. The first secretary (preferably *Times* correspondent Philip Graves) would meet the press and propaganda requirements of London, the Persian Gulf, Mesopotamia, and the Arab world. The second secretary would advise Sykes and Graves on activities most likely to conflict with the government of India in addition to supplying both the Anglo-Indian and vernacular presses in India. The third secretary (preferably Alfred Parker, former governor of Sinai) would be responsible for organizing and collecting native agents in Egypt, Syria, and the Hejaz for purposes of intelligence and propaganda. No mention was made of activities in Mesopotamia, save of a "traveler" officer for the bureau who would tour Mesopotamia, India, and the Persian Gulf, reporting back to Cairo via the established British authorities in those regions. Liaison offices for the new unit were also proposed for London (to the Committee on Imperial Defence), Basra (to Cox, the chief political officer), and New York (to remain in touch with Arabs in America and disseminate useful propaganda there). Under this arrangement, Allied attachés were to be kept abreast of the type of propaganda contemplated for distribution, in case deletions or revisions should prove necessary.[32]

Sykes, while aware of Clayton's contacts with the Admiralty, saw both advantages and disadvantages to its control. He personally admired the man in charge at Naval Intelligence, Admiral W. R. ("Blinker") Hall, but was very suspicious of his colleague, Lieutenant Cozens Hardy, whom he regarded as conniving and ambitious. Sir Mark resented his frequent refusals to dispatch communications directly to Clayton rather than through regular Foreign Office channels. He also viewed the Admiralty as a staid, discredited department owing to its recent debacle in the Dardanelles, whose voice would carry little weight on political questions.[33] However, Robert Fitzgerald at the War Office was also pressuring Sykes for an official connection with the proposed bureau. As bait he dangled the extensive facilities of Military Intelligence (code systems, agent networks, myriad intelligence machinery, etc.). But the War Office could hardly compete with the navy's coffers.

For his own part, however, Sykes came to the conclusion that the proposed bureau should remain under Foreign Office control. He preferred to remain in London as Clayton's "receiver" in order to "put the case for you to the statesmen."[34] Sykes looked to the new bureau as an instrument to induce cooperation among the various departments through formulation of a uniform Arab policy. Authorities in London could eventually be expected to defer to the new agency, thereby ensuring the diplomatic consistency so desperately sought.

Such optimism may have been warranted theoretically. But London and Cairo were too distant and situated too differently relative to the war for strategic priorities to develop in tandem. And divergence was assured once the decision was made to base the new agency in Cairo, for Clayton had plans to mold the bureau in his own cast. Cairo's intelligence chief had already gleaned a group of candidates from various departments who possessed considerable background and expertise in the Middle East. Desiring a special status for this new bureau, he took preemptive steps to save the unit from the grasping talons of other covetous departments, whether in London or in Cairo itself. He envisioned considerably more freedom of action for the proposed unit than Sykes had in mind. In a note to Admiral Hall, Clayton confessed that his ideas were "somewhat different from those of Sykes in that what I want to start is a Bureau here which will be a center to which all information on the various questions connected with the Near East will gravitate."[35] Clayton preferred to set aside specific discussion of the proposed bureau's function and scope, fearing it might result in unnecessary restrictions. He also thought Sykes's push for the agency in London had needlessly "alarmed the various authorities at home, and led them to think that a more far reaching organization is contemplated than might be desirable."[36] Clayton thought it would be far better if the new unit's scope were left vague so as to suit whatever contingencies might arise. Its proper limits would become obvious once its officers had gained experience and its potential had become more apparent. Most significantly, Cairo's intelligence chief argued that, aside from nominal supervision from the Foreign Office (through the high commissioner), the new bureau "should be rather an independent body" in the collation, interpretation, and dissemination of political intelligence and propaganda. Accordingly, he offered an unofficial understanding with Naval Intelligence, advocating placement of an Arab Bureau representative "in your system" and "in touch with your people." For this purpose he suggested Professor David Hogarth.[37]

Clayton's desire to secure as long a tether as possible is certainly understandable from his vantage point. While convinced that such a unit would have to be based in Cairo to be of any real use, he was anxious to avoid the pitfalls attending official association with any large department. A close working relationship with Admiral Hall, despite official Foreign Office aegis, offered the dual advantage of liaison assistance in the Red Sea with minimal interference from London. Hall had already assured Clayton of his desire "not to centralize Intelligence in the Near East in London but to feed you everything we get and regard you as the principal Intelligence center for that part of the campaign. This seems to me the only successful plan, as you have people on the spot who are able to assess any information at its proper value."[38] These efforts by the Admiralty, which, in Sykes's words, "barged in and seized me and the Bureau," were blunted once Whitehall vetoed the suggestion of an Arab Bureau representative to Naval Intelligence. The link, however, between the new unit and the intelligence departments of both the army and navy persisted, albeit in shadowy form, throughout the war.

The Foreign Office meanwhile continued to wrestle with the details of the bureau's constitution and functional scope. The lords at Whitehall remained uncertain as to the proper position of the new organ in the wartime scheme of things. Early in January, High Commissioner McMahon was consulted on the question of whether the proposed bureau would overlap the function of any existing organization. His reply assured Foreign Secretary Grey that it would not and backed Sykes's prodding for prompt action on the matter.[39] Indeed, one member of Clayton's nascent intelligence cadre characterized McMahon's mood as "very anxious about the development of the . . . Bureau."[40]

One problem, of course, was how best to provide the new agency with the pedigree to execute its functions without sacrificing either its secrecy or its theoretical neutrality among the various departments. According to Sykes's plan, all departments (including the Foreign Office) would be kept "simultaneously informed" on matters of intelligence, while propaganda would be generated in Cairo and distributed via regional political officers. The objects of this system were to circumscribe preferential treatment for one department over another and to elicit cooperation from them all. The question of propaganda, however, ran afoul of Indian protests almost immediately. No provision had yet been made for censorship roles for Mesopotamian commanders and the government of India, to which the content of propaganda was always a matter of the most profound importance. High Commissioner McMahon, under whom the new bureau would be placed, insisted that it not be compromised by outside interference and that a commanding but liberally constructed mandate, loosely supervised by Whitehall and the residency, offered the best solution: "Nothing but dire confusion can come of things which are entirely within the province of the Foreign Office being partly managed by other departments whose concern they are not."[41]

Early in January 1916, an interdepartmental conference consisting of Arthur Hirtzel (India Office undersecretary), Lancelot Oliphant (from the Foreign Office), General George Macdonough (chief of Military Intelligence), Maurice Hankey (secretary of the Committee of Imperial Defence), Admiral Hall, and Sykes was summoned to Whitehall by Asquith to consider the question of Sykes's bureau. Miraculously, approval was soon granted, with a few changes. The original title, "Islamic Bureau," was transformed to the less provocative "Arab Bureau" out of deference to Indian sensitivity. The agency was established as a branch of Cairo's political and military intelligence network but was uniquely responsible to the residency through Clayton. Ultimate control of the bureau rested with the Foreign Office. Its primary function would be to harmonize British political activity in the Near East through the centralization of intelligence collection and interpretation respecting the Arab world and to keep the Foreign Office, the Indian Office, Aden, the War Office, and the government of India "simultaneously informed on the general tendency of German and Turkish policy." In addition, the new bureau was authorized to generate propaganda in favor of Great Britain among non-Indian Muslims "without clashing with the susceptibilities of Indian Moslems and the Entente Powers."[42] The Foreign Office came to the sound conclusion that some discretionary authority over sensitive intelligence and propaganda should be kept in London. Oliphant was especially emphatic that Whitehall keep the other offices informed and not merely be one of them.[43] In the wake of the Committee on Imperial Defence meeting of 7 January, a directive was issued to the effect that all reports compiled by the Arab Bureau be dispatched "to this office only, whence they will be distributed."[44] Such reports were to be transmitted to Whitehall through the Egyptian residency.

Given the centrifugal tendencies of British bureaucracy in the Middle East at this juncture, this mandate was certainly ambitious enough. Indeed, in certain respects this format made eminently good sense. Many of the bureau's future activities, after all, would require logistical capacities for which close cooperation with the military authorities in Egypt would be essential. Moreover, if the new Arab Bureau failed to work closely with GHQ Intelligence, much duplication and inefficiency doubtless would result.

But close proximity to Cairo's intelligence establishment had drawbacks as well. The potential for departmental intrigue and encroachment was unarguably great. Many of the explosive political questions that the Arab Bureau would be called upon to address involved decisions best made at the most detached diplomatic levels. McMahon's pledges to Hussein provided one example of the unfortunate consequences that can stem from an injudicious grant of diplomatic license. Perhaps most significantly, the decision to incorporate the new bureau into Cairo's intelligence network had the ineradicable effect of identifying it closely with wartime Cairo's view of the Arab world. While this association gained credence as the war progressed, the process was to a certain extent self-fulfilling. Although anxious to offer up the Arab Bureau as a panacea for its complex difficulties in the region, London was unprepared to nurture it through to maturation as an effective adjunct to the Foreign Office. Instead, the new Arab Bureau was thrown headlong to Cairo's wolves, in turn to be dismembered and reconstituted under a new master. Even Mark Sykes, Clayton's putative sponsor in London, formally distanced himself from the bureau to appease a hostile viceroy and India Office. This was an auspicious turn of events for Clayton. Sir Mark's irrepressible pomposity would only have hastened the bureau's descent from the lofty heights he had envisioned for it. Hereafter, Clayton fed him bureau reports with which to spice up his Arabian Report to the CID, but ceased to regard him as the unit's mentor across the water. Increasingly, it seemed, it was Clayton's show. Subsequently, the evolving Arab Bureau would be perceived less as an arbiter than an advocate, adding to the confusing chorus of advice from which bad decisions were inevitably drawn.

Clayton in Cairo and his superior, F. Reginald Wingate in Khartoum, were already coming to regard the new bureau as their own. "The main idea," wrote Clayton to Wingate in February 1916, "is that, in practice it should be independent and furnish information of all kinds, rather than express views, though I presume it would naturally draw conclusions from the information it obtained."[45] Cairo's intelligence chief clearly shared Sykes's appreciation of the fine line that distinguished an informational body from an advisory one. Governor-General Wingate responded with the speculation that the new agency would prove useful in helping to "influence the opinions of India and Mesopotamia."[46] These two men saw the Arab Bureau as a conduit through which their own perspective on Arab policy might penetrate and transform attitudes hostile to the initiation of a more forward Arab policy, less through persuasion than by invocation of the powerful sanction that had underwritten its birth. The sirdar would have preferred that the Arab Bureau be placed under the War Office, fearful perhaps of nettlesome interference from Whitehall.[47] Clayton was also chary of Foreign Office supervision, especially where it concerned India Office access to bureau communications. Accordingly, he often communicated privately to the Admiralty and the War Office, thereby skirting the gaze of the India Office. This drew predictable complaints from the Indian undersecretary, which prompted the War Office to suggest the Arab Bureau confine itself to proper channels. Clayton responded that, while he would comply, "I think it is as well to have some unofficial channel of communication as it is frequently desirable to send information for the private information of the D.I.D. or D.M.I."[48]

McMahon's expectations, as Egypt's high commissioner, were hardly so grandiose, but he was extremely protective of his new unit and determined that it not be subsumed by the intelligence organization being transferred to Egypt in the wake of the Dardanelles evacuation. He was particularly worried over the status of Colonel Samson's Intelligence Bureau, newly arrived from Salonika. Wiring the Foreign Office, McMahon requested verification of rumored curtailments in Arab Bureau activity or, worse, termination of the agency before it had even begun its work. The response of Arthur Nicolson, permanent Foreign Office undersecretary, was soothing, assuring the high commissioner that, on the contrary, the trend would be "quite the reverse," despite impending troop reductions in Egypt.[49]

The bureau's official chain of command did not fully reflect political realities in Cairo. As a Foreign Office adjunct, the Arab Bureau fell under the theoretical authority of McMahon. But Clayton, first as director of military intelligence and then as chief of intelligence for the Egyptian government, was ex officio head of the agency and in regular (and often furtive) communication with Wingate at Khartoum. Successive Arab Bureau directors worked at Clayton's direction with minimal interference from McMahon, whose tenure in Cairo was, at the best of times, fitful and indecisive. Invested with scant direction from London in his negotiations with the Sharif of Mecca, he came to rely increasingly upon subalterns whose experience with and knowledge of Arabia were far more extensive than his own (e.g., Clayton and Ronald Storrs, his oriental secretary). As a neophyte in the art of oriental diplomacy, the high commissioner often chose to defer to the judgment of such officers in the conduct of his relations with Arabia. Rather than direct the course of events, poor McMahon presided over them and ultimately bore much of the blame for the results. Early in 1916, he remained ensconced at the residency, beset with the task of forging a politically defensible and militarily viable Anglo-Arab alliance. Predictably, he came to look upon his new Arab Bureau in the manner of a drowning man upon his life ring. As summer approached, he could no longer ignore Wingate's looming presence on the Cairo scene and seemed uncertain as to the source of the tune to which the new bureau would most likely march, formal arrangements notwithstanding.

The atmosphere in Cairo, therefore, was conducive to the bureau's development along the independent lines Clayton envisioned. But the loosening of London's ties was followed by gradual reattachment to a new center of regional influence located in Khartoum. With McMahon's later departure and replacement by Wingate, the melding of the Sudan school and the Arab Bureau neared completion. McMahon, though unequal to the task before him, remained the only manifestation of Foreign Office authority to which the bureau was mandated to answer. Many of the officers rising to positions of responsibility at the bureau had Sudan experience in their backgrounds. But the gravitation of the Arab Bureau toward the Sudan and then Cairo (once Wingate was installed there) was inevitable in light of the function it was called upon to perform. Moreover, its expertise was coveted by both Clayton and Wingate to reinforce their emerging conception of Arab policy at the expense of political adversaries in Mesopotamia, India, and the Egyptian high command.

In any case, by the spring of 1916 the new Arab Bureau had, in Clayton's words, "suddenly materialized" in Cairo.[50] This is most certainly overstating the case, because many of the new agency's officers had been on the scene for months as part of Clayton's burgeoning intelligence staff. Hogarth, employed there by Admiralty Intelligence, had sent word to London late in 1914 requesting assistance, which prompted the dispatch of a remarkable group of adventurers. George Lloyd, Leonard Woolley, and T. E. Lawrence were ordered to proceed to Cairo under Stewart Newcombe's command, whereupon they were to report directly to Clayton. Departing Marseilles on 9 December, they had reached Egypt before Christmas, joining comrades Aubrey Herbert, Storrs, and Philip Graves. They dubbed their little group "the intrusives" and set upon myriad tasks: gathering intelligence, interrogating prisoners, concocting propaganda, monitoring internal security in Egypt, and infiltrating enemy territory with agents. In these endeavors they were ably assisted by Turkish experts such as Wyndham Deedes of Military Intelligence and Robert W. Graves of the Eastern Mediterranean Special Intelligence Bureau.

As soon as the Arab Bureau was founded, however, rival departments began staking their claims on this close-knit group. "A great war," noted Deedes, "is being waged over my body."[51] Clayton left his position as director of military intelligence and assumed control over political intelligence and the new Arab Bureau. But the line between the two spheres would remain a fine one, at least until the official merger of Maxwell's and Murray's commands into the Egyptian Expeditionary Force and the removal of its headquarters to Ismailia later in the year. As official civility eroded between the army and Clayton's organization, the Arab Bureau became a de facto pariah, caught between both groups. Yet the esprit that characterized the "intrusives" was resilient enough to withstand the squabbling of superiors. Despite official detachment, experts such as Deedes and Robert W. Graves were prevailed upon to "do, besides other duties, work indistinguishable from that of the Bureau and in cooperation with it."[52]

Alfred Parker was tapped to be the bureau's first director. But shortly after the outbreak of the Arab Revolt in June 1916, he chose to forgo the honor and join the fray. Duly transferred to the Red Sea port of Rabegh as political officer, he began to assess the situation in the interior in order to "gain valuable information about the country and its people."[53] Other bureau representatives—Kinahan Cornwallis, Gertrude Bell, and G. W. Gerrard—were dispatched to Jeddah, Basra, and Port Sudan, respectively. This left Hogarth in charge at Cairo, directing a streamlined complement of fifteen officers and half a dozen clerks and typists. Because Hogarth's expertise was often in demand elsewhere, Cornwallis returned later to assume the posts of acting director and, eventually, director.

The Arab Bureau was housed in three rooms of the Savoy Hotel in Cairo, although billeted next door at the Grand Continental. The Savoy was one of those peculiar, hybrid architectural creations, blending Orient and Occident, so common in India and Egypt. Built by an English company in the mid-nineteenth century, it was known originally as the New Hotel and later as the Continental-Savoy (for the two were adjoining). It soon became a rival of Shepheards, the khedive choosing to house guests there for the Suez Canal opening in 1866. The Savoy soon became the giddy center of the city's whirling social life in the years before World War I. The complex sported an exotic air in which seemingly anything from boa constrictors and caged leopards to old issues of the *New York Tribune* and *Daily Mail* were available for purchase from the veranda, while acrobatic baboons performed on the backs of donkeys for passersby. With the military invasion of its facilities in 1914, the Continental-Savoy became a martial hub, "jammed with staff officers with suede boots, fly whisks and swagger sticks."[54] Here Hogarth amassed a library that would eventually total over three hundred volumes on Middle Eastern topography, ethnography, history, and theology. From these sources and reports submitted by traveling agents who ranged from Basra to Addis Ababa, officers assembled handbooks on numerous regions, including profiles of prominent political personalities, ethnic rivalries, and trade prospects. In addition, military and political intelligence summaries encompassing developments from Persia to Morocco were published by the bureau for internal consumption. Hogarth's unit thus developed into an analytical clearinghouse, rendering the reams of reports and studies both more manageable and comprehensible. It also was called upon to perform many perfunctory duties for the high commissioner, such as translating letters from the Sharifian government to the residency and transmitting replies to C. E. Wilson in Jeddah. And while messages to McMahon from Arabia or Wingate were transmitted via the bureau, it is interesting that Hogarth failed to clear his messages to Khartoum or Jeddah with McMahon.

Bureau officers also monitored intercepts of enemy wireless messages from Syria and Medina. The results were then forwarded to Wilson in Jeddah, preceded by the phrase, "Information has been received," to indicate the source. So concerned was Hogarth that this capability not be compromised that Wilson was warned not to pass such intelligence along by any means other than ships' captains.

Yet despite its best efforts, the bureau remained distinctly unesteemed in the citadels of the Egyptian high command. Notwithstanding the fruitful collaboration of Hogarth's unit with supposedly rival personnel, General Murray's ill-concealed hostility grew more intense as the Cairo intelligence community became more labyrinthine. The Arab Bureau seemed to some a disruptive and unnecessary inconvenience. Its arrival on the Cairo scene was deemed an augury of the eventual consolidation of manifold intelligence functions in Egypt. Clayton, particularly, was an object of suspicion at GHQ despite his orders to cooperate closely with Army Intelligence. Murray was so determined to erect a *cordon sanitaire* around the new unit that when Cornwallis was named acting director in the autumn of 1916 he was deprived of his army rank and forced to enlist Foreign Office intercession to regain it.

The commander in chief's distrust of Clayton was rooted partly in his suspicion of Wingate. Indeed, Murray seems to have regarded Clayton as little more than Wingate's factotum in Cairo. McMahon did little to allay this impression and may possibly have contributed to it.[55] Moreover, Murray's chagrin at being rebuffed in his offer to supervise military operations in the Hejaz in June 1916 (a responsibility subsequently handed to Wingate), and his annoyance at Clayton's occasional shielding of confidential telegrams from his scrutiny, also seemed linked somehow to the sirdar. Finally, bad blood lingered between rival intelligence organizations of the Egyptian Expeditionary Force prior to their amalgamation under Murray's aegis in the spring of 1916. Murray's intelligence section was centered at Ismailia, concentrating on the movement and composition of Turkish forces, while Maxwell's was in Cairo, under the command of Clayton, addressing problems of the Egyptian interior and Arabia. Clayton's sponsorship of the new Arab Bureau, therefore, seemed ominous in Ismailia. It also soured relations between Murray and McMahon. Since Foreign Office supervision of the Arab Bureau was never made sufficiently clear to the members of contending bureaucracies, it became simply another intelligence unit among the many in Cairo, serving to muddy already murky waters. Internecine jealousy prevailed despite the presence, in Wyndham Deedes's words, of "ample [intelligence] for both."[56]

To Wingate, this lamentable state of affairs stemmed from conflict between the residency and GHQ that the Foreign Office simply refused to address. While insisting that coordination and cooperation were essential in order to streamline decision-making in this theater of operations, Whitehall refused to vest McMahon with the authority to bring Murray into line. The sirdar dubbed Clayton "the unfortunate shuttlecock" in this volley of administrative badminton. Important issues, he charged, were "obscured by personal jealousies and ambition—a condition of affairs which is of very rapid growth in the intrigue-soaked soil of Egypt."[57]

A critical problem was the fundamental disagreement between McMahon and Murray regarding the significance of the impending Arab Revolt itself. From the beginning, military authorities in Egypt had been skeptical of its strategic soundness, especially if run militarily from Khartoum. Wary of association with potential catastrophes in the wake of Gallipoli and Kut, GHQ preferred to maintain a healthy and uncooperative distance. Clayton was warned by an Ismailia confidant "that no officer in this office was to assist Hogarth in any way. I managed to get this somewhat modified so that Lawrence assists in all but where action is necessary and Hogarth is permitted to consult me."[58]

Such beginnings were hardly auspicious for the Arab Bureau. Consequently, during those first tenuous months of the Arab Revolt, the prospects for success in Sharif Hussein's campaign were not good. The army withheld its cooperation, except in the most perfunctory courtesies. Egypt seemed indifferent to the rising, and the Indian government leery of it. Shortly following his arrival in Cairo, Hogarth recognized that if the Arab Bureau were ever to live up to expectations, remedial steps would have to be taken immediately. In his first report from the bureau in May 1916, Hogarth pleaded for closer cooperation between his agency and military intelligence while also arguing for his unit's semi-independent status. The siege mentality had already begun to take its toll in bureaucratic confidence. In making the case for a permanent career director, Hogarth touched upon his fear that the Arab Bureau risked being sucked into the remotest recesses of the military establishment with "the obvious danger that the work of the Bureau will not be sufficiently detached and evident for its utility to be known outside." This new agency needed a directing champion to stand up for it "first and foremost," lest it "drop out of existence."[59]

2

PROFILE OF A
"BRILLIANT CONSTELLATION"

In the study of any governmental body, scrutiny of members' backgrounds is useful in order to gain insight into their selection and the experiences from which important perspectives were drawn. With the Arab Bureau, however, certain difficulties render this task more complex.

First, the composition of this agency was very fluid, with some members joining merely to carry out a specific assignment or research project before departing for a new unit and locale. So it is debatable whether much esprit d'corps ever coalesced at all, given the transient nature of many involved with the bureau's work. Bureaucratic identity was further clouded by the intimate participation of individuals not officially assigned to it. Officers such as G. S. Symes (Wingate's private secretary at the residency), Robert W. Graves, Wyndham Deedes, and Leonard Woolley from Military Intelligence and the Eastern Mediterranean Special Intelligence Bureau, although officially detached, worked closely with the bureau, especially after Wingate's reorganization in early 1917. This was, of course, a natural outgrowth of a maturing Cairene intelligence network, where information from respective agents was garnered to a single purpose and utilized with a minimum of duplication and friction. The eventual marriage of Military Intelligence with the Arab Bureau and other intelligence bureaus by late 1917 enhanced efficiency and minimized political conflict. However, the various agencies in Egypt had never been very rigid as to personnel or purview. While the new arrangement imparted greater departmental distinction, the artificial boundary separating the Arab Bureau from the nascent Hejaz operations staff was, at best, a blurred one. The example of Alan Dawnay, who was affiliated with both branches, is illustrative.

Circumstances surrounding the bureau's establishment reflected the anomalous position it occupied in the overall British administrative scheme. Clayton soon recognized that if many of its intended functions were to be effectively performed (and adequately disguised), members of the bureau not already affiliated with a military unit would have to be provided a commission. This not only facilitated the inconspicuous movement and activity of bureau officers in military circles, but also served to mask the true nature of their work—especially that of civilians like Hogarth, mustered into the bureau with the rank of naval reserve commander but never officially inducted.

Most of the bureau's company were plucked from intelligence and military units throughout the British services. Hogarth and Gertrude Bell came from Admiralty Intelligence; Clayton, Cornwallis, and Symes from the Sudan; George Lloyd from the Mediterranean Expeditionary Force, which had foundered in the Dardanelles; Alfred Parker and Lawrence from the War Office; A. B. Fforde from India; and, later, Harold Fenton Jacob from Aden. This mélange proved so difficult to finance through departmental solicitation that bureau officers were paid by the department from which they originally hailed, with Egypt assuming the responsibility for housing costs and furnishings and the Exchequer picking up the balance. Hogarth was forced to procure volumes for the bureau's Savoy Hotel library with his own funds. This unseemly haggling, which often arose over the most petty bureau expenses, provides further evidence of just how untimely the concept of a centralized, coordinating intelligence agency was.

Monthly bureau reports offer hints of the specialties into which the unit subdivided. Although the Arab Bureau was too sparingly and mercurially staffed to avert frequent reshufflings in assignments, the monthly record at least affords suggestions regarding the personal interests and proclivities of some officers. Philip Graves and H. Fielding worked with Lawrence, prior to his departure, on propaganda publications, later to be joined by Lieutenant Harry Pirie-Gordon. Captains Lloyd and C.A.G. Mackintosh concentrated on matters of regional finance and trade. Lieutenant L. F. Nalder was stationed as the bureau's liaison contact with the Red Sea Patrol, but would later work on studies of Yemen and Asir. William Ormsby-Gore, following a brief stint as supply officer for the Hejaz, delved into questions about Palestine's economic and agricultural prospects and about Zionism (of which he later became an enthusiastic adherent). Fforde wrote on political and military developments in Yemen and Aden in addition to acting as the Indian government's official representative on the bureau's staff. Osmond Walrond specialized in developments within the Syrian exile community in Cairo. Lieutenant L.W.W. Buxton journeyed to and reported on Abyssinia.

Of course, Hogarth and Cornwallis addressed the more pressing and contentious policy questions as they arose. While both men were called upon occasionally to travel to Arabia or Palestine, Cornwallis more frequently journeyed to the Hejaz to assess the situation firsthand or to act as personal liaison between Cairo and C. E. Wilson's staff of military advisers there. When British relations with the sharif or Emir Feisal became too strained, or a particularly ambiguous policy required personal "explanation" (as did the Sykes-Picot Agreement and the Balfour Declaration), Hogarth would be dispatched. He also traveled intermittently to London to parlay the bureau's perspective on events. But while in Cairo, Hogarth kept the Savoy humming along in its research, dealing directly with High Commissioner McMahon and Oriental Secretary Ronald Storrs, summarizing and evaluating accumulated political and military intelligence, assisting in translation, offering policy input, and generally following Clayton's lead.

Of course, the bureau's roster and duties would change much as the front grew more distant from Cairo. Hogarth, Clayton, Cornwallis, Graves, and Pirie-Gordon eventually expanded the bureau's activities into Palestine with Allenby's army. George Lloyd and Ormsby-Gore would return to London. A very disgruntled Fforde would request transfer out of Cairo. Their replacements, especially in the bureau's latter days, were drawn from Wilson's Arabian contingent and included the likes of W. A. Davenport, Dawnay, and Herbert Garland, who eventually became director.

Of most of the other individuals who served with the Arab Bureau—the officers who worked at the direction of Hogarth, Cornwallis, and Clayton—little or nothing has survived. Indeed, with the notable exceptions of Clayton, Lawrence, Bell, Lloyd, and Parker, no biographies have been written of the bureau's members. But some biographical information does exist in general works concerning its more prominent members (its core, as it were), which is worth noting.

Gilbert Clayton was probably the most influential advocate of the Arab Bureau in the Near East and its chief defender against outside detractors. He was educated at Isle of Wight College and the Royal Military Academy at Woolwich, receiving a commission in the Royal Artillery in 1895. His first overseas post was, aptly, Egypt, where he availed himself of the opportunity to master Arabic before joining Kitchener's expedition up the Nile. After earning several British and Egyptian decorations and being mentioned in dispatches, Clayton became a captain in 1901. One year later, he left the Egyptian artillery for service as a civil administrator in the southern Sudan until repeated malarial attacks forced his return to Cairo. Upon his arrival, Clayton joined the general staff of the Egyptian Army as a deputy assistant to the adjutant general. In 1908, he returned to the Sudan as Wingate's private secretary and was subsequently transferred to the Sudan Government Service. Five years later, Clayton returned once again to Cairo to serve a dual function as liaison between the consul general (Lord Kitchener) and the governor-general of the Sudan (Wingate) and as chief intelligence officer for the Egyptian Army under General Maxwell. For these new responsibilities, Clayton was promoted to colonel. His biographer has termed this position "one of the most important and influential" in the Middle East at the time. Clayton's tie to the governor-general was strong, Robert O. Collins has suggested, as he was "chained to the Sudan service by a jealous, and rather parental Wingate."[1] Indeed, it seems the sirdar was often careful to remind Clayton of this bond in the most unequivocal terms.[2] The attachment was not to be geographically strained until the latter's departure for Palestine as Allenby's chief political officer in early 1918. In the twenties, London once again called on Clayton for help in mediating the dispute in Arabia between King Hussein and Ibn Saud.

Of all the officers involved in the operation of the Arab Bureau, Clayton was probably the most indispensable, for it was he who stood up for the agency's interests during the frequent departmental disputes that arose during the war. What limited success the bureau enjoyed was due to Clayton's adroit management of sensitive relations between Khartoum, the residency, and the Egyptian high command. While it seems doubtful that any individual, however diplomatically gifted, could have successfully bridged the chasm of distrust between Cairo and Delhi, at least Clayton was able to maintain an equilibrium that facilitated bureau activities requiring the cooperation of numerous administrative arms. He also employed this talent in his direction of personalities, with the same notable success. With the collection of strong and individualistic characters who staffed the Arab Bureau, this ability assumed special importance. Lawrence, writing in his own inimitable style, sketches an apt portrait:

> Clayton made the perfect leader for such a band of wild men as we were. He was calm, detached, clear sighted, of unconscious courage in assuming responsibility. He gave an open run to his subordinates. His own views were general, like his knowledge; and he worked by influence rather than by loud direction. It was not easy to descry his influence. He was like water, or permeating oil, creeping silently and insistently through everything. It was not possible to say where Clayton was or was not, and how much really belonged to him. He never visibly led; but his ideas were abreast of those who did: he impressed men by his sobriety, and by a certain quiet and stately moderation of hope. In practical matters he was loose, irregular, untidy, a man with whom independent men could bear.[3]

David George Hogarth was the philosophical and spiritual cynosure of the Arab Bureau, and he exercised profound influence over its development. A prominent archaeologist, he was the preeminent savant on the Middle East to whom the British government turned during the war. As keeper of Oxford's Ashmolean Museum from 1909, and author of numerous books and articles on the ancient Near East, his scholarly credentials were unimpeachable. Hogarth is said to have been an accomplished linguist who mastered French, German, Italian, Greek, Turkish, and Arabic.

Hogarth had a history of contact with Britain's intelligence community prior to World War I. British intelligence had long used academia as a recruiting ground, and in Hogarth they acquired a gem. Here was a man who had worked extensively in Asia Minor, Greece, Crete, and Syria with such renowned scholars as Sir William Ramsey and Sir Arthur Evans. His father was closely acquainted with the noted Professor Palmer, who died in Syria while on an intelligence mission. Hogarth himself was close to Dr. David Margoliouth, chair of Arabic at Oxford and founder of his own philosophical school of Arabists and students. Margoliouth was, in turn, connected to the head of the London School of Oriental Studies, Denison Ross, who became special adviser to the director of Military Intelligence, which had been busy since 1896 evaluating and recruiting likely candidates for intelligence work in the Middle East. Not coincidentally, Hogarth's father was a close friend of the Reverend Henry Thomas Armfield, father-in-law of "Blinker" Hall, the first director of Naval Intelligence.[4] As early as 1911, according to H.V.F. Winstone, Hogarth engaged in clandestine intelligence work for the Admiralty with colleagues Lawrence and Woolley, spying on German engineers at work on a railroad near their archaeological digs at Carchemish in Syria, noting routes, gauges, strengths, and possible weaknesses of the line. Yet the subject of Hogarth's prewar intelligence activities continues to provoke spirited debate. Lawrence's most recent biographer, for instance, claims there is absolutely no evidence of the professor's employment by Naval Intelligence before 1915, beyond the fancy of Winstone's imagination.[5]

By the outbreak of World War I, Hogarth was already personally acquainted with many of the intelligence officers with whom he would work. His abandonment of the secure, cloistered life of an Oxford don for the itinerant life of an intelligence operative is not so difficult to understand, despite the scanty information that survives concerning his private life. The opportunity to travel once again in the East while continuing the scholarly research that was the center of his life must have been alluring. It is also likely that Hogarth had served as a consultant for the War Office for some time before the war, anticipating hostilities with the Ottomans. An overriding patriotism and conservative conviction in the future of the empire (a faith he would eventually forswear) certainly figured prominently in this decision: "[U]nless everyone in the country who had had any special qualification put it at the service of the country, we couldn't get through, and I put mine with one sole object—to beat the Bosche! and keep Britain where she was before the war."[6]

The distinguished career that preceded Hogarth's wartime service was embellished with varied awards and recognition. He was educated at Winchester and his beloved Magdalen College, Oxford, where he became a fellow of the British Academy. For three years he was director of the British School at Athens, after which he embarked on journeys of exploration in Asia Minor and Syria. Hogarth conducted extensive excavations there as well as in Egypt, Cyprus, Crete, and Melos. Among his many published works, the more notable are *A Wandering Scholar in the Levant* (1896), *The Nearer East* (1902), *The Penetration of Arabia* (1904), *The Ancient East* (1914), and *Kings of the Hittites* (1926).

Hogarth's stature in British policymaking circles is difficult to overstate. His counsel carried considerable (although not always irresistible) weight with superiors. But his close identification with Cairo, Clayton, and Wingate worked unquestionably to taint the objectivity of the professor's judgment in the view of many officials in London, Basra, and Delhi. Hogarth's intimate association with and sponsorship of Lawrence also reinforced this image. But to Wingate, who came to rely heavily on Hogarth's advice, the assistance was invaluable: "I cannot speak too highly of Hogarth's work in the Arab Bureau. His detailed knowledge of Arabic, sound judgment and general scholarship, have been of the greatest assistance to us and if, . . . you require expert local advice you cannot do better than send for him."[7] To Lawrence, he was far more: "Not a wild man, but Mentor to all of us was Hogarth, our father confessor, and advisor, who brought us the parallels and lessons of history, and moderation and courage. To the outsiders he was a peacemaker . . . and made us favoured and listened to, for his weighty judgment. He had a delicate sense of value and would present clearly to us the forces hidden behind the lousy rags and festering skins which we knew as Arabs."[8]

T. E. Lawrence remains a difficult figure historically, one whose larger-than-life image obscures hindsight. Certainly, his life and psyche have been meticulously dissected and chronicled in a manner usually reserved for history's elect few. Unfortunately, it would be easy to magnify Lawrence's role in the Arab Bureau beyond what the evidence indicates—a trap into which many historians have carelessly fallen. Still, certain select observations are worth making here.

Lawrence's arrival at Oxford had the fateful result of acquainting him with Hogarth at the Ashmolean. He eventually became the good professor's protégé while matriculating at Jesus College, totally infatuated with the depth of Hogarth's writings and expansive knowledge. Connections that have been drawn between their relationship and Lawrence's desperate want of a father figure seem reasonably well founded.

As an aspiring archaeologist, Lawrence made his first trip to the Middle East in 1909. The following year, the avuncular Hogarth arranged a Magdalen traveling scholarship for him so he could accompany a new

British Museum expedition to the excavations at Carchemish. Here he
worked sporadically for the next three years, first with Hogarth and then
with Woolley, whom he would work with later in Cairo intelligence.

These were formative years for Lawrence. At Carchemish, he acquainted
himself with Arab culture and language—and perfected his uncanny knack
of getting on with the Arabs and eliciting their devotion, which was to prove
so critical to his later success. According to some writers, the Carchemish
experience was also his initiation into intelligence work. While scholars
disagree about this dimension of Lawrence's work in Syria, some have
argued (as stated above) that the archaeological expedition had objectives
other than the study of Hittite civilization. Lawrence's interest in a railroad
span over the Euphrates has drawn particular notice. Yet the evidence that
his curiosity sprang, at this stage, from intelligence work remains conjec-
tural, for he would later dismiss news of the bridge's completion as "of
little military importance."[9] In January 1914, Lawrence worked alongside
Stewart Newcombe on a geographical survey of a portion of the Sinai
peninsula (essentially the Negev) that had been missed by two earlier
British surveys, one completed by the Egyptian government and a second
completed by Lt. (later field marshal) Herbert Kitchener in 1872. The
survey was conducted under the archaeological rubric of the Palestine
Exploration Fund. Lawrence and Newcombe acquired a great deal of vital
cartographic and geographic data for British intelligence before the venture
was terminated by Turkish authorities in early 1914. Lawrence spoke
accurately when he observed, "We are obviously only meant as red
herrings, to give an archeological colour to a political job."[10]

With the outbreak of World War I in August 1914, Lawrence was
frustrated in his enlistment attempts owing to his slight stature. But through
Hogarth's intercession he finally gained a commission with the geographical
section of General Staff Intelligence at the War Office. The officer commanding the section, Col. Coote Hedley, appreciated Lawrence's extensive
knowledge of the Near East (especially Syria) and so recommended him to
the new intelligence section being gathered by Clayton in Cairo. There he
joined other personalities: Aubrey Herbert, Newcombe, Woolley, Philip
Graves, and Lloyd.

Lawrence's duties in this new section, housed at the Savoy Hotel, were
varied and included both mapmaking and interrogation of Turkish prisoners. His work with the Sinai survey also made him the ideal liaison officer
between the survey and Military Intelligence and, later, the Arab Bureau.
He also acted as intermediary between the survey, the Admiralty, and the

Mediterranean Expeditionary Force under Sir Ian Hamilton; he was also responsible for collection of data for maps, records, and reproductions. Finally, Lawrence became the administrative link between GHQ and the Egyptian government press.[11] In his frequent letters to Hogarth he was often disdainful of this new role: "The Egyptian army officer is pathetically ignorant of across the border. Woolley sits all day doing precis and writing windy concealers of truth, for the press. . . . Newcombe runs a gang of most offensive spies . . . I am map officer and write geographical reports, trying to persuade 'em that Syria is not peopled entirely by Turks."[12]

Apparently, Lawrence burst upon the Cairo scene with an enthusiasm and abilities far beyond the expectation of his rank. Appalled by the lack of knowledge and preparation that assaulted him from every quarter, he reveled in the role of pesky maverick—tweaking the staid, upturned nose of officialdom at every opportunity. He and his colleagues proudly dubbed themselves the "intrusives," a cognomen that they also adopted as a telegraphic label. Indeed, Lawrence was able to exert an influence far beyond the limitations of his rank, chiefly because of his relationship with Hogarth and his early success in ingratiating himself with Clayton and Ronald Storrs. Both of these advantages worked to enhance his position as events developed. Hogarth later called him "a moving spirit in the negotiations leading to an Arab Revolt and the organizing of the Arab Bureau."[13] In this same spirit, Hogarth later wrote of Lawrence's "singular persuasiveness" and of the young subaltern's sense of purpose. Even at this early stage, it seems, Lawrence was "pulling the wires."[14]

Once Clayton's official connection with the Egyptian Expeditionary Force was severed in 1916 and Lawrence came under the command of Colonel Holdich (the new director of Military Intelligence), he found his situation intolerable. This was the result of antagonism between Clayton and General Murray's staff, who had insisted he be "driven out." Not to be left languishing behind in what he regarded as an inferior cadre, Lawrence schemed to obtain a transfer to the Arab Bureau, despite the determination of Holdich to keep him at Ismailia. "I interpreted this," Lawrence wrote, "not without some friendly evidence, as a method of keeping me away from the Arab affair." He continued: "I decided that I must escape at once, if ever. A straight request was refused; so I took to strategems. I became, on the telephone . . . quite intolerable to the Staff on the Canal. I took every opportunity to rub into them their comparative ignorance and inefficiency in the department of intelligence (not difficult!) and irritated them yet further by literary airs, correcting Shavian split infinitives and tautologies in their reports."[15] This impudent behavior produced the desired results: in the autumn of 1916 Clayton was notified by the Foreign Office that Lawrence's transfer was impending.

Once his die was cast in the sands of Arabia, Lawrence maintained steady but distant ties with the bureau and would never assume a full-time post there. Reports sent back to the Savoy and infrequent trips to Cairo were his only contacts with that base. Some of those reports, one of his biographers has contended, were doctored at the Arab Bureau before being passed on, so as to embellish Lawrence's reputation (e.g., the capture of Aqaba).[16] Robert Graves later confirmed this, as Lawrence "could not be sure how acceptable the truth would be, or how well his secrets would be kept."[17]

Few officials concerned with the Arab question were neutral about Lawrence. Although generally recognized as extraordinarily able and exceptionally knowledgeable about the Middle East, he did not lack detractors. Those on General Murray's staff were alienated by Lawrence's "cheek." Mesopotamian authorities also grew offended at his high-handed arrogance, revealed during a visit there in the spring of 1916. Even some of Lawrence's compatriots, working with him to effect the Arab Revolt, were unimpressed by his postured élan. Lieutenant Colonel Wilson in Jeddah wrote angrily to Clayton: "Lawrence wants kicking and kicking hard at that, then he would improve. At present I look upon him as a bumptious young ass."[18]

But Lawrence remained an important agent in the field; he enjoyed the confidence of Arabian princes, the fortitude of British pluck, and the borrowed anonymity of the bedouin. These considerable attributes were not unalloyed, however, as his fondness for political gamesmanship often left the indelible impression that the Arab Bureau was an ancillary organ to the pursuit of Lawrentian designs.

Kinahan Cornwallis, an eventual director of the Arab Bureau, devoted himself to its operations. He was born in New York to an American mother and a British father who was a journalist and writer. He was educated at Haileybury and Oxford (University College), where he obtained a second-class degree in jurisprudence and Arabic. Cornwallis's service background had its roots in the Sudan Political Service and in the office of the civil secretary, and he spent four years posted at Kassala. He subsequently became assistant private secretary to the governor-general in Khartoum. In 1912 Cornwallis was borrowed by the Egyptian government for service in its Finance Ministry, eventually becoming a permanent member of the Egyptian civil service. He joined Clayton at GHQ Intelligence in 1914, eventually succeeding Hogarth as director of the Arab Bureau in late 1916. He remained at this post until leaving Cairo to become civil governor of Beirut in 1919 and then moving to the Middle East department of the Foreign Office. In May 1921, Cornwallis was attached to King Feisal in Iraq, where he worked in the Interior Ministry for the next fourteen years. Nominated to be ambassador to Baghdad in 1941, Cornwallis fought a courageous holding action to retain the Habbaniya air base against Axis sympathizers until the arrival of a relief column. Transferred to Cairo in 1946 for work on a commission to negotiate the impending Anglo-Egyptian Treaty, he was compelled by ill health to retire home to England.

Little survives about Cornwallis beyond the official documents that bear his signature and the monthly reports that he submitted from the bureau to the residency.[19] What is clear, however, is that he was the person most responsible for the daily operations of the bureau, the anchor for the accumulated efforts of Clayton and Hogarth, and a primary executor of policy. In this he was undeniably proficient. Indeed, Wingate regarded Cornwallis as "the first of the young proconsuls of the future."[20] Lawrence's appraisal was likewise complimentary and typically incisive: "a man rude to look upon, but apparently forged from one of those incredible metals with a melting point of thousands of degrees. So he could remain for months hotter than other men's white-heat, and yet look cold and hard."[21]

One of the first men selected for the Arab Bureau was Capt. Philip Graves, a journalist in both Cairo and Constantinople before the war. Forty years old when he was recruited by the bureau, Graves had first traveled to Egypt as correspondent for the *Egyptian Gazette* in 1906, where he shared a flat with Storrs. "Besides being an admirable companion and a master of his absorbing craft," noted Storrs, "his esteem for me would have risen to affection if I had been capable of developing from a friend into a news fact."[22] As Constantinople correspondent for the *Times*, he had personally witnessed the Young Turks' overthrow of Sultan Abdul Hamid. Graves was valuable to Hogarth for many reasons. In addition to his connections with Storrs, he was the nephew of Robert W. Graves, former consul general at Salonika and later an important officer in Deedes's special intelligence unit. He was Oxford educated, with a knowledge of both Turkish and Arabic, and possessed a familiarity with the reorganized Ottoman Army far superior to any existing War Office handbook on the subject: "and from him [Graves] and Turkish refugees he [Clayton] was able to compile accurate information on the state of the railways and quantities of artillery, ammunition, and men that the Turks could bring against the Suez Canal."[23]

Following the war, Graves penned a biography of Sir Percy Cox in addition to other works concerning the Middle East. But it was his journalistic expertise that most recommended him to the post at the bureau. Not surprisingly, much of his time there was spent in the propaganda section. Originally, Clayton had planned to pair him with Lawrence (another writer with a flourish), but with the latter's disappearance into the Arabian wilderness chief propaganda duties devolved upon Graves. After a respite in England in 1918, he rejoined the Arab Bureau's Palestine branch as an assistant political officer, where he worked closely with his uncle in Clayton's political mission at Bir Salem. He finished out the war in the Holy Land.

Capt. George Ambrose Lloyd, M.P., another prominent figure often mentioned in connection with the Arab Bureau, had a more patrician background. He was the youngest son of Sampson Samuel Lloyd and Jane Emelia Lloyd, heiress to the Lloyd banking fortune. Educated at Eton and Trinity College, Cambridge (though taking no degree), Lloyd chose the death of his parents as the occasion to embark on a stint of eastern travel. Upon his return, he tried his hand in the family firm but soon grew restless, finally resolving to enter a career of public service. Later he was appointed honorary attaché to Constantinople, where he made the acquaintance of Sykes and Herbert. In 1907 he was named special commissioner to inquire into the future of British trade with Turkey, Mesopotamia, and the Persian Gulf, a region in which he would always retain an enduring imperial interest. Lloyd entered parliament in 1910 as a West Staffordshire Conservative, spending recesses traveling throughout Europe, Africa, and the Near East. He was an unapologetic supporter of military preparedness and the French alliance, and undertook rudimentary officer's training at Woolwich before joining the Warwickshire Yeomanry in August 1914. His war service led him to the Dardanelles as a general staff intelligence officer, and then to a fact-finding mission to Basra. Shortly afterward he was dispatched on an investigative mission to the Hejaz and assigned briefly to the staff of the Arab Bureau. Lloyd was therefore well acquainted with the economics and politics of Anatolia and Mesopotamia. He was less conversant with Arabia and Syria. While he possessed considerable knowledge of the Turkish language, he spoke no Arabic.[24] His chief value lay in his extensive familiarity with the intricacies of economics, trade, and finance, especially relating to imperial trade routes in the Near East. He was a staunch proponent of the "all red overland route to India."[25] In many ways, Lloyd was philosophically different from the bureau as a whole. He was very Europocentric in his strategic thinking and a firm believer in the necessity of the Anglo-French entente, suspicious of any policy that threatened to disrupt the alliance: "Europe is the *main main* show. Don't introduce into that already utter struggle, unless you are forced to, any new elements that could weaken us there . . . by causing friction between ourselves and France. . . . Syria is the one question that might—is it worth it?"[26] While his stay in Egypt was interrupted, Lloyd remained in contact with Hogarth and Clayton during his absences. His Francophile sentiments underwent some erosion as a result. Lloyd later became governor of Bombay Presidency and in 1925 succeeded Allenby as high commissioner of Egypt. He held this post until stormy relations with the Foreign Office prompted his resignation two years later. Back in Britain, he participated in numerous patriotic associations such as the Navy League and the Empire Economic Union. Eventually elevated to a peerage, as Baron Lloyd of Dolobran, Lloyd was appointed leader of the House of Lords shortly before his death in 1941.

The officer chosen in February 1916 to represent the government of India at the Savoy in Cairo was one Alfred Brownlow Fforde, a member of the Indian civil service and former magistrate in the United Provinces. Although his initial reception at the Arab Bureau was cordial enough ("They are all good fellows here") and Cairo had communicated that it was entirely satisfied with the choice, the new member was well aware of the friction that marred the Cairo-Delhi relationship.[27] Dissatisfaction with Fforde surfaced shortly after his arrival. "You may be interested to know," he remarked to Hirtzel, "that I am not the man wanted by the High Commissioner."[28] Fforde sensed that McMahon (or, more particularly, Hogarth) would have preferred an officer with some Arabian experience— and the high commissioner was somewhat indiscreet about that preference. An irritated Hirtzel pointed out that Sykes himself had approved the appointment and that, in any case, an officer was needed who was sensitive to Indian conditions and needs, rather than some dreamy scholar of Arabia. Besides, Hirtzel noted, "The Indian Representative in the Bureau was appointed not to please Sir H. McMahon but to please the G.[overnment] of I.[ndia]."[29] Hirtzel suspected that McMahon was conniving behind the scenes to replace Fforde with a more fraternal substitute and so tried to stir the India Office to action. But Thomas Holderness, permanent India Office under secretary, convinced that the under secretary was overreacting to a private letter, wrote soothingly that no such change could be contemplated officially without prior notification. Hirtzel was not so sure: "I do not press it. But the reason why I suggested it was the hint that the thing was to be arranged privately. I do not feel certain that we shall hear of any change until it is accomplished fact."[30]

So before long, Fforde was made to feel uncomfortable in the company of the high commissioner and his new Arab Bureau. By the early summer of 1916, Cairo was already requesting his replacement by Harold Fenton Jacob, an old Aden hand. While A. H. Grant of the Indian Political Department responded approvingly to Hogarth on this matter, Hirtzel continued to object. This proposal, he complained, seemed the result of the tactless pressure intimated to earlier by Fforde. Besides, he felt Jacob had been "isolated too long" and had forgotten such peculiarly Indian priorities as concern over Indian Muslim opinion.[31]

The remainder of the war must have been an unfulfilling period for Fforde. Much of his time was taken up with writing to his superiors to request leave and haggling over discrepancies in his pay. Jacob's departure from Aden was long delayed, as India had suddenly found him indispensable. Fforde applied for private leave in September 1917 and was finally replaced by Jacob some time thereafter. India's first representative received a generous (if not heartfelt) commendation for his work from McMahon shortly before the latter's departure from Cairo, declaring that Fforde "has been most useful throughout."[32]

Some of the members of the Arab Bureau must remain obscure footnotes to a tangled tale. These were the officers who labored on projects drawn from the fertile minds of Hogarth, Cornwallis, Clayton, et al. These men laid the tedious groundwork from which superiors compiled voluminous analyses and summaries for British policymakers, but they left few traces—signatures affixed to reports or initialed margins—to link them to a particular sphere of investigation or policy recommendation. Secondary sources can offer only tantalizing glimpses into the versatility of this group. There was the barrister H. Fielding; Alfred Guillaume, later a renowned Arabic and Hebrew scholar; Osmond Walrond, Kitchener's former assistant; Harry Pirie-Gordon, archaeologist and correspondent for the *Times*; and numerous others who remain nondescript—Groves, Wordie, Gerrard, Cadogan, Buxton, Macmichael, Mackintosh, and Macindoe—men gathered from a dozen or more different military units to collectively expedite and transform British policy toward the Arabs.

As H.V.F. Winstone has observed, these men were products of the English public school, weaned on the gospel of empire. As one might suspect, most leaned toward Toryism—being "of the Milner and John Buchan brand, devotees of the Round Table, somewhat Francophobe and decidedly clever."[33] Perhaps more bitterly than any other writer, Winstone disparages the activities of the British intelligence community in Cairo and, by imputation, the Arab Bureau, which was spawned by it. He has referred caustically to "the antics in Cairo . . . which were to result in high-level political and military dissension in war, in the making of illegitimate promises, and the creation of a nation-state which would plague mankind for ever after."[34] In one fell swoop, this author lays the collective sins of British politicians and diplomats at the feet of this comparatively tiny and putatively sinister company of men. Of the men themselves, Winstone avers, "Never before or since has there been so tragi-comic or on occasions, so farcical an episode in the recorded history of war. But these were not ordinary soldiers. In the main they were civilians dressed in uniform, usually ill-fitting and ragtag."[35] Despite the bureau's many critics, it remains difficult to quarrel with Gertrude Bell's use of the appellation "brilliant constellation" to describe this remarkable group.[36]

In late 1917, Hogarth penned a few lines of doggerel to characterize the personalities of those with whom he worked at the Arab Bureau. While the original prose differs somewhat from the version later reproduced by Storrs, the eccentricity of the group is conveyed by both:

> Do you know the Arab Bureau?
> asked Hogarth; and answered:
>> Clayton stability,
>> Symes versatility,
>> Cornwallis is practical,
>> Dawnay syntactical,
>> Mackintosh havers,
>> And Fielding palavers,
>> Macindoe easy,
>> And Wordie not breezy;
> Lawrence licentiate to dream and to dare
> And yours very faithfully, bon a tout faire.[37]

3

GROWING PAINS

The Hajj, Rabegh,
and Monsieur Bremond

In June 1916 Sharif Hussein of Mecca raised the standard of revolt. In the frenetic weeks preceding this event the Arab Bureau was busy plumbing the depths of scholarly arcana for the most basic anthropological and geographic information about the Turkish territories. At the time, the British were alarmingly ignorant with respect to geographic and political conditions in the Arabian peninsula. Few Europeans had even glimpsed the fastnesses of this desert wilderness. Thus, with Hussein's seizure of portions of the Hejaz coast, a golden opportunity beckoned for the British to gain firsthand experience. To this end, agents were dispatched to the coast both to monitor the status of the revolt and to funnel back data to be digested and compiled at the Savoy. Cornwallis was posted to Jeddah, and Lt. Col. Alfred Parker to the town of Rabegh. This deployment was no simple task, since the Arabs were justifiably suspicious and forbade British officers from investigating inland beyond their bases on the coast. Ultimately, however, as the Sharifian government came to appreciate the need for qualified instructors, such barriers were skirted. An extraordinary cadre of British demolitions and weapons experts was gathered, and they proved invaluable in sustaining bedouin forces in the field and harassing the Turkish railway to Medina.

However, the relationship of this group to the Arab Bureau was not clearly defined at first. Lawrence, for instance, was deputed to the bureau following his return from Arabia in the autumn of 1916. Capt. Herbert Garland, who led many demolition forays against the Hejaz railway, replaced Cornwallis as the bureau's director after the armistice. Parker, who supervised British liaison in Rabegh, continued to report primarily to the Arab Bureau—despite the protests of Lieutenant Colonel C. E. Wilson, acting British agent at Jeddah and Britain's official representative to the sharif's government, who commanded the unit of advisers. Wilson was a patient and conscientious if somewhat naive figure, who devoted himself to the sharif's cause as if it were devoid of any dark geopolitical underpinnings. One contemporary who worked closely with Wilson described him as a "dapper, soldierly little figure" who "looked tired, like a man grappling ceaselessly with insoluble problems. Indeed, he had a thankless task which he employed with unfailing good humor."[1] While McMahon exercised control over political aspects of the Arab Revolt, he usually communicated with the sharif and members of his government through Wilson. Yet the British agent (as previous governor of the Sudan's Red Sea province) came officially under Wingate's command, despite the sirdar's refusal to assume overall military supervision. While this became the source of considerable confusion, reports from this Arabian advisory group eventually reached the bureau to be rendered down in that agency's summaries.

While not completely unanticipated at the Savoy, the outbreak of the revolt caught many off-guard. Earlier that month, Storrs and Cornwallis journeyed to the Hejaz to confer with the sharif but were forced to settle for inconsequential talks with his youngest son, Zeid. Cornwallis remained for a time at Jeddah, whence he reported the new Sharifian government "in a state of chaos."[2] Hogarth dubbed the rising ill timed and potentially ill fated: "The revolt was genuine and inevitable but about to be undertaken upon inadequate preparation, in ignorance of modern warfare, and with little idea of the obligation which its success would impose on the Sherifial family . . . too much has been left to the last moment and to luck . . . it is hard to see how any sort of order can quickly come out of the chaos which will ensure their success."[3] The bureau's director later expanded on this admonition, circulating a note that stressed the probable consequences of failure. Britain risked excoriation in the Muslim world for cynically exploiting Islam for sinister purposes and might be pilloried in the end as "a faithless friend and a feeble enemy." British prestige in the region, Hogarth warned, would suffer grave damage as a result.[4]

The more the bureau acquainted itself with the state of affairs in Arabia, the less sanguine it became. Cornwallis reported the Hejaz in a state of confusion, with "no one who has any idea of organisation" and a political atmosphere riven with intrigue.[5] The fact that the bureau did not quite trust the sharif or his aides is evidenced by the breaking of the "secret code" used between the sharif and his Cairo liaison, Mohammad al-Faruqi. Thereafter, regular summaries of such correspondence as well as material gleaned from covert surveillance were sent to Wingate in Khartoum.[6]

The incessant wrangling among the various departments involved left the question of which branch should help Hussein in abeyance. After White-hall's rebuff, Murray washed his hands of the Hejaz. Wingate refused to assume overall military command unless awarded sweeping *political* authority as well. McMahon simply lacked the expertise to manage affairs in the absence of sufficient power to bring the various departments into line. Consequently, responsibility for staff functions of supply, ordnance, and transport connected with Arab Revolt devolved to the Arab Bureau. These duties were outside its province and sorely tested the mettle of an already overworked and understaffed group. Not only did intelligence and propaganda activities suffer, but the supply problem in the Hejaz grew ever worse.

Events moved ahead swiftly. Mecca surrendered to its nominal keeper on 15 June, Jeddah on the sixth, and, in rapid succession, Rabegh, Lith, Taif, and Yenbo. But despite these initial successes, the sharif's momentum was largely spent by autumn. Medina and its railroad supply line continued to hold out, while the British pipeline to the bedouin armies frequently turned up empty. Required munitions, monies, and sundry supplies simply were not collected and dispatched with any regularity. Clayton's departure for London in the early summer further aggravated the situation, as Cairo's intelligence chief had taken responsibility for fulfilling all such requests from the Hejaz. In his absence, confusion reigned as GHQ was suddenly deluged with entreaties from "various sources."[7] Besides being called upon to screen such requests in advance, the bureau arranged for transport from

Egypt to the Hejaz ports. Acknowledging the developing wrangle in Cairo, Hogarth conceded that the bureau was ill prepared to cope with these new demands and cited obstruction from GHQ as a contributing factor: "The departure of Clayton at a very inopportune moment, and certain difficulties between authorities here which became more strident as soon as he was gone, has caused delay in arriving at this obvious settlement. The C in C [Murray] seems never to have realised Clayton's position in regard to you and by certain action, he temporarily threw out of gear the whole machinery of our communication with you."[8]

In a move guaranteed to heighten tension further, Wingate stepped up his own campaign for control of British operations in Arabia. By means of frequent transmissions to his superiors, the sirdar succeeded in gradually undermining support for McMahon while evading the high commissioner's protests against the steady erosion of his authority. By midsummer, Wingate was complaining to his superiors in London that despite his own advocacy of centralized control, "very opposite views are held by some authorities and I fear that is the source of trouble at the present moment in regard to the Hedjaz."[9]

Wingate was keenly interested in Arabia and the future of British fortunes there. The sirdar had fixed on the same strategic imperatives that had for so long guided the hands of British policymakers of the old Egyptian school. While often frantic in his efforts to elicit support for Hussein's rebellion, Wingate was unsympathetic to what he regarded as illusory Arab aspirations. Therefore he was often disingenuous in his dealings with the sharif. He saw the revolt as an opportunity, both to neutralize an important potential source of Turkish support and to inscribe on a palimpsest a new political order—a pan-Arabian union under the protection of and dependent upon Great Britain. This proposed Arab confederation he compared to the greater Bulgaria that Russia had attempted to fashion in the preceding century at the expense of the Ottoman Empire. Indian apprehension over pan-Islamic revivalism he regarded as baseless. Britain, after all, was already experienced in the sustenance of client states saddled with sufficient safeguards to preclude evolution into the menace that the Indian government seemed to fear. Wingate was no more enthusiastic than the viceroy to promote the growth of Arab nationalism; indeed, he disdained the concept. But with the war in Europe locked in bloody stalemate, the aftershocks of the Dardanelles debacle still lingering, and the advance of the Indian Army stymied before Kut, the prospect of a clarion call to jihad from a replacement sharif in Mecca

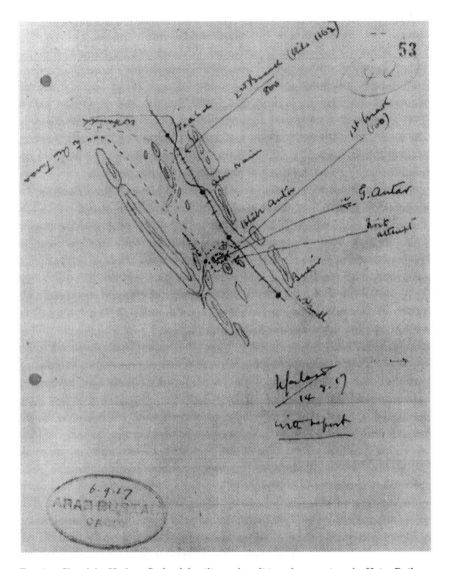

FIG. 3. Sketch by Herbert Garland detailing a demolitions foray against the Hejaz Railway. Complaining that the local Arabs (the Ageyl) were "extremely difficult to manage," Garland confessed that "it is a mistake to suppose that the British officer does control them." (from the Arab Bureau files)

loomed large. This revolt by the incumbent Keeper of the Holy Cities would preempt such a calamity. Throughout Wingate's correspondence during 1916, one theme recurs with unmistakable emphasis: the urgent need for quick action. As long as the Hussein-McMahon Correspondence conveniently provided the groundwork, the sirdar saw no need for further hesitation or restraint—territorial squabbles with the French notwithstanding. The sharif's revolt should be given whatever support was required to ensure success. Whatever additional pledges might prove necessary along the way might be justified in the name of expediency. Of course Delhi would howl, but later they would be made to understand. While rebutting charges that he actually sought a consolidated Arab kingdom, the sirdar explained: "but it has suited me, as I believe it has suited all of us, to give the leaders of the Arab Movement this impression and we are sufficiently covered by the correspondence which has taken place to show that we are acting in good faith with the Arabs as far as we have gone—It may be difficult to make either the Foreign Office or the Indian Government appreciate the rather subtle distinction, but I think we ought to be given credit of a certain amount of ordinary common sense and prescience to which a prolonged residence in these countries entitles us."[10] Wingate was convinced of the efficacy of this strategy and grew infuriated over the muddle in Cairo, for fear the sharif's revolt might die on the vine. Repeatedly bemoaning confusion and intrigue in Cairo, he complained that "there is too much anxiety on the part of various people concerned to have a finger in the pie for personal motives."[11] To his executive officer in the Sudan, Sir Lee Stack, the sirdar was even more blunt, regretting the apparent accession of "all sorts of Dicks, Toms, and Harries, none of whom understand much about what they are dealing with."[12]

So the very internecine squabbles that chronically plagued the British command structure continued to hamstring the Arab Bureau. Not only was it now compelled by force of circumstance to perform functions far beyond the scope of its original design, but, as Clayton's fief, it was caught up in the tripartite struggle between Wingate, the residency, and the Egyptian high command.

The extent to which Wingate directly influenced Clayton's performance is unclear. In many instances, the sirdar issued scarcely veiled directives to the bureau that transgressed the bounds of administrative propriety. But Clayton's communications to Khartoum were often similarly risky. In his private notes, Clayton was often careful to urge discretion; "I should get into very hot water," he warned, "if it were known that I had sent them to anyone else." To Cairo's intelligence chief, Murray's lack of cooperation was tantamount to negligence and clearly calculated to make McMahon pay dearly for his untoward ambition. While Clayton was for the most part sympathetic to the problems of the high commissioner, he remained skeptical of Sir Henry's capacity to take charge as he should. Although hopeful that Colonel Wilson's impending arrival from Jeddah would light a fire under him, misgivings persisted. "Entre nous," he confided to Wingate, "he does not drive the F[oreign] O[ffice] hard enough."[13]

Hogarth's position at this juncture is more difficult to pin down. He also was sympathetic toward McMahon and the crisis he faced. It is clear that he regretted Whitehall's ungenerous dismissal of the high commissioner later that year. He fully expected McMahon's replacement (Wingate) to be followed to Cairo by a retinue of Sudanese officials, and this he found disquieting. He was also apprehensive because Wingate was, as yet, an unknown quantity to him: "The change of High Commissioner will not make it any easier for me to leave till the new man has been some time in the saddle. I've known him on and off for . . . years, but what he will really be like in international affairs I don't know. It will depend very much on who runs him. He'll bring some of his own people along at the first, and knowing what they are like, I expect a battle royal."[14] Yet the bureau's director did not oppose the idea of Wingate assuming overall supervision of Hejaz affairs. Indeed, shortly after the outbreak of revolt on the peninsula, Hogarth wrote to him urging that unified control be swiftly implemented.[15] Such sentiments are not necessarily incompatible. Hogarth may well have desired the greater organization and efficiency that unified command would bestow while keeping Wingate at a distance. He may have feared that the sirdar would be more difficult to "run" than McMahon. In any event, once the change took place in Cairo, Hogarth adjusted quickly and was later often found at Wingate's elbow, advising on Arab policy.

To the British agent at Jeddah, General Murray was clearly the monkey on the back of the nascent revolt. Wilson's numerous letters to Khartoum complained bitterly to Wingate about the critical shortage of provisions and munitions: "it is General Murray who is the stumbling block and the cause of the whole trouble, of that I have not a doubt and if he played the game all would even now be well. I only hope to heaven that his conduct is eventually fully disclosed."[16] But Wilson found little sympathy during his visit to the residency in the autumn of 1916, where he received a blistering reprimand from McMahon for problems in the Hejaz. Clayton (who was present) reported to Wingate that the high commissioner's callous upbraiding of "the wretched Wilson" was "very unjustifiable and most unfair" and conducted in a very "ill-considered and unmilitary way." Once again, the specter of Murray hovered over Clayton's version of the encounter: "It was most unfair and seemed pretty evident that GHQ had got up the whole thing with a view to evading any criticism as to delay in meeting the Sherif's demands and in supporting him, which might hereafter arise."[17] Clayton was confident, however, that the position of the Arab Bureau was secure despite the logistical confusion, and that "what has gone from here has been due to their efforts." Again he begged Wingate's discretion, as "mischief untold" would result from an untimely revelation of his breach of confidence.[18]

It is difficult to overstate the significance of the Khartoum connection. Despite official secrecy, the deepest recesses of the residency were accessible to Clayton and, by inference, to the sirdar. The correspondence confirms this speculation. It became clear to all that McMahon was under a great deal of pressure from the Foreign Office. The latitude he had enjoyed in his milestone correspondence with Sharif Hussein had come under serious attack in London; this goes far to explain his persistent inability to bring contending factions into line. As the dog days of summer retreated before autumn around Whitehall, the high commissioner grew daily more expendable. "Sorry for Sir H. McM," Hogarth would later write, "he has never had a fair chance."[19]

Wingate's star was on the ascendant, rising from the enormity of the Sudan. Effective military control was already his, manifested in Wilson and the advisers under him, while the Arab Bureau (under Clayton's direction) handled intelligence and propaganda from Cairo and supply from Suez. GHQ bristled with jealousy, and the residency was lapsing into redundancy. As the sharif's fortunes began to wane, Wingate awaited the call to assume direction of the campaign for which he had long been preparing.

The unfortunate conjunction of this supervisory disarray and a rapid deterioration of the Hejaz military situation brought the Arab Revolt to the brink of disaster in late 1916. As early as July, warning signs had begun to temper the elation attending the revolt's initial successes. Lawrence warned in a widely circulated memo that a Turkish attempt to recapture Mecca was imminent and recommended the immediate British reinforcement of Feisal at the port of Rabegh.

Rabegh was strategically situated along the main road from Medina to Mecca that the Turks would be most likely to follow in the event of a sortie. It also possessed the only readily available water source along the route. Emir Feisal's bedouin force garrisoned the town amid surrounding tribes that were only marginally sympathetic to Hussein's rebellion. Lawrence suggested the dispatch of a single, "preferably Mohammedan" infantry brigade to shore up Feisal's sagging morale. Although professing an appreciation of the military and political complications such a move might cause, Lawrence offered a Hobson's choice: "It is a matter for H.M.G. to decide . . . whether this would not be preferable to the very serious situation which might result from the total collapse of the Arab Movement."[20]

This talk of the movement's "collapse" became all too frequent during the latter months of 1916—so much so that Wingate offered contingency plans to McMahon in the event of such a disaster.[21] Yet Lawrence's proposed remedy sparked such debate that the practical effect on decision-making with regard to Rabegh was stifling.

The Rabegh crisis began at a time when the Arab Bureau was groaning under colossal administrative burdens and desperate staff shortages, especially after Hogarth's departure in August. For some months, he had been pushing for the appointment of a permanent director, for he preferred to free-lance and led far too itinerant an existence during the war to keep the bureau functioning as an integral unit. Besides, the professor was no administrator, preferring instead to immerse himself in the research to which he was so eminently suited. Alfred Parker, Lord Kitchener's nephew and a former governor of Sinai, was seriously considered, as was Lieutenant Harold Fenton Jacob, a noted field officer in Aden. In the end, the responsibility devolved (rather by default) upon Hogarth's younger deputy, Kinahan Cornwallis, a man whom the Foreign Office believed was "not equipped with sufficient guns for the part."[22] Cornwallis, however, while proving equal to the task, complained bitterly to Wingate that the Arab Bureau was hopelessly understaffed. This infuriated the sirdar: "and this is to my mind incomprehensible when they have such an enormous number of experienced men to draw on in Egypt—there is no doubt there is something very wrong in our organisation, or want of it."[23] By late September, the Arab Bureau's situation had become critical. Clayton appreciated Hogarth's temporary return to assist and was hopeful that important research left unfinished in the wake of immediate pressures and reduced staff might now be continued. Procuring an extra officer for political work, he complained, "is like drawing a tooth."[24]

In September, Parker was dispatched by the bureau to Rabegh as a political officer. Aside from keeping Cairo abreast of Turkish movements in the vicinity of the port, his task was to establish a badly needed intelligence network. His initial reports were not sanguine, warning that, "If Turks advance and attack Rabegh under present conditions, they are likely to be successful."[25] Parker became an ardent advocate of reinforcement, but only if in sufficient force to ensure success and only with the Arabs' knowledge and consent. His appraisal of the bedouin army was as discouraging as his military prognostications: "Should [the Turks] advance in force it is possible that they will take Rabegh, and it is conceivable that the event of Rabegh falling Arab opposition to the Turks may entirely collapse."[26]

The strategy of reinforcement, while originating (oddly enough) with Murray, enjoyed the added support of Col. Edouard Bremond, commander of the French military mission in the Hejaz, and the mercurial Wingate. The new high commissioner, given less chaotic circumstances, probably would not have agreed, for it put him at odds with his principal advisers at the Arab Bureau. But Arab morale was crumbling under the threat of a Turkish thrust and the unnerving attacks of a few enemy aircraft. While a diversionary attack on the Hejaz railroad north of Medina by Abdullah's bedouin provided some relief, there remained the question of how to secure that port in the interim and whether or not to land British troops to do it. Initially, the sharif was not opposed to the suggestion, perhaps deeming this measure the lesser of two evils. His receptiveness touched off immediate debate in Cairo and Arabia as to whether the proposed contingent should be British or Muslim in composition.

Several members of the Arab Bureau cautioned against the use of British troops so close to Islam's holiest shrines. Aside from GHQ's protests that no troops were readily available for the duty, there was the expected Indian anxiety over the consequences that such a decision would provoke. But other considerations intruded as well. George Lloyd warned that the introduction of Christian troops into the Hejaz would destroy Hussein's credibility with local tribes, playing into the hands of enemy propagandists and spawning large-scale defections.[27] William Ormsby-Gore agreed, cautioning that if London approved the introduction of British forces into Rabegh, aside from evoking Indian revulsion and irreparably damaging Hussein's aspirations to the caliphate, "we must be under no delusion as to the consequences either in India or in the Hejaz itself and upon the British troops, once landed, will fall the burden of maintaining the Sherif now and possibly hereafter."[28] Wilson at Jeddah shared this view—as did Lawrence, converted upon his return from Arabia in October. The bedouin would react hysterically, he now insisted, and "scatter to their tents again, as soon as they heard of the landing of foreigners in force."[29] Moreover, Lawrence argued, the Turks could not capture Mecca without fatally endangering their communications. Short of a substantial reinforcement of their forces at Medina or an extensive blockhouse system strung out along the way, such a campaign would likely court disaster.[30]

Hogarth also advised against any such move. And like others at the bureau, his reasons derived from expediency, fear of adverse political reaction, and the numerous practical objections to a landing. First of all, it would render ludicrous an earlier Indian government proclamation renouncing direct military intervention in the vicinity of the holy cities, and place Delhi in "an invidious position." Enemy propaganda that cast suspicion on Britain's territorial motives would probably erase any chance that the vacillating and powerful Harb confederation would join the sharif's movement. Further, citing the travel accounts of the great Sir Richard Burton, Hogarth belittled the strategic importance of Rabegh itself and pointed to the existence of less-traveled but nonetheless usable mountain routes skirting the port that the Turks could always employ. Besides, he insisted, Mecca was not the psychological cynosure to Muslims as was so prevalently assumed. With or without it, the revolt would carry on, while most of the Islamic world remained disinterestedly quiescent. Put simply, the advantages that such a landing would confer were not "commensurate with its disadvantages." Proceeding in the practical vein, Hogarth contended, "I hold that some day the inviolability of Mecca and the Hejaz must be signally infringed in order to purge Islam of its medievalism, and neutralise for ever its potentiality of being an armed conspiracy. But it is not at this moment that we can afford to initiate such a change by affronting the Moslem world."[31] To writers swept up in the perception of the Arab Bureau as a coterie of romantics promoting the fortunes of Arab nationalism, this passage must surely give pause. Hogarth's arguments against a landing at Rabegh stemmed from his concern for the Arab Revolt and the necessity of its continuance. Yet his cool disdain of Muslim feelings about the holy cities reflected a measure of contempt rather than sensitivity toward Britain's Arab allies.

India's representative to the bureau's staff was predictably pessimistic in his reaction to the proposal, stressing that a landing would represent a crossing of the Rubicon in Arabia. He felt the line between indirect and direct intervention would be irrevocably crossed and popularly interpreted as "the next step towards control over the Holy Land." If the gamble were successful and the Arab Revolt survived the shock, India could do nothing but go along with it: "But a reverse to British arms in the Holy Land would be disastrous. Far better risk the collapse of the revolt than risk that."[32]

Yet the plan to safeguard Rabegh had its proponents, whose arguments carried the added weight of strategic immediacy and personal observation. Parker dismissed political arguments opposed to a landing as "unconvincing." The sharif already had accepted Christian gold and arms in any case, and if the temporary nature of the occupation plan were adhered to, British withdrawal would provide "ample refutation of the suggestion that the British wish to establish themselves and finally take possession of the Arab holy countries."[33] The argument that a British presence at Rabegh would destroy Arab morale was also specious, he insisted: "It is a delightful theory and will give pleasure to any Arab enthusiast but it does not bear clear reasoning and cold fact."[34] Parker worried that the interminable vacillation that dogged London's handling of the Rabegh question might tempt a Turkish coup de main there and so erase the gains of summer. Either the port should be strengthened by "foreign troops," or the enemy's attention should be diverted immediately toward their rail lifeline. Failure to act decisively, he warned, risked a "debacle of the Arab cause," adding: "What may possibly hold the Turks back from advancing on Rabegh is inability to grasp that we can be so foolish as to let them take it if they like."[35]

Another powerful supporter of a landing was Wingate, who was determined to prevent any lapse of Sharifian control over Mecca. He dismissed the probable deterrent effect of Muslim troops, since Indian participation had been all but ruled out. But one suspects he was loath to accept responsibility for the proposed venture, for he himself restricted troop availability by insisting that the Sudan had none to spare and would release a contingent only if suitable English replacements were transferred there (a request that he knew full well to be impossible). Once the sharif had decided to allow British troops into the Hejaz, the sirdar grew suspicious. Wingate told Wilson that the turnabout was the result of the unwise and pernicious counsel of pro-Turkish religious elements bent on leading Hussein down the path of destruction.[36] Shortly after his arrival in Cairo as the new high commissioner, Wingate wired to Whitehall: "I fully appreciate the political objections to the despatch of Christian troops to the Hedjaz, but I consider they are secondary importance to the risks involved by the collapse of the Arab revolt."[37] It is interesting to note that this message was not relayed to India, at the behest of the new high commissioner.

Rabegh ultimately received reinforcement in the form of an Egyptian artillery brigade and a small squadron of aircraft, dispatched in November. The long-awaited Turkish thrust never materialized beyond an unnerving but inconsequential sortie. And while the bedouin did not get on well with the Egyptians, the aircraft and artillery did impart a measure of psychological security.

Despite the official decision not to land British troops at Rabegh, reinforcements were sent to Suez and held at the ready until the Anglo-Arab seizure of Wejh in early January, when increased attacks by Abdullah along the Hejaz railway obviated the need for them. But the crisis dramatically illustrated the grave consequences of dual control over Hejaz military operations. Exercising its authority (or lack of it) through the residency, the Foreign Office injected itself directly into the Rabegh debate. As Whitehall maintained itself as the sole channel for the issuance of such decisions, indecision reigned. Parker's anomalous position is also revealing. Prior to his departure for Cairo, Wingate stood in official command of European advisers. But his authority over Rabegh's political officer seems to have been less certain, for Parker reported first and foremost to the Arab Bureau. Wilson complained to Wingate that Parker "knows you are in charge of operations and yet always wires to Arbur [Arab Bureau's telegraphic name] or Cornwallis."[38] Sykes observed that the proper authorities should have "taken the matter in hand in a businesslike way," and attacked one residency cable in particular:

> In it Sir Henry McMahon tells Lord Grey that the Sirdar has told him (Sir Henry McMahon) that he (the Sirdar) proposed to tell Colonel Wilson to tell the Sherif certain things, but that he (Sir Henry McMahon) had made certain alterations in the text of the message which the Sirdar desires Colonel Wilson to convey to the Sherif and that the Sudan concurs in the amendments.
>
> It is very lucky for us that for the moment nothing is happening in Arabia that requires either thought, decision or action, since, if there can be thirty telegrams a week about nothing, it would require a nice collation to figure out how many telegrams would be neces- sary if something urgent were afoot. . . . This is contrary to all

sense and experience. It is urged with all seriousness and earnest-
ness that the moment has come to set matters right once and for all
in regard to Arabian policy and management.[39]

But despite the muddle, Hogarth's mood was upbeat. Rabegh was safe,
and the revolt still alive. With Wingate's arrival, Cairo would truly be the
nerve center of Hussein's revolt. Having been unprepared for the hasty
manner in which the sharif had begun his insurrection, the professor was
pleasantly surprised at its longevity: "All round, however, the coast is
clearing and my own particular little war is going quite well in its own
strange way. It is the Asian Mystery that it has lived till now! December
will make six months and I hardly dared to give it three."[40] The enemy
must have appreciated the contribution of Hogarth and his colleagues at
the Arab Bureau to sustaining Hussein's resistance, for in November the
Savoy Hotel was ineffectually bombed by German aircraft.

A more immediate problem arose with the impending pilgrimage, or hajj.
Once the blockade of the Hejaz coast had been imposed, the event was
severely curtailed—at least until the sharif's revolt succeeded in capturing
and securing sufficient territory to permit its commencement. Predictably,
this stirred rumblings in Delhi, where it was feared Cairo had handed
Indian Muslims more ammunition with which to attack the Raj. The viceroy
was adamant in insisting that "we have in the Haj the most natural and
effective agency for bringing public opinion over to the side of the Sherif—
that is if they return without grievances."[41] The Arab Bureau was in general
agreement with this assessment. But Cornwallis, on assignment in Jeddah,
warned that the preparations necessary for a successful pilgrimage were
simply not being taken. Citing the risk of a debacle to Sharifian prestige
and British fortunes in the Arab world generally, he admonished, "the
Arabs leave much to Allah, and must be saved from themselves."[42]

Aside from the logistical and political headaches that were bound to
attend a wartime hajj, there was the additional problem of a policy
established by British officials restricting pilgrim traffic to Arabia from
Egypt and the Sudan. These restrictions stemmed from apprehension over
the possibility of infiltration by enemy agents during the exchange of such
large numbers of people and of possible recruitment by the Turks of
pilgrims, for work as agents in British territories. In the Sudan, Wingate
had already subjected pilgrims to "moral disinfection" at specified depots
upon their return from Arabia. Clayton had long been critical of formal

proscriptions as productive only to enemy propagandists, preferring the employment of somber dissuasion (coupled with Wingate's quarantine system) to restrict the flow of the faithful to Mecca. Cornwallis agreed, arguing in the summer of 1916 that such limits to access be lifted. He insisted that if a pilgrimage were attempted, it must be one worthy of the name for any enhancement of the sharif's prestige to result.[43] This end was desirable from a much wider perspective than that of Arabia—it had possible positive ramifications in India as well. Consonant with this, the Arab Bureau opposed the Egyptian government's perennial solicitation of a *fatwa* from the Egyptian mufti as a means of discouraging pilgrim traffic. If limits had to be imposed, Clayton and his colleagues preferred to blame them on the transportation shortage. But Ronald Graham at the Foreign Office objected to these suggestions. Such a course, he stressed, would only bring down calumny on the Egyptian authorities for being unable to provide adequate transport. As for the *fatwa*, Graham argued that it provided a necessary salve for the Muslim conscience and was thus effective in inducing Egyptians to remain contentedly at home. "The Arab Bureau," complained Graham, "in its anxiety to help the Cherif, appears to me to ignore the situation in Egypt on this pilgrimage question, and I look upon certain of the Bureau's suggestions with serious misgivings."[44] The onus for preparing contingency plans to this purpose devolved, however, upon that same Arab Bureau.

Further compounding difficulties in the fall of 1916 were Delhi's misgivings about the wisdom of entrusting Indian pilgrims to the care of the fledging Sharifian government. As the strategic situation worsened in the vicinity of Rabegh, the viceroy asked Cairo whether he should allow pilgrim ships to leave. McMahon responded with tentative approval "as long as there is a reasonable chance of success."[45] For its part, the bureau was determined to pull off the hajj if at all possible. The Savoy instructed Wilson, as the British agent, to ensure that the sharif's bedouin were vigilant toward the activities of Turkish sympathizers during the pilgrimage season, and especially watchful of Egyptian agitators. Captain N.E.E. Bray of the Bengal Lancers was dispatched to assist Wilson in the creation of a successful native intelligence network to aid this effort. In addition, Cornwallis spent time in Jeddah expediting pilgrimage arrangements. The Arab Bureau was clearly anxious to please—fully realizing that a successful hajj would be of immeasurable value in helping to vindicate the sharif's position abroad and in neutralizing the effects of enemy diatribes against him. "We must pull off this pilgrimage," wrote Clayton to Wingate, "which will do much to establish the Sherif."[46]

For the sake of Indian opinion, a journey was staged by four selected Indian officers in order to provide the Muslim press with the salutary material necessary to ply support among India's Muslims. But even with this interest in common, misunderstandings persisted between the bureau and Delhi. The Savoy was anxious to obtain the resulting accounts from the officers as well as general impressions from returning pilgrims.[47] In the sense that no untoward incidents marred the hajj of 1916, the Arab Bureau had indeed piloted a stricken craft through treacherous waters. In Cairo, measures were taken to drive this point home with a draft communiqué from the residency, attributing a generous measure of credit for this success to the exertions of the British government. The communiqué, actually written by Hogarth for McMahon, hastened to conclude that "the contrast between the order and security of this pilgrimage and the hardships and dangers of preceding ones is widely commented upon by those who have experienced both. It does honor to the Sherif and affords a good augury for future pilgrimages under the new ruler of the Hedjaz."[48] While the Indian officers' reports were gratifying, Cairo's request for a report of general pilgrim reaction from India went unanswered. Sykes was particularly bitter about this, charging that the successful pilgrimage had been deliberately ignored in the government-censored Indian press, although given wide play elsewhere—in Egypt, Tunis, Algiers, and Morocco. India meanwhile dispatched a simple note in response to such claims: "Whereas Egyptian pilgrims seem to have been profuse in their open acknowledgments of the arrangements made by the Sherif, Indian pilgrims who have returned to India seem to have kept their opinions to themselves and the subject is conspicuous by its absence from the pages of the Moslem press."[49] Sykes regarded this version as fanciful indeed, suspecting that the pilgrims' impressions simply had not been solicited and suggesting that "even now some steps might be taken by the Indian Government to make capital out of the affair."[50]

The autumn of 1916 also marked the start of French participation in the Hejaz campaign. The French mission was commanded by Bremond, who, with a force that ultimately numbered almost four hundred Berber troops, embarked upon a militarily outstanding campaign of harassment against the Turks. The British did not invite this Allied contribution, but felt compelled to accept the French offer so as not to give diplomatic offense. Besides, with the Rabegh crisis looming that September, the chance for any additional trained troops in the Hejaz (they would be based at Yenbo) was not to be lightly cast aside.

While Hogarth was apprehensive about any French involvement in Arabia, Clayton was not—at least not initially. Bremond, he informed Wingate, "is a strong, keen, practical man and will I hope introduce a spirit of 'ginger' which is sadly lacking."[51]

From the outset, however, the Anglo-French partnership in Arabia was fraught with suspicion and intrigue. Sykes insisted that the British and French military missions cooperate harmoniously to hasten Hussein's conquest of the Hejaz. Perhaps anticipating the problems that would later arise, the Foreign Office wired assurances to the residency regarding the purpose of Bremond's mission: "French Government have given official assurance that strict instructions have been sent to Colonel Bremond that he is to act in complete accord with British authorities in Cairo to render all possible facilities and not to intervene in internal administration of the New Arab State nor in any questions affecting political status or territories on Red Sea littoral."[52] It was one thing for Whitehall to elicit such guarantees from the Quai d'Orsay. It was quite another to actually police the behavior of Bremond and his unit in the distant Hejaz. Scarcely a month later, relations between Wilson and Bremond had begun to sour. In his Arabian Report, Sykes noted this "great suspicion and misunderstanding" and coyly hinted that well-placed "tactful instruction" to British officers involved, exhorting frankness and comradeship, might help ease the alarming buildup of inter-Allied tension.[53] Commenting on this state of affairs for the India Office, Hirtzel (the office's under secretary) charged Cairo with reckless Francophobic intriguing. "It would seem desirable," he wrote, "to send some staff instructions to Cairo where (it is understood) they think Anglo-French [cooperation] at an end."[54]

The outlook for fruitful Anglo-French collaboration in the Arabian peninsula was never very good. British informants in Mecca learned of the sharif's displeasure at this development and of his determination to mislead and obstruct French activities whenever the opportunity arose. McMahon was quick to inform Foreign Secretary Grey of this.[55]

Differences in strategic perceptions also emerged. Bremond favored the employment of substantial numbers of British, French, and Indian troops in the Hejaz fighting, a course that the Arab Bureau opposed almost to a man. More serious perhaps was Bremond's persistent discouragement of plans to expand Hussein's revolt northward. Any success the Sharifian forces might enjoy in the direction of Syria (as the Arab Bureau hoped so fervently) would only complicate French ambitions in the Levant once peace was at hand. Instead, Bremond sought to redirect the focus of Hussein and his sons to the conquest of Medina and the Hejaz railway. Even with these rather limited objectives, however, the Savoy perceived the Frenchman's resolve as suspect.

In November, George Lloyd traveled to Arabia to report firsthand on conditions there. The choice of Lloyd for such a mission was a curious one. He spoke no Arabic but had impressed Wingate with his business acumen. He also had a keen eye for the financial perspective so apt to elude soldiers and academics. His mission also seems to have been connected with the impending dissolution of the Ottoman Bank in Jeddah and its prospective replacement by another institution.

In late October, Cornwallis submitted a report on the Ottoman Bank to the residency that highlighted the need for action. With the expulsion of the Turks from Jeddah, the customary European extraterritorial capitulations lapsed and were supplanted by the Shariah law of the new Sharifian regime, which of course proscribed usury. Ignorant of European requirements, the new Arab administrators were unprepared to exercise their authority in order to safeguard European interests. In this uncertain environment, financial interests at the port were threatened by both the absence of those safeguards and the possibility of dangerous "fanaticism." Jeddah was also the major pilgrim depot and therefore needed a banking institution. Yet the Ottoman Bank, despite being an Anglo-French concern, was a Turkish institution that had to be dissolved or at least reconstituted under a more innocuous title. Pursuant to this, Cornwallis urged a quid pro quo with the sharif: that Colonel Wilson be vested with consular authority in exchange for the "many benefits conferred on him by Great Britain." This jurisdiction should properly include license to: "settle all cases, civil and criminal in which British or British protected subjects are concerned . . . either between themselves or with the natives of the country or with subjects of other nations."[56] Lloyd's departure from Cairo shortly thereafter, despite contrary signals, was prompted by this report. While an enthusiastic booster of Lloyd, Wingate was opposed to reestablishment of the Ottoman Bank because he felt its officials were primarily involved in the promotion of French, rather than British, economic interests. Rather, he argued, establishment of a British bank was desirable both from the standpoint of currency circulation and for the protection and maintenance of the Manchester cotton trade in the Red Sea.[57] In addition, it soon became apparent that Bremond had no intention of confining his activities to the narrow assurances given by Paris. In early November the Arab Bureau learned from Wilson of attempts by the French commander to persuade Hussein to establish a new bank in Jeddah controlled by French capital. In turn, the British agent made a counterproposal for the introduction of a British bank. "The latter course," wired Cornwallis to Khartoum, "seems desirable from every point of view."[58] Lloyd's subsequent investigation concluded that Bremond's initiative had higher sanction—from none other than Aristide Briand, the French premier. Lloyd urged that Whitehall not permit this and hinted that "scope for a British bank might be arranged." Wilson was similarly adamant, urging Grey to adopt "a firm line in the matter," and warning via Wingate's relay "that should a French or semi-French bank be established in the Hedjaz at the present juncture it will give the French an economic and political hold in an area in which it was understood that British influence was to be paramount."[59]

Sykes viewed these appraisals as unnecessarily alarmist and brash enough to precipitate a rupture with Bremond and his superiors. He was not even convinced of the need to establish an exclusively British concern at Jeddah. Indeed, reacting to Cornwallis's October note, Sykes advised, "No bank at all would be best."[60]

Lloyd's reports also pointed out what he sensed to be the larger design behind the French overture. Bremond, Lloyd charged, was conniving for an offer from the sharif to become banker for the Sharifian government. In this way, "they could gracefully concede, and we could say nothing." This was ominous, Lloyd stressed, as only a British firm could provide a secure conduit for the Hejaz subsidy. Besides, a British firm would guarantee the preeminence of the pound sterling and the rupee in Red Sea trade. French success in the banking ploy would result in widespread currency conversion to units familiar to French merchants and alien to Indian traders, a prospect to be avoided in any case. Aside from the continued resistance of the Arabs to Turkish occupation, Lloyd regarded this question as "the most important one before us in the Hijaz at the moment."[61]

Lloyd was then reassigned to the staff of the Arab Bureau, and his reports on conditions in Arabia certainly did nothing to reduce that agency's intrinsic suspicion of the French. The criticism of Bremond was not restricted to the Ottoman Bank affair. Lloyd claimed that his impression, gained partly through personal interviews with Bremond, was that the French most desired to maintain the status quo in Arabia—that is, the continued Turkish resistance at Medina. Well aware of the opposition and suspicion with which their aspirations were regarded in Syria (which would only be strengthened by successful expansion of the revolt northward), Bremond obstructed. He also feared this would deprive France of her coveted role of liberator in the Levant. Bremond, Lloyd claimed, had expressed on more than one occasion his wish that the sharif not take Medina. "Briefly speaking," the financier concluded, "they do not wish the Shereef to fail, but would rather that his movement failed completely than that it should succeed too signally."[62] Bremond evolved into something of a political gadfly, raising frequent objections to the sharif with respect to pilgrimage arrangements, customs levies, and permission to set up French wireless facilities. Hugh Pearson, an assistant to Wilson in Jeddah, complained to the Arab Bureau that "Bremond is becoming rather difficult and is constantly springing harm on the doings of the Sharifian Government, which really do not concern him, and it will be an excellent thing when Medina falls and the mission has no longer any excuse for staying." Cornwallis conveyed this assessment, along with his concurrence, to Clayton.[63] Lawrence was also active in spreading tales of French perfidy, relaying to Wilson accounts of his conversations with Abdullah, Hussein's second son, in which were recounted scurrilous messages from the Frenchman warning that the British were conniving at encirclement of the anticipated Arab state. British occupation of Baghdad, Gaza, and Aden were cited as portentous examples.[64] Before long, distrust of the French pervaded the highest levels of the Foreign Office, infecting even the Francophile Sykes. During an April visit to the Hejaz with his counterpart Georges-Picot, he confessed to Wilson that "Picot was apparently of the same mind as Bremond, was anti-Sherif and appeared not to wish the Arab Movement to succeed."[65]

Picot's attitude, to Wilson's mind, was attributable to a generous dose of "Bremond poison" administered after the Frenchman's arrival. By early May, Sykes had reached the conclusion that the French mission "should be wound up." Graham, at the Foreign Office, informed Wingate of identical sentiments the very day Sykes's assessment was received. French officials, he complained, were blatantly anti-Arab and divisive: "Their line is to crab British questions, to the Arabs, throw cold water on all Arab actions, and make light of the King. . . . They do not attempt to disguise that they desire Arab failure . . . I find my chief difficulty in improving the feeling between the Arabs and the French owing to the deliberately perverse attitude and policy followed by Colonel Bremond and his staff."[66]

Friction between the Savoy and the French also arose over the formation of an Arab Legion, a subject on which the bureau had already tussled with

India. As this was a force to be mainly composed of Arab prisoners of war recruited from (among other sources) Indian prison camps, Clayton and his colleagues had misgivings about Sykes's and Picot's promotion of the legion as an Anglo-French project. Picot's superiors were hesitant to permit Britain to assume the exclusive role of Arab sponsor; nor was the Quai d'Orsay willing to allow the formation of such a force without the constraining input of Paris regarding its deployment. The concept of a legion, wrote Clayton, "was seized on by the Authorities in London and Paris as a sort of political card, with a view to its being the outward and visible sign of Arab nationality fostered by the Entente."[67]

Clayton appreciated the benefits that might stem from an effective legion. "The presence of an organized body of Arab troops, however small," he noted, "with the Army in a future advance into Syria would be of great *political* advantage and be an inducement to desertion from the enemy ranks" (emphasis added).[68] He was anxious for the legion to be ready to join Feisal's advance northward into Transjordan with tribes of the Harb confederation. But he also insisted that Britain maintain control of the new unit, in terms of both composition and deployment. French participation, he felt, might provide boundless opportunities for mischief, present obstacles to the legion's deployment outside the Hejaz (in Syria, for example), and supply Paris with an ideal vehicle for political proselytizing in the region. Quite predictably, Lawrence also opposed the concept, convinced that injections of regulars into Feisal's bedouin army would vitiate the movement's distinctively "Arab" character and so adversely affect morale. It might also be added that units headed by regular Arab military officers might have been considerably less susceptible to Lawrence's charismatic "leadership." Lloyd was similarly cautious, advising that dual control be terminated and supplanted by one or two "Arab corps" absorbed into the Egyptian Expeditionary Force. The new legion's officers, assembled first at Wejh and then Aqaba but as yet unbloodied, thought of nothing, asserted Lloyd, "but politics and private intrigue and on present lines we shall make a complete failure."[69] Wingate, though unbothered by the risk of French scheming, was concerned that dual control would badly hamper recruitment.

Protracted negotiations over the future of the Arab Legion frustrated Clayton's attempts to dispatch that force to Feisal. Failure to accommodate Picot's demands toward this project would seriously discredit him in Paris at a time when he was urging his government to accept revisions in the Sykes-Picot Agreement respecting Arabia. If this should happen, Sykes warned, Picot's influence would evaporate before the more obstructionist "Bremond party," which "will be a permanent and powerful factor."[70]

Meanwhile, the anomalous legion transferred to Aqaba, where it languished until a system of more indirect Anglo-French aegis was instituted, under minimal European direction. Still, it failed to live up to the grandiose expectations Sykes had held for it. Clayton's evaluation was especially pessimistic with respect to the officers, whom he assessed as "undisciplined, unskilled and, so far, show but little real keenness." By year's end, he was ready to support its disbandment. The legion, he wrote to Sykes, was not worth the money or the time.[71] That much-trumpeted force, camped at Ismailia with scarcely five hundred men and afflicted with sagging morale, was finally dubbed a failure and sent off to Aqaba to be absorbed into one of Feisal's regular units.[72]

The Arab Bureau's stormy relationship with the Bremond mission foreshadowed more serious confrontations later over the territorial future of Syria. Yet this Fashodist attitude is attributable less to reflexive Francophobia than to genuine concern that the French were plotting to usurp political primacy in the region. The bureau reflected Cairo's view that this was a position to which Britain was uniquely entitled by virtue of her military and financial exertions. Lawrence's hostility to the Levantine ambitions of France grew increasingly vituperative as the war progressed. This has since conveyed a misleading impression of the bureau's strategy toward Paris. The opposition to French designs that those at the Savoy grew to share with their bedouin allies was not the result of empathy with the sharif and his sons. Indeed, Hussein often attempted to play off the British against the French. It is demonstrable that the bureau's officers saw no future in the realization of Arab nationalist aspirations, for they were far more sophisticated than the popular label of "enthusiast" suggests. Indeed, alongside their collective experience and competence, their French counterparts were but poor competitors.[73] That Lloyd's report, reinforced with the support of Wilson and Cornwallis, soured Sykes and his Foreign Office colleagues on Allied collaboration in Arabia is not to be doubted. Yet, suspicion toward the French, long extant in Cairo and dormant in London, provided fertile ground in which the seeds of doubt, sown by the bureau, could germinate and take root. The complex Middle Eastern political scene was rife with opportunity for intrigue and duplicity due largely to the unlikely alliance of France and Great Britain in a region that had traditionally been a hotbed of imperial competition: "Fashoda is consciously or unconsciously in the thoughts of British and French in the Orient. Offence is seen where no offence is meant. Suspicion spreads to European and native alike and the result is disastrous for all concerned."[74]

4

THE WAY OF
WRONG IMPRESSIONS

The Arab Bureau and the Raj

The reaction of Indian officials to the concept of an Arab Bureau was not initially adverse. Certainly India Office under secretary Arthur Hirtzel recognized Delhi's shortcomings in coping with enemy propaganda against the Raj. Dubbing Sykes's idea "sound," he conceded, "There is no doubt that we do not use our opportunities either for obtaining information or for influencing opinion and that, on the contrary, through inadvertence which ought to be impossible—we allow opinion to be influenced against us."[1] Despite this admission, however, Hirtzel was prepared to exert his influence to limit the bureau's independence. Interdepartmental jealousy played a part in this. If the new agency were to attempt coordination of intelligence and propaganda activities toward the Arab world, he felt a neutral, detached status was essential. Early in 1916 the India Office began to cast a jaundiced eye toward the new Arab Bureau and became increasingly nervous that India was surrendering a measure of control to military authorities in London and Cairo. "I am much disturbed," Hirtzel noted, "by Colonel Clayton's telegram to Mark Sykes about the Arab Bureau. The proposal that it shall be only nominally under the Foreign Office and its London representative should be on the staff of the D.I.D. will meet with the strongest opposition here. . . . This is much too important and delicate a business—from the Indian point of view—to be controlled by any body except that which is officially responsible for the foreign policy of H.M.G."[2]

Late in 1915 Indian opposition to Sykes sprang from several quarters: the Indian government, the Mesopotamian high command, and the India Office. Most complaints struck a common theme: Sykes's perceived hostility toward the Indian administration and his persistently unrealistic view of British diplomacy. An earlier visit by Sir Mark to India and Mesopotamia had unfavorably impressed officials there. His reports back to the Foreign Office "are so visionary and strategically impractical," complained General Lake, commander of Indian forces in Mesopotamia, "that we should not have recommended him for the work."[3] One suspects Sykes's Francophile tendencies worked against him as well, there and among officials in Cairo. In any event ultimate Indian acceptance of the bureau came only after Sykes stepped down as its presumed director.

Indian suspicion toward the Arab Bureau had deeper roots, however, than administrative jealousy or personal antipathy. Even as officials in Delhi were fretful over the possible loss to Cairo of political authority in Mesopotamia, they also harbored serious misgivings as to the wisdom of encouraging an Arab revolt at all. The viceroy was horrified at the prospect of a unified Arab state on India's flank, athwart its line of communication. Its view toward a new bureau fated to play a pivotal role in such a revolt was one of suspicion, heightened both by Sykes's association with it and the proposal to center its activities in Cairo. The government of India had disdained the military usefulness of the Arab tribes with which its forces had come in contact. This attitude nourished hostility, coupled with worry over the possible repercussions of the Arab Revolt among Indian Muslims and the prospect of an impending Arab political entity that would include at least portions of Mesopotamia. Neither specter was one that Delhi wished to propitiate by encouraging revolt among the Mesopotamian tribes. Well-traveled officers who would have been of considerable use in a liaison capacity with Iraqi tribes were conspicuously unemployed to that end.[4] Rather than promote close cooperation between expeditionary forces and the Arab tribes of the lower Tigris, British commanders were content to buy them off with direct subsidies, thereby securing their lines of communication. But this policy only encouraged tribal divisiveness and predation, as many recipients used the subsidies to increase their own local power. In the Hejaz, by contrast, financial support of Sharif Hussein provided the necessary if evanescent inducement to marshal a substantial force of tribesmen against the Turks. So in this way the widening political rift between the perspectives of Cairo and Delhi had acquired a psychological dimension as well. The Indian government mistook Egyptian attempts to effect an Arab uprising as indicative of a deeper disjunction in strategic attitude. Such schemes were deemed politically dangerous, futile, and liable to worsen an already exaggerated view of Arab nationalism. "India seems obsessed," Clayton confided to Wingate, "with the fear of a powerful and united Arab state, which can never exist unless we are fools enough to create it."[5]

Early in 1916 another series of events occurred that illustrated the growing divergence in attitude. Working from Cairo, Clayton concocted a scheme with Aziz Ali al-Masri, an Egyptian of Mesopotamian ancestry released from Turkish captivity and subsequently employed by the British, to travel to Mesopotamia with several compatriots in order to establish contact with disaffected tribes and secret nationalist cells within the Ottoman army. They hoped to garner widespread support from local tribes and improve the position of the besieged British garrison at Kut al-Amara. While the Foreign Office approved the scheme, General Lake and the India Office blocked it until such time as the relief of Kut was impossible. Once again Whitehall chose not to assert itself with Delhi, and the project was aborted.

The debate that swirled around the formation of the Arab Bureau sheds light on the degree to which the government of India feared the loss of its own authority with the Mesopotamian tribes through the activities of a branch bureau to be set up in Basra. Differences in policy were fundamental. Indian and Mesopotamian authorities questioned the entire direction of British policy in the Middle East. The Hussein-McMahon Correspondence, in their view, came close to surrendering the Mesopotamian domain, which Indian officials had come to look upon as a future acquisition of the Raj. In addition, encouragement of an Arab revolt against a sitting Islamic caliph boded ill for Anglo-Muslim relations on the subcontinent. Wingate and Clayton, however, saw no contradiction in these ends and justified their tactics along imperial lines. To them the very notion of Arab political unity was absurd. The sirdar took pains to assure War Office Intelligence that Delhi's views were not lost on him: "The surrender of Indian interests in Mesopotamia is to be deprecated as much from a British Imperial as from a purely Indian standpoint; and in view of the express recognition of these interests by responsible Arab leaders it is not anticipated they will raise obstacles to the institution of a system of local semi-autonomous government in those regions under our immediate control and supervision."[6] Of course Wingate was referring to Hussein's acquiescence to special postwar administrative measures in the vilayets of Basra and Baghdad, given Britain's peculiar interests there. Certainly from the residency's standpoint, McMahon had successfully covered all bets through such provisos. Yet in India these arguments were unconvincing. Wingate contended that British direction of Arab political destiny would in fact reduce the Islamic threat to imperial and (by inference) Indian interests. At the India Office, Hirtzel grew impatient with this line: "Kitchener's policy of destroying an Islamic state merely for the purpose of creating another, has always seemed to me disastrous, from the point of view no less of expediency than of civilisation."[7]

For its part, Cairo was anxious to put aside such differences for the sake of the war effort. Both Wingate and Clayton hastened to stroke ruffled feathers and urge union against the Turk under the guiding hand of the Cairo Arab Bureau. But confusion quickly surfaced as the India Office attempted to transmit to India the precise limits of the new bureau's authority. Initially the viceroy was told that its Basra branch would be incorporated into General Lake's own intelligence organization as a distributing agency for Cairo-inspired propaganda (the use of which would be left to Lake's discretion). But on 26 April the India Office informed Lord Hardinge that the new Arab Bureau "is the central organ through which His Majesty's Government will lay down policy and principles." Further, General Lake was directed to "work in strict conformity with indications received from Cairo." Some latitude on his part would be permissible in adapting policy to local conditions, but only "where absolutely necessary."[8] While admitting that his initial enthusiasm for the bureau had evaporated, Hirtzel wrote that Lake should be given clearly to understand that he was to work "in *subordinate* coordination and not on equal terms with the Cairo Bureau."[9]

This broader scope of authority appeared to extend far beyond the propaganda organ originally contemplated, and it sounded alarms in Basra and Delhi. From this directive it seemed as if both Indian power centers were being nudged out of decisions concerning Mesopotamia—even denied the courtesy of consultation. Lake responded quickly and directly that "It must be remembered that the environment and point of view of Cairo differ widely in many respects from ours in Irak. Certainly hitherto the experiment made in attempting to handle affairs of Irak through Cairo without previously consulting us can hardly be regarded as fortunate."[10] Lake went on to cite the areas of disagreement that had arisen as a result of this "experiment": objections to Mesopotamian references in McMahon's pledges to the sharif; the affair of the Mesopotamian officers and their abortive mission to Basra; and the employment of Sayyid Talib, a prominent Basra politician, to promote British fortunes in Mesopotamia. While expressing hopes that recent visits to Basra by Lawrence and Lloyd had helped to allay "wrong impressions" concerning Mesopotamian operations, Lake suggested that a multiparty conference of Middle Eastern officials might go far toward ironing out what problems of policy remained.[11] From Delhi came an equally direct if less tactful protest. "We have come to the conclusion, after the experience of the last few months, that it is not suitable to make the Arab Bureau the mouthpiece of His Majesty's Government's policy and principles as regards the Arab Question."[12] While Lake's conference never came about, Austen Chamberlain eased tensions considerably with a clarifying telegram to the viceroy on 27 May. "Policies and principles," the secretary of state for India reassured Lord Hardinge, meant overall Arab policy, not local Arab policy, leaving Lake free to decide which material provided by Cairo might be suitable for use. As for the Arab Bureau, its role was to be that of an informing agency, transmitting tenets of policy formulated in London and obligated to routinely consult with both the India Office and the government of India.[13] Its officers were to be placed directly under Cox's command (as chief political officer), and all communications to Cairo would pass through him. The skeptical viceroy posited that unless the bureau's activities were limited just to propaganda, it would be difficult to ascertain whether bureau communications reflected London's true wishes or Cairo's particular point of view.[14] Neither were Hirtzel's suspicions dispelled by this change of heart at Whitehall. "The whole position of the Arab Bureau," he minuted, "and everything connected with it is unsatisfactory."[15]

In its eagerness to placate India, the Foreign Office in effect reduced the Basra branch of the Arab Bureau to little more than a propaganda unit. In the process, the bureau's mission was irredeemably compromised. The goal of coordination and control, sought in order to minimize administrative conflicts and formulate a consistent and rational Arab policy, could not now be reached. The Mesopotamian campaign would continue along its narrow, insular course, unconcerned with Cairo's priorities. Although the War Office had viewed Indian mishandling of the Kut disaster as serious enough to strip military control of the Mesopotamian campaign from Delhi in April 1916, India's influence was still sufficient to retain a stranglehold on political affairs in that region. The facade of harmonious cooperation, so fancifully imagined by Sykes, was crumbling. Hogarth remained anxious to repair the breach, adding in his second report from the Arab Bureau: "I have so drafted the Report as to meet Indian objections, as far as I understand these, i.e. I have tried to show that the Bureau have not acted as a 'mouthpiece of H.M.G.'s policy,' but has confined its energies to collecting and distributing Arab Intelligence, and giving advice on Arab matters."[16]

The viceroy successfully insisted on the appointment of a member of Lake's own intelligence division as a bureau officer at Basra. A Major Blaker was given the appointment although already on intelligence assignment from the War Office. As for a liaison officer to keep Cairo informed, the viceroy opposed any assignment at all. Contending that such an officer would be "dangerous unless under close control," he preferred that all communications to this branch be forwarded direct from London.[17]

Clayton staged a coup of sorts with the appointment of Gertrude Bell to Mesopotamia as Cairo's representative. Bell was unassailable in her credentials and suitably Cairene in her sympathies. Her knowledge of Mesopotamian and central Arabian tribes, augmented by extended travel and a succession of distinguished scholarly works, was not easily challenged. And her views concerning ambient political wrangling were quite clear. She recognized the futility of attempting to extract meaningful policy consensus from "strictly watertight compartments" as well as the important role to be played by administrative branches in order to "establish and maintain a close understanding of one another's doings."[18] She was a past master in the use of personal communication to overcome bureaucratic inertia and employed it to great effect in disarming the hostility with which she was initially confronted. Her intimate friendships with Lord Hardinge and *Times* correspondent Valentine Chirol proved valuable assets in this regard. Bell sincerely desired to play a role in effecting a rapprochement between Delhi and Cairo, for the sake of the war effort: "There is so much, oh so much to be thought of and considered—so many ways of going irretrievably wrong at the beginning, and some of them are being taken and must be set right before matters grow worse."[19]

As much as she desired cooperation between the branches, however, Bell remained a staunch advocate of Egyptian control of Arab affairs in Mesopotamia. While she got on splendidly with Chief Political Officer Cox, she quickly acquired a hearty contempt for the Mesopotamian high command, particularly General Lake. She began serving in Mesopotamia at a very inauspicious juncture for Anglo-Indian arms, just prior to the disaster at Kut. Writing to Lawrence shortly before the latter's departure for Basra, Bell confessed that "on general lines my own view with regard to this country is that the administration ought to be under Egypt, not under India and that view is confirmed by all that I hear in Basrah. . . . We don't need another watertight compartment."[20] She was similarly critical of the Mesopotamian intelligence division, which she regarded as second-rate and unequal to the opportunities that real cooperation with the tribes might offer. Force D's failure to exploit tribal disaffection had been criticized by Cox, who was himself exasperated with Lake's headquarters. This marked the beginning of an enduring partnership between Bell and Sir Percy, who eventually inveigled her transfer to his own personal staff. She remained in close touch with Cairo, however, using her new position to pass on political information that otherwise would have had to go through Cox. To this end Bell conspired with Hogarth to exchange "personal judgments" via the circuitous Suez-Gulf troopships, thereby avoiding Mesopotamian censors. This she regarded as her "right" as Cairo's representative and believed that, while it would probably be recognized as such in time, "if asked for now it would arouse suspicion."[21]

Bell's contribution to the Arab Bureau's Mesopotamian branch was no mean one. Shorn of its intended role as a coordinating agent in Mesopotamia, this agency stagnated prior to her arrival. Little or no information was forwarded to Cairo or London, and scant propaganda was generated. The attitude of the local authorities toward it was resentful and suspicious. Bell stepped into a caldron of splenetic pettiness. An India Office commendation of her performance conceded this: "They lectured her on the Indian Official Secrets Act and actually censored her letters. For a woman of her *status* the position must have been uncommonly galling; but she put up with it and I imagine that the improvement in the political attitude of Basra to Cairo and H.M.G. is largely due to her work."[22]

Bell provided a touch of éclat to the Mesopotamian intelligence scene— she was a font of energy and scholarship. Her familiarity with the local vernacular provided a new dimension to political intelligence there. The eloquent reports and memoranda that flowed from her hand were scrupulously to the point and seldom ventured into the realm of political polemic; this was a graceful abdication indeed in a time when there was no lack of bureaucratic bickering. For such a delicate role, Clayton could scarcely have made a better choice. As the war in Mesopotamia wore on, however, Bell slowly lost touch and sympathy with contacts at the Cairo Arab Bureau. Undoubtedly this metamorphosis was at least partly tied to her adulation of Cox. Over time it became steadily more apparent that the bureau was losing a valuable voice of Cairene reason in Mesopotamian military and political councils, a voice muted under the burden of Cox's growing hostility toward that agency. Hogarth, acknowledging Bell's descent "fully more and more under the influence of her chief," thought a timely furlough might yet bring her back into the fold—"but she won't leave her present lord."[23]

The mounting paranoia in Anglo-Indian circles about the Arab Bureau during the first half of 1916 is not difficult to understand. At just about the time Delhi was losing control of the Mesopotamian campaign, officers from Cairo appeared on the scene to inquire after conditions along the Tigris. One was George Lloyd, then serving with the Royal Sussex Regiment. He had been dispatched as a possible replacement for Bell (a move that, because he did not speak Arabic, never came about). He was extremely knowledgeable in financial matters and had conducted several missions in Arabia prior to his formal assignment to the staff of the Cairo Arab Bureau. His report to Cairo in May 1916 was hardly flattering. Bemoaning the poor communications, inept leadership, and penurious supply of Force D, Lloyd concluded that the army had "been doubly cursed with a Commander in Chief with too little grip and a Finance member called Mayer with too much."[24] Major Blaker, he continued, was ignorant of Arab affairs and often preoccupied with other duties, and so would most likely assume a nominal role while Bell handled substantive matters of the branch bureau. In light of this, Lloyd also felt that some sort of independent communication with Cairo was essential but believed such license would ultimately evolve from the relationship between Bell and Cox.

Lloyd also left his own imprimatur on the report. With a lengthy caveat he warned that Britain had best prepare itself for postwar economic developments in the area. He clearly regarded the Arab Bureau as a permanent institution (to the befuddlement of Cox, for the Foreign Office had yet to declare it so). The Arab Bureau's formal Mesopotamian role as an organ of propaganda was merely "ephemeral," Lloyd reminded Cairo. If

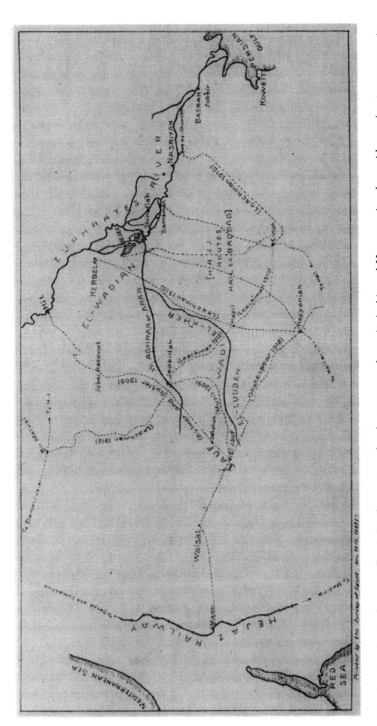

Fig. 4. Map by the Survey of Egypt detailing routes taken by prewar explorers in Arabia and Mesopotamia, along with prominent caravan routes. (from the *Arab Bulletin*)

it were to have any lasting importance, it must broaden its activities to "become a kind of museum of up-to-date knowledge in affairs geographical, political, economic, and archeological." In this region more than any other, "economic pressure and the grip of markets . . . share in the political plough." Spheres of economic influence were meaningless if left unsupported by the commercial wherewithal to hold on to markets. In efficiency of Mesopotamian economic penetration, Lloyd concluded, Britain had compared unfavorably in the past with Russia and Germany and should begin planning now, via the intellectual resources available to the Arab Bureau, to earmark the "best commercially penetrative arteries."[25] Lloyd's conception of the bureau's postwar role illustrates the priorities of the man more than of the agency. Lloyd was a banker, not an Arabic scholar, and as such he leaned toward a dispassionate, econometric perspective. Such arguments were seldom expressed by other bureau officers as a rationale for their administrative existence; in fact, to have entertained such thoughts at that time would have been unjustifiably optimistic. The defeat of the Turks, perforce, had to command first priority.

The arrival of T. E. Lawrence and Aubrey Herbert in Mesopotamia that April further poisoned relations between Cairo and Delhi. While Lawrence has been erroneously tagged by Winstone as a member of the Arab Bureau at this time, he most assuredly was not assigned to it until late autumn.[26] Rather, he was then a junior officer in the mapmaking section of Military Intelligence. His mission to Basra was bizarre. Authorized to expend up to £1 million, Lawrence's task was to bribe the Turkish commander before Kut into allowing Townshend's Sixth Division to peacefully disengage and retreat. Aside from the presumptuousness of this scheme, its execution in Mesopotamia was ill timed, coming on the heels of the affair of al-Masri and his Mesopotamian officers. In addition, Sykes had recently passed through the area en route to India, decrying everything Indian and managing to offend virtually every Indian official with whom he came in contact. Wyndham Deedes, a Turkish expert assigned to Murray's intelligence staff, originally had been tapped for the mission but declined it in disgust after Lake's refusal to treat with al-Masri. Lloyd was also considered but again his ignorance of Arabic intervened. The choice of Lawrence was made largely at Deedes's behest.[27]

In addition to this attempt at bribery, Lawrence was instructed to test Mesopotamian waters for a reintroduction of al-Masri and his comrades to make contact with disaffected elements in the Ottoman army. Lawrence proved an even more tactless emissary than Sykes, sowing the seeds of a bitter antagonism that one observer alleged was to have "serious effects on British policy in the Middle-East."[28] In a blistering report he detailed the appalling conditions on the Mesopotamian front. Nearly every facet of the campaign, from logistical planning to intelligence, was, in Lawrence's view, riven with incompetence, mismanagement, and neglect. A contemporary serving in Basra confessed: "We dared not show it [the report] to the C in C, but had to water it down. . . . I have regretted ever since that I never kept a copy of the original; it was Lawrence at his best."[29] This impetuous subaltern from Cairo, never one to suffer fools gladly, only succeeded in earning the undying enmity of the Mesopotamian high command. While this mission was conceived by the War Office and executed through Military Intelligence, the Arab Bureau was held responsible for Lawrence's abrasive behavior. Administrative divisions often were not as clearly discernible as they might have been; but this mattered little in Basra, where military authorities tended to view all of Cairo through a single lens.

The attempt to bribe Khalil Pasha, the Turkish commander, into relaxing the stranglehold on Kut failed miserably. Cox thought the scheme preposterous from the outset and quickly disassociated himself from it. Al-Masri's renewed attempt to establish contact with compatriots serving with the Turks likewise came to grief. Here again Cox suspected that Cairo's real motive was to rid Egypt of nettlesome "gas-bags who are impatient there."[30] But Lawrence came away rather confident as to Sir Percy's real sympathies, stressing that while Cox opposed any premature forfeiture of British designs in Mesopotamia, he clearly differed from Delhi in the extent to which he was willing to cooperate with Arab insurrectionists. Lawrence wired to Deedes that Sir Percy "does not know how Cairene he is" and concluded that "he does not understand our ideas but is very open and will change his mind as required."[31]

Lawrence did much to obstruct constructive intercourse between Cairo and Delhi. Whether or not his mission was truly an attempt by the new Arab Bureau to erode Indian authority is immaterial, for it was perceived as such—as an effort conceived by that Arabophile cabal in Cairo. "The whole affair," argued Arnold Talbot Wilson (Cox's chief assistant), "was unfortunate from first to last" and, like Sykes's earlier visit, "did little to endear the Arab Bureau or its representatives to the Indian or Mesopotamian authorities."[32] The viceroy's suspicion was rekindled by Lawrence's activities, and by Cairo's tactless failure to apprise him of the nature of the mission.[33] Lord Chelmsford, the new viceroy, afterwards tried to restrict independent action by the Basra bureau, especially with regard to propaganda that Delhi regarded as inflammatory.

The bureau was also at loggerheads with the Indian government over its uncooperative response to the creation of an Arab Legion. When Sykes conceived the idea in early 1916 he naturally looked to India as a promising source for legion recruitment (i.e., the POW camps). Accordingly, McMahon requested that India dispatch suitable prisoners for service in the Hejaz, especially officers and artillerymen. In addition, the high commissioner asked that Delhi relay certain messages from al-Faruqi (Hussein's representative in Cairo) to the prisoners, designed to encourage their defection. But shortly afterward Wingate received a disappointing telegram (via Arbur) from the viceroy: "I shall be glad to know whether these proposals have the approval of H.M.G. and yourself, before doing more than taking preliminary action here."[34] Sykes was also perturbed by the "slowness" with which the government of India was complying with McMahon's request.[35] When the prisoners finally did arrive at Rabegh in late 1916, their condition and deportment did not meet the approval of Alfred Parker, who had been ordered to receive, train, and assimilate them into Sharifian units. In a highly critical report, which eventually reached the attention of the Foreign Office, he lashed out at Delhi for the selection of ignorant, uncooperative, abused, and otherwise unsuitable POWs. Most of these Arabs were Turkish sympathizers forced off the train at Bombay at bayonet point. Indian authorities, Parker charged, had made no attempt to weed out undesirable prospects and maintained an atmosphere of semisecrecy around the entire operation. One prisoner was actually wounded at the rail siding when he resisted. Upon arrival in Arabia many of the prisoners refused to disembark, claiming that they were told before departing India that they would not be compelled to fight for the sharif or anyone else. In general, Parker charged, these men were not only uncooperative but openly hostile. And he did not hesitate to point the finger of blame: "The manner in which these things occurred [in India], conjoined with the bayonet episode already mentioned, was calculated to arouse every suspicion and render the matter incredibly difficult."[36]

Of course such behavior was consistent with the viceroy's attitude toward the Arab Revolt and his obvious reluctance to encourage Mesopotamian Arabs from striking common cause with the sharif. But Delhi insisted that Cairo had not requested preliminary screening of potential recruits, stipulating only that they be "fit for further service." As for the bayonet incident, India's Foreign Department insisted that it had followed an attack on one of the guards at the railhead by one of the ejected prisoners.[37]

After reading Parker's report, Sykes was beside himself. The problems that had arisen with the proposed legion were vexing enough without the additional woes inflicted by an uncooperative viceroy. In a scathing minute Sykes dubbed Parker's version "a miserable story," adding: "The cause of this is want of a coordinated policy between India and Egypt. This has been the cause of much misunderstanding and could undoubtedly be remedied. I suggest that this fiasco might be made use of, as a ground for close cooperation on both sides."[38]

Given the serious problems that developed between Delhi and Cairo over the original scope of the bureau's function, it hardly seems surprising that controversy also surrounded the issue of the Arab Bureau's postwar future. Early in 1916 officials in Cairo (notably McMahon and Clayton) lobbied strongly for Foreign Office recognition of the need for such an agency, even after victory was assured. The high commissioner stressed that it would be indispensable to a government facing various and complex political questions in the Near East following the war. Wingate added his voice, writing to Balfour of the ease with which such an organ could be productively assimilated into the postwar Egyptian intelligence apparatus. Early on, Clayton prompted Sykes to press the question home at Whitehall. "The necessity of the Bureau continuing at the end of the war," he warned, "must not be lost sight of."[39] In a similar vein, Cairo's office of Military Intelligence wired Nicolson at the Foreign Office that such an agency, properly constituted, would be invaluable not only in addressing the complexities of future problems but in combating the activities of "many secret hostile agencies."[40]

To the India Office and the viceroy's government such ambitions were frightening. To them it appeared that officials in Cairo, discontented with merely running the Arabian sideshow, hankered after supreme authority on Middle Eastern questions. In India's view, what Clayton and Wingate actually wanted was a sort of junior Foreign Office established in Cairo, with a comprehensive purview over political questions in the Middle East. India feared interference in the future administration of Mesopotamia; repeated pressures for concessions to Arab nationalists; and promulgation of an Arabian policy untempered by Delhi's counsel. Besides, the concessions that such a bureau, emboldened by permanent status, might proffer to the Arabs and the French were perilous to contemplate. Hirtzel noted disconsolately that "the idea of a permanent Arab Bureau of the future is not attractive."[41] Holderness echoed the suspicion that "what is in the back of people's minds is that the Bureau may be the germ of a future foreign office, which at present Cairo backs," adding that insofar as the government of India was concerned, support for it was "essentially a temporary measure [and] . . . does not commit us to supporting it after the war."[42] Such formidable opposition was difficult to ignore; and while it appears that both Lawrence and Bell conveyed to Cox the impression that the bureau would become a permanent fixture on the Near Eastern imperial scene, this was not the case. In midsummer of 1916, a memo written by Cox on the functions of the Basra branch had included in its introduction the statement that, aside from the connection of the "Eastern Bureau" (as it was sometimes circumspectly labeled in Mesopotamia) directly with the war effort, "it is intended that the Bureau shall be a permanent institution for use after the peace has been proclaimed." Cox had apparently been told this by Lawrence.[43]

At the end of 1916, as Wingate was planning to revamp intelligence operations in Cairo with Clayton as his new chief of staff, Delhi's apprehension grew. That this measure was essential to rid Cairo's intelligence community of internal rivalry was not to be questioned. Yet Hirtzel reacted suspiciously to War Office approval of the scheme for fear that might prove an augury for postwar organization of Middle Eastern intelligence generally, dominated by a new intimacy between the Arab Bureau and Military Intelligence. "This is another step," he warned, "in the direction of creating an Egyptian Foreign Office."[44] But it was a step that London was not yet prepared to take. In a secret letter from the Foreign Office to the Exchequer at the end of August concerned primarily with the bureau's anticipated expenses, it was revealed that "Lord Grey will agree not to press for the permanent establishment of the Bureau at this stage, though he may be compelled to do so later."[45]

There the matter rested until after the war when the matter of the Arab Bureau was reviewed afresh, sparking a new firestorm of controversy. En route to India from Cairo early in 1916, Bell (herself a strong proponent of an enduring Arab Bureau) described the essential ingredient without which permanent establishment would have had little meaning: "We want to establish here a permanent Intelligence Bureau for the Near East, which shall endure after the war is over—it would be invaluable; but it could not work properly without the sympathy and help of India."[46] Such succor Delhi was far too suspicious and parochial to provide in 1916. At war's end it would be even less disposed to do so. India's rejection of the Arab Bureau concept ensured that Cairo's Savoy Hotel would be relegated to the status of one of Bell's "watertight compartments." This inability to attract acceptance in the East rendered the Arab Bureau more controversial and, therefore, more expendable in a postwar world.

The actual outbreak of the Arab Revolt further exacerbated Delhi-Cairo tensions. An immediate point at issue was the extent to which Britain might permissibly use the naval power of the Red Sea Patrol to assist the Sharif of Mecca and to safeguard communications and shipping in the Red Sea. A military occupation and search of Jeddah was contemplated, to scuttle suspected Turkish mine-laying and submarine operations. The subsequent naval bombardment of that port, followed by a naval blockade of the Hejaz, was stridently resisted by the government of India as a contravention of previous pledges guaranteeing the inviolability of the holy places. Once again fear of Indian Muslim outrage had aroused the Cassandras in Delhi.

The declaration made by the viceroy himself on 2 November 1914 renounced the use of any military force in the vicinity of the holy places unless the hajj itself were interfered with. This fact was brought to the attention of Cairo intelligence, the issue eventually falling to the Arab Bureau to reconcile. Contained within a bureau summary of documents related to events leading up to the outbreak of hostilities on the peninsula are copies of two Foreign Office telegrams (dated 18 October and 14 November, respectively) that to a great extent nullified the Indian declaration. Noninterference was pledged and aggressive intent forsworn "unless necessary to protect Arabian interests" against Turkish aggression "or in support of any attempt by the Arabs to free themselves from Turkish rule." The following comment in the report elaborates on the source of the confusion: "It is important to note that this last declaration gives a much freer hand for Military and Naval action than the earlier Proclamation. In Cairo the Foreign Office declaration of November 14th had always been regarded as the governing decision while at the time of the outbreak of the Sherif's revolt the proclamation of November 2nd was still regarded as binding by the Indian Government."[47]

For purposes of convenience the British Red Sea Patrol was split into two squadrons, one based at Ismailia and one at Aden. The northern squadron policed the Red Sea coast off Asir and Yemen to the Aden protectorate. Communications between Aden and Cairo were poor at the best of times, and their respective spheres ill defined. As late as mid-1915 Aden still operated on the assumption that Indian maritime authority in the Red Sea extended as far north as, and included, Jeddah. In March of that year the viceroy had gone so far as to proclaim (without any advance warning to or consultation with Cairo) a commercial blockade against Egyptian millet sent to Jeddah's pilgrims, claiming that much of it was falling into the hands of the Turks. Such was the sorry state of imperial communications. On 31 March the Foreign Office finally ruled that Cairo should have political control over the Hejaz and its ports, from Aqaba to Lith. There the matter rested until the incident at Kunfidah in the summer of 1916.

The prosecution of an Arab revolt would have been difficult enough with unified direction. But the diffuse character of British political authority on the peninsula itself lingered long after the Arab Bureau gathered at the Savoy. Resulting complications soon became evident. The Sharif of Mecca was but one cog, albeit the most significant one, in the machinery of rebellion. At about the same time, British representatives from Aden to Mesopotamia labored to arrange cooperative risings in Asir and Nejd to augment the one planned for the Hejaz. While Ibn Saud coyly maintained his distance, the Idrisi of Asir agreed to join against the Turks. A treaty guaranteeing that ruler's autonomy in exchange was initialed in April 1915. Cairo would probably never have received word of this treaty had not both McMahon and General Maxwell specifically asked to be kept informed of negotiations with the idrisi and Ibn Saud. They were in due course informed—over two months after the fact, on 7 June.

Another key weakness in such proceedings was that definitions of spheres of influence were usually based upon imprecise geographic designations (e.g., Hejaz, Asir, Nejd) whose borders varied widely depending on the perspective from which they were addressed. This made them useless as practical diplomatic parameters. British ignorance of internal Arab politics was to spawn many costly diversions and result in a general weakening of the tribal effort against the Turks. These regions shared disputed boundaries; worse, British representatives such as Jacob in Aden, Philby in Nejd, and Wilson in the Hejaz increasingly found themselves in the thankless role of boundary advocates for particular monarchs in their correspondence with superiors. Within this atmosphere, the Kunfidah incident was probably inevitable.

Kunfidah was a town under Turkish occupation to which both the idrisi and the sharif had laid claim. On 12 June 1916, just days after Hussein opened the revolt in Mecca, Lieutenant Nalder (who often acted as the Arab Bureau's liaison with the Red Sea Patrol) wired Commander Turton of the HMS *Northbrook* an account of an interview he had conducted with the idrisi at Gizan a few days before. After being promised cables as proof that Hussein had actually risen against his Turkish overlords, Asir's skeptical monarch (who had himself led a revolt against the Turks some years before that had been suppressed with Hussein's assistance) quickly promised to launch offensives against Turkish garrisons in Mohail, Abha, and Kunfidah, ostensibly to prevent those Turkish troops from attacking northward toward the Hejaz. Nalder's curious comment to Turton was: "To this no objection can be made, but it might be necessary to in the future warn the Idrisi that the value of his offensive might be lessened if it were carried out in directions which the Sherif might regard with suspicion."[48] Dangerous foundations had been laid in this reckless emphasis on marshaling as much tribal force as possible for use against the Turks, without regard to the compatibility of Britain's Arabian allies. The myopia was aggravated by, and to a certain extent the result of, the murky nature of political control through which Cairo had to grope for proper execution of its Arab strategy. At the end of March, on the heels of the residency's own overtures to the idrisi through the intercession of a sympathetic idrisi kinsman, the Arab Bureau submitted a report that pretended to address the labyrinthine complexity of South Arabian politics. Its tone revealed just how seriously the threat of such divisiveness among putative allies was coming tõ be viewed in Cairo: "The subsequent differences between the Sherif, the Imam and the Idrisi may well be left for themselves to settle, their inevitability is a sure safeguard against the existence of a United Arab Empire which is the dream of the Sherif and which might become as great a menace to British interests as the present Ottoman Germanic rule."[49] This represents a theme that recurred often in bureau reports and memoranda. It reflected Cairo's conviction that the Arabs (including the Sharif of Mecca) could be militarily exploited with a minimum of risk—certainly nothing remotely comparable to the peril of a truly united Arab political entity. With the possible exception of Ibn Saud, Arab political potential was regarded with scorn. In this respect, Cairo's view was not unlike India's. Clayton and his bureau were convinced that Arab martial spirit, once aroused, could be politically neutered and harnessed to assist the war effort. Once the Arab Revolt had spent itself, the tribes could be counted upon to turn on one another again, providing the political vacuum into which Britain might opportunistically step. The affair at Kunfidah amply demonstrated that this prospect was not preordained. In the bureau's view British interests lay in sublimating tension between the various Arabian potentates while maintaining a useful balance of power between them. Such Machiavellian deviousness hardly seems characteristic of Arab "enthusiasts."

The British Resident at Aden, perhaps sensing trouble in Nalder's report (which was not, incidentally, forwarded to Cairo), wired the Political Department at Delhi for instructions, and received the following reply: "If Idrisi is going to move against Lahaiya, Abha, and Kunfidah, his action will be against the Turks and in conformity with his treaty with us. In extending his limits to these places or others definitely in Turkish possession we can support him."[50] In due course the HMS *Minto* of the southern patrol appeared off Kunfidah and proceeded to pass along observation information to the idrisi's forces, offering whatever assistance he might require in the manner of transportation for his tribesmen. This is remarkable in light of the fact that Aden was warned of impending trouble. Aboard the *Northbrook*, Turton warned the resident that the idrisi had developed a proprietary interest in Kunfidah and that should the sharif also view that port as within his own operations' sphere and decide to launch an independent offensive toward it, "the most serious position between the Sherif and the Idrisi is likely."[51] Meanwhile, Cairo's view seemed muddled: "Consensus Cairo Political opinion seems to deprecate strongly any interference with Sherif's plans and actions. Tribal sympathies Kunfida area not known to be fixedly either pro-Sherif or pro-Idrisi."[52]

Despite ample evidence that some sort of allied altercation at Kunfidah was imminent, no move was made by Cairo or Aden to restrain either monarch from offensive action against the town. Cairo's reluctance probably stemmed from its clear lack of justification. After all, the sharif was nominal leader of the Arab Revolt, while the idrisi had yet to score any notable successes against the Turks. On the other hand, Aden actually engineered the Asiri capture of the town. On 18 July British naval units bombarded Kunfidah. Shortly thereafter the Turkish garrison surrendered, and the idrisi's tribesmen were brought ashore in craft lowered from British ships. British officers accompanied them, presiding over the raising of the Asiri banner over the Turkish fort.

News of this coup de main aroused Hussein, who swiftly dispatched Nasir Bey toward Kunfidah from Lith with a force of Sharifian tribesmen. Catastrophe was averted only by the presence of the British naval force, which actually threatened to intervene on the idrisi's behalf if the garrison were attacked. Both McMahon and Wingate, aware of the gravity of the situation, sternly urged Hussein to restrain his aggressive lieutenant. The whole affair left British officials in Cairo red-faced, as it appeared Aden had staged a fait accompli at Kunfidah. But the spectacle of Hussein humbled by his rival, the idrisi, was clearly impossible for the Arab Bureau to tolerate. Once a semblance of order was reestablished, the idrisi was informed on 7 August that he had three days in which to evacuate his contingent prior to Sharifian occupation.

While a relatively trivial affair, the Kunfidah incident had several significant consequences. First and foremost it underscored the risks inherent in dual political control along the Red Sea littoral. Aden's (and by inference India's) reckless game of one-upmanship, played without prior consultation with Cairo, seemed inexcusable. Yet it was hardly incomprehensible in light of the state of affairs on the peninsula. The ignominious withdrawal of British forces from Lahej to the Aden citadel in 1915 had created a desperate appetite there for some success comparable to that realized by the Arab Bureau in the Hejaz. Writing from Jeddah, Wilson termed the Kunfidah affair "a real bombshell," while Wingate suggested in a postscript to Clayton that any repetition of such events in the future "will not enhance our prestige with the Arabs or the Sherif."[53] The Arab Bureau's judgment was even harsher, contending that this "unfortunate incident" had "paralyzed ever since the effective cooperation of these two Arab notables."[54] What chance had existed for passable harmony between Hussein and the idrisi seemed to have vanished with the forced evacuation of Kunfidah. The subsequent British occupation of the Farasan Islands (to preempt a feared Italian thrust) wounded the idrisi even more, despite the subsidiary treaty hastily drawn up to mollify him. Back at the Savoy, Cornwallis recognized that relations between the two had soured and pressed Hussein for some gesture of magnanimity (such as a face-to-face meeting) that might prompt a reconciliation. The sharif, however, was not moved. The importance of seriously addressing such problems as the interpersonal relations between South Arabian potentates suddenly assumed added significance at the Arab Bureau: "The recognition of the Sherif by the Idrisi as the leader of the Arab movement can better be left until such time as it will have a genuine meaning based upon mutual understanding between the two chiefs."[55] In early 1917, the Foreign Office finally recognized the folly of dual authority in the Red Sea and placed the entire Arabian coast (including Aden) under Cairo's political control.

The bureau had long been critical of the Indian government's ignominious forfeiture of the initiative in South Arabia. The Turkish rout of British forces before Lahej in early 1916 and their subsequent self-internment within the citadel of Aden precipitated a collapse of local morale. This state of affairs was particularly galling to British officials there, who were left impotent in the face of Indian refusal to sanction any counterattack northward. In Cairo this reluctance was scorned as injurious to their efforts to entice the rulers of Asir and Yemen to join in revolt against the Turks. An Indian expert on South Arabian affairs, Lt. Harold Fenton Jacob (who often cooperated with bureau research in this area), warned that neither the idrisi nor Imam Yahya of Yemen would likely commit himself heavily to the sharif in the face of British inertia at Aden. Failure to recapture Lahej would fatally discredit those would-be British protégés. If the Turks were left to themselves now, even if dislodged from the region later by Allied victory elsewhere, the imam would avail himself of the opportunity to "deride our pretensions to even our own hinterland," Jacob warned. Inaction would mean that Britain's representation as a government "will be lost within our border" of South Arabia.[56]

Even though India had been shorn of political authority in the region, *military* supervision was retained. This dual control was clearly unsatisfactory insofar as Cairo was concerned. "But it should be clearly pointed out," George Lloyd advised, "that the time for a change has come; either in the whole mental attitude and method of India towards Aden or its transference to a more enterprising, sympathetic and up to date authority."[57] Yet Indian opposition to a forward policy in South Arabia remained formidable despite Cairo's assumption of political control. Delhi worried that such a move might undermine the precarious neutrality of Imam Yahya, whom it regarded as the key native power in the region. It was equally unapologetic toward officials in Cairo and Aden who were flirting (albeit inconsequentially) with a rival tribal confederacy in the Yemen led by a pretender to the imamate. In the viceroy's view this was simply another hint of the disaster that loomed over the extension of Cairo's authority: "In view of impending catastrophe of transfer political control of Aden to Foreign Office we hesitate to press our advice regarding situation with developments in which we shall presumably not deal but we feel convinced Imam is keynote to situation which might well be left to develop for the present without our active intervention."[58]

Officials at the Arab Bureau dissented emphatically. Lloyd was particularly insistent that Britain treat with the imam's rival lest an opportunistic Italy steal the advantage and do so itself, spreading Rome's sphere of influence across the Red Sea from Eritrea. Besides, he added: "We have here a proposal that fits in with both our Military and Political policy. What we have done in the Hejaz with the very worst type of Arab warriors, we should at least succeed in doing in the Yemen with the best fighting tribes of Arabia . . . , the present absurd Aden situation should rapidly be liquidated."[59]

The imam's stock had long since crashed in Cairo, where his early sufferance of Turkish garrisons was read as bald opportunism posing as tortured neutrality. The obdurate yet sloppy policy of the Indian government, timorous of alienating this aging potentate, was detectable in an earlier telegram from Delhi to Balfour, which "displays more compressed ignorance to the facts than could without long practice have been put into a similar number of lines."[60]

Although Cornwallis was in general accord with the spirit of Lloyd's assessment, he was more cautious as to the manner in which this policy should have been executed. The bureau's director saw a familiar pattern emerging: solicitous chiefs queuing up for the imperial dole with little to offer in the way of reciprocity. He counseled extreme caution to Clayton before considering wholesale material support of this would-be imam and his supposed confederacy. First, the true influence of this pretender among the hill tribes should be ascertained. If the results proved promising, a coordinated, responsible plan of action should be submitted *before* the dispatch of any monies. Most importantly, no assistance should be sent unless British forces could make some sort of successful military demonstration from Lahej. "It is important," Cornwallis warned, that "we should do something more active against the Turks than subsidize other people to fight against them."[61] Now in residence at the Arab Bureau, Jacob was likewise skeptical of any such scheme, even allowing for the stimulant of an offensive from Aden. The Yemeni pretender (of the idrisi's clan) was simply a parvenu, and the Italian threat was neither new nor worrisome. He also felt that to break faith with a negotiating imam now would only leave Britain vulnerable to charges of duplicity and further damage her prestige.[62]

Ultimately, nothing ever came of these musings, for the Arab Bureau could not arrive at unanimous consensus on whether to chance an open break with the imam. Following the evacuation of Turkish forces from Arabia in 1919, the Savoy hoped to salvage some sort of nominal suzerainty for Hussein in Arabia, as a sop to that unhappy monarch. Such a title would have been meaningless, as the imam, the idrisi, and Ibn Saud likely would have suffered no loss of temporal power as a result. But in the absence of those rulers' consent, such hopes were vain ones indeed. "I

cannot help feeling," Herbert Garland (the bureau's last director) confessed, "that no interpretation of the word 'nominal' can be evolved which
in actual practice will really satisfy rulers who are ever on the watch for
tangible and material advantages."[63] The confederation that the bureau
envisioned for the Arabian peninsula would have to be even "looser" than
they had desired or expected, for they would have to rely on pilgrimage
facilities to enhance the sharif's dwindling prestige as Keeper of the Holy
Cities.

5

WRAPPING BANANAS

The Arab Bureau's Propaganda Dimension

Early in the war, British planners made effective (and often shameless) use of propaganda overseas to evoke sympathy for the Allies and hostility toward the Central Powers. Anonymous Belgian civilians gained immortality as martyrs against the barbarities of "the Hun." The skill of British propagandists in turning the tide of American opinion especially has been widely acknowledged. The bogus Bryce Report was so successful in arousing hatred against the Germans, notes Phillip Knightley, that it ranks as "one of the most successful propaganda pieces of the War."[1]

So to apply similar methods to resurrect the image of "the unspeakable Turk" did not bring on a crisis of conscience at Whitehall. That image had been in steady decline in Britain since the late nineteenth century and Gladstone's thunderous denunciation of Turkish behavior toward Christian civilians in Bulgaria. But in the Middle Eastern theater of war, a successful propaganda campaign would have to be tailored to specific British interests in the region at the time. First, Whitehall was determined to blunt the pan-Islamic appeal of the Ottoman sultan/caliph to the Turks, Asians, and Muslims living under British rule. Second, it sought to arouse sympathy (or at least neutrality) for Sharif Hussein and his revolt among all Muslims of the region. The government of India was particularly concerned that the first objective be reached. This anxiety was not as hysterical as it might seem at first glance. The volatile Khalifat movement that swept through India in 1919 seemed to vindicate Delhi's wartime judgment. The viceroy was distinctly less receptive, however, to propaganda that glorified any native revolt against established authority—even Turkish authority.

From the early days of the war, German experts worked assiduously alongside their Turkish allies, disseminating pan-Islamic propaganda to the acute discomfiture of officials in both Cairo and Delhi. A hand-picked staff of experts in both cities liberally dispensed gold and intrigue and even dispatched far-ranging furtive military missions in Persia and Afghanistan in efforts to undermine the Entente in the Muslim world. These machinations were inspired by Baron Max Von Oppenheim, who rashly divulged German intentions to Emir Feisal in Damascus in 1915. "We want," stressed the baron, "to make rebellions of Moslems against Christians" in Egypt, India, the Sudan, and North Africa.[2] Major Hennessy, an early and transient member of the Arab Bureau, saw much to emulate in Von Oppenheim's work and exhorted his colleagues to "copy the Germans," adding that they should "let it impress this fact deep in the minds of the people of all Moslem countries that there is only one real Moslem power capable of understanding and directing Moslem ambitions and ideals and that power is England."[3]

It seemed obvious to Gilbert Clayton that this new campaign of "offensive propaganda" against Berlin's Pan-Islamic Bureau should be orchestrated from Cairo, owing to the presence of "various journalists we could use" such as Doctor Shahbandar of al-Mokattam. Besides, he felt that the British might as well begin honing the propaganda weapon for later use "when the war is over and all the seditious elements of the Committee of Union and Progress and all other similar societies are thrown upon their beam ends and have to seek new fields of activity." Clayton claimed to have "new evidences" that two of these fields had been and would be Egypt and India.[4] High Commissioner McMahon concurred in this view. Both men hoped fervently that the newly constituted Arab Bureau might prove the vehicle "to counter propaganda which now and hereafter threaten to injure our position in the Eastern world."[5]

The Arab Bureau took this injunction seriously, pursuing a plan calculated to incite Turkish revolt without stirring up Arab nationalism; to promote Hussein as a legitimate usurper with viable authority over Mecca, but lacking the authority of a new caliph of Islam; and to direct the mobilization of Arab opinion toward the Allied cause and away from specious evocations of Turko-German jihad. These objectives, while not overwhelmingly successful (or even achievable) through the propaganda medium, nonetheless spoke to a genuinely perceived peril to the Arab Revolt's prospects and the pressing need to galvanize or at least distract Muslim opinion behind it. Urgency seemed greatest outside the Arabian peninsula; and since India was deemed especially susceptible to pan-Islamic appeal, Wingate averred: "It is for this reason that I have advocated so strongly the continuance, with redoubled effect, of the counter-propaganda which the Hejaz movement has so opportunely afforded us and which we must now support at all costs to resolve to make a success."[6] This propaganda campaign was also intended to dovetail with bureau efforts to alert superiors and colleagues to policy matters and impress them with their agency's far-ranging activities through an internal publication.

The most direct means by which the Arab Bureau parlayed its own viewpoint in the highest political circles was the *Arab Bulletin*, the confidential official summary of Near Eastern developments as interpreted by the agency. Its contributors were generally from within the bureau: David Hogarth, T. E. Lawrence, Philip Graves, Gertrude Bell, George Lloyd, and colleagues, although on occasion insights were solicited from other quarters such as the Egyptian residency or the Jeddah Agency. The *Bulletin* included regional political and personality profiles in addition to military assessments of troop strength, dispositions, and movements, often accompanied by firsthand accounts of fighting in Arabia from British observers. Reaction to developments in Arabia from throughout the Muslim world was also carefully monitored in the *Bulletin*.

In qualitative terms, the bureau's medium exceeded expectations. "I am immensely struck," wrote Wingate, "with the excellence of the bulletins and the clear and concise way in which the matter is recorded." But the goal of maintaining its secrecy would prove more problematical. And Sykes was not averse to blocking its circulation in London if the news was insufficiently optimistic.[7] Its distribution was supposed to have been severely restricted, with just over a score of copies printed per issue and dispatched to the Foreign Office, the War Office, the Admiralty, the government of India, and other diplomatic stations in the region. Certain individuals received copies directly: Colonel C. E. Wilson, Ronald Storrs, Sir Percy Cox in Basra, Alfred Parker, Sykes, Clayton, and Lawrence—a select group to be sure.

In reviewing the run of the *Arab Bulletin*, several facts are remarkable. One is its wide scope. Reports analyzed cultural, ethnographic, religious, and geographic conditions in addition to political and military intelligence directly related to the war effort. They ranged from Morocco to Abyssinia to Malaya and the remotest recesses of Islamic penetration, in order to determine not only political climates but also pertinent personalities and trends. But of course the emphasis remained, first and foremost, on the course of the Arab Revolt and its larger ramifications and prospects. The second feature of the *Bulletin* that strikes the critical historian is its signal avoidance of some of the most nettlesome contemporary issues confronting the British in the Middle East, particularly proposed policies toward the French and the Zionists. The Arab Bureau was established originally to act as an intelligence repository from which advice on policy formulation would presumably flow. Yet for the historian combing the files for the bureau's perspective on such questions, the *Arab Bulletin* is disappointing fare indeed.

The reason for this is quite simple. Shortly after its inception the confidentiality of the *Arab Bulletin* was fatally breached. Sykes had never been a pillar of discretion insofar as this publication was concerned. In August 1916, he asked Hogarth to send thirty additional copies (over the original consignment of five) to London. Hogarth replied that further information was required, such as for whom the documents were intended, but sent them anyway.[8] Over one year later, apparently appalled at the consequences of his recklessness, Sykes asked that distribution be restricted once more to five copies because the *Bulletin* was then being read by over ninety people in London and "issue can only be controlled by number of copies."[9] An irritated Clayton replied: "I was under the impression that circulation was limited to very few selected persons in high office and publication was regarded as strictly secret. If this is not so, as is indicated, publication must cease to be a complete presentation of facts."[10]

In point of fact, the *Bulletin* had long since ceased to be "a complete presentation of the facts," due not to Sykes's indiscretions in London but to prior French and Italian knowledge of its existence and content. This was discovered by McMahon rather by accident in the summer of 1916 when the French chargé d'affaires, Monsieur de France, revealed knowledge of the *Bulletin* to him. The high commissioner, in turn, asked Hogarth how this unfortunate situation had come about. The Arab Bureau's director revealed that the Italian attaché in Cairo, a Mr. Vitali, who apparently had free rein of Egypforce's intelligence section at Ismailia, had seen a copy of the *Arab Bulletin* there. He in turn informed Monsieur St. Quentin, the French attaché, who then stormed into the Savoy to berate Hogarth for concealing the publication from him. Hogarth confessed to McMahon that he had been placed "on the horns of a dilemma" but felt compelled to divulge the truth to St. Quentin because "it seemed to me less harmful to let St. Quentin see the file than to leave him aware of its existence and suspicious about his exclusion from the sight of it."[11] This disclosure had the effect of negating much of the *Bulletin*'s potential usefulness and neutralizing an otherwise powerful lobbying tool for the bureau in London. Consequently, the text of the *Arab Bulletin* was shorn of potentially abrasive political overtones. One officer who had served with the bureau confessed after the war that:

> The constant wish of the French and Italians to see the Bulletin made it impossible for us to discuss certain problems in it at all, and rendered drastic expurgation necessary in the case of most of the rest. As a result, it can hardly be regarded as an impartial review of the Arabian situation, in reference particularly to Syria and Asir. It tended more and more to confine itself to noncommittal appreciations of the spheres in which our Allies are not immediately interested, and to general reviews of intelligence of historical, geographical and even scientific interest.[12]

In 1919, once the Turks had been defeated and the attention of Europe's diplomats focused on the convoluted problems of the peace, the suggestion was made to reconstitute the *Bulletin* behind a new facade—actually just a new name, which would convince prying eyes that the *Bulletin* had been terminated. Various titles were suggested: *Middle-Eastern Bulletin, Political Notes on the Middle-East,* and *Middle-East Gazette.* Ultimately *Notes on the Middle-East* was agreed upon.

A squabble soon erupted, however, over which department would distribute it. This seemed important in light of the embarrassing situation that had developed with the *Arab Bulletin*. The *Bulletin* had known many distributors in the past. Probably because of Hogarth's close ties with the

Admiralty, the *Bulletin* originally came to London through Naval Intelligence. Shortly thereafter the publication was addressed to Sykes, who incorporated sections of it into his Arabian Report. He in turn submitted it to the Committee on Imperial Defence. By the end of the war, the *Bulletin* was being sent directly to War Office Intelligence and thence to the various interested departments. Finally, in 1919 with the creation of the new *Notes*, the Foreign Office resolved not to lose again the exclusive rights to its distribution. Indeed, wrote Hubert Young from Whitehall, "I do not quite understand why the W.[ar] O.[ffice] retain an interest in either the Arab Bureau or its publications."[13]

Another mounting problem early in the war was the alarming and effective employment of pan-Islamic propaganda by Turko-German intelligence. A special Pan-Islamic Bureau had been established in both Berlin and Damascus to capitalize on the regional mass appeal of the Turkish caliph. To British and especially Indian officials, this tactic was political dynamite. Pan-Islamic societies were rife throughout the Muslim world but especially in Afghanistan and India, where the prospect of Islamic revivalism was chilling. The Afghan emir, Delhi suspected, aspired to the caliphate himself. (He was, in fact, later discovered to be collaborating with secret Indian societies in the dispatch of agents disguised as pilgrims to the Hejaz; their mission was to stir up discontent against the sharif and funnel religious monies to the Turkish war effort.) Along the canal front the Turks employed several tactics to encourage Arab cooperation, including tax remissions and large bribes. This became evident after additional information was obtained from Turkish prisoners following the repulse of their offensive against the canal in 1915. These developments, observed Wingate, "all go to show that there is a very distinct and definite Arab policy emanating from Berlin, and that our enemies will not stick at spending largely in order to obtain their object."[14]

An intelligence officer in Clayton's command submitted a note on the pan-Islamic movement in late 1915 suggesting the creation of a British-controlled medium by which to counter such efforts. Wingate, however, shared the apprehension of many of his colleagues toward the notion of a pan-Islamic bureau, fearing that such a pretense would only enrage Muslims. Far better to refine a special anti-pan-Islamic section of the Arab Bureau, employing several Muslims to advise and assist. In any case: "The propaganda part of the business would . . . come within the scope of the Arab Bureau and it is understood that such propaganda would be directed by people well-acquainted with Moslem opinion in the various British dependencies as well as with the aims and activities of the different sections of Pan-Islamists."[15] So in addition to the organization and collation of intelligence and research information, the Arab Bureau was engaged in the concoction and distribution of Allied propaganda. This material was disseminated by both covert and overt means, usually in a manner designed to deflect recognition of the bureau's hand in various propaganda publications.

First and foremost among these was the pictorial tabloid *al-Haqiqa* (the Truth), conceived in early 1916. This journal was published in London and devoted primarily to martial illustrations, accompanied by legends in several vernaculars such as Arabic, Persian, and Hindustani. In its planning stages, the pictures in *al-Haqiqa* were supposed to represent two major themes: "(a) those shewing Great Britain as the friend of Mohammedanism, and (b) those shewing the Naval and Military strength of Great Britain and acts of individual heroism."[16] As the need for some type of effective counter to Turko-German propaganda in the Arab world became more apparent, support grew in Cairo for some sort of immediate action. In February, McMahon suggested that the newly formed Arab Bureau would be the best source of suitable material for the new publication.[17]

The first issue of *al-Haqiqa* (of which ten thousand copies were printed) received negative reviews in Cairo despite the fact that Storrs (McMahon's oriental secretary) had submitted some of the material used in it. Lawrence was particularly ungenerous: "Re the HAKIKAT . . . the blocks and the ideas are excellent; and the calligraphy the worst I have ever seen; in fact it was Kakagraphy (apologies to Storrs). If the thing is to continue they must get a better man to write it."[18] But Storrs was aware of the shortcomings of this propaganda effort: "We . . . had no text-book upon which to base our methods. All we knew was that careful and progressive handling of public opinion was no less difficult than necessary among peoples of alien race, language, and religion. Articles, diagrams effective in Europe often produce a negative sometimes even a contrary result in the East. Some of the most repulsive . . . excited admiration rather than horror."[19] For example, India was particularly anxious that reports of the Arab Revolt's progress be carefully censored, for while details of Turkish shelling of the Kaaba (Mecca's foremost shrine) might play well on the continent, it might "arouse India and seem to substantiate [the] accusation that [the] Arab Revolt endangers sanctity of [the] Holy Places."[20] Similarly, tales of Palestinian pogroms and massacres of Armenians ran the risk of casting the Turks in a locally favorable light. When local sensibilities had to be appeased, British officials were not above soliciting help from the editors of the Egyptian newspaper *al-Muqattam,* a publication heavily subsidized by the British.

Further problems arose in the manner of *al-Haqiqa*'s distribution and availability to projected readers. The range of the magazine's dispersal was theoretically wide, extending throughout Egypt, the Sudan, Basra, and Aden. In addition, copies were shipped from Suez to various points along the Hejaz coast and smuggled into Syria and Palestine. Following shipment from London, *al-Haqiqa* was deposited in two commercial houses in Egypt, at Alexandria and Port Said. Beyond this initial stage, however, no adequate distribution network existed. Because shipment cases were often inadequately marked, ten days were usually lost between the time of *al-Haqiqa*'s arrival in Egypt and its proper dispatch to the residency and the Arab Bureau for distribution elsewhere. The remaining copies were simply turned over to news vendors to hawk on the streets of Cairo at an inflated price. Unsold copies were ultimately distributed free of charge to the public.

In the early stages Storrs was responsible for distribution, but this duty was later deputed to Lawrence. Still, the system remained inadequate. An insufficient number of copies "reach the native population whom it is most desirable to impress," complained Clayton. One of the reasons for this, he opined, was *al-Haqiqa*'s eventual free distribution: "The Egyptian does not understand that it is possible to give away something for nothing."[21] Philip Graves, a correspondent for the *Times* who worked in the Arab Bureau's propaganda section, felt the distribution bottleneck might have been overcome simply by making the Arab Bureau the sole (and more selective) distributor, because "the oriental is inclined to disdain what is, so to speak, thrown at him."[22] Such wholesale distribution of the paper, the bureau feared, had discredited it in Arab eyes by giving it the look of a cheap propaganda sheet.

Wingate agreed that the Savoy should handle all distribution and that the tabloid would probably fare better with a modest price attached to it. Eventually, sale and distribution in Egypt was allotted to the Egyptian Commercial Intelligence Bureau while the Arab Bureau continued in the role of official *al-Haqiqa* translator and occasional contributor of pieces solicited from sympathetic Arab writers with whom it was in contact. Free distribution was restricted, however, to specific locations such as banks, waiting rooms, and the like. Copies were spread about Egypt in a less conspicuous manner to public institutions, churches, and schools. A typical regional allocation was broken down like this: (1) Egypt and the Arab Bureau (for distribution in contested or hostile territory), 10,000; (2) Aden and the government of India, 1,000; (3) Somaliland, 250; (4) Mesopotamia, Basra, the Persian Gulf, and Force D, 4,000; (5) Persian Gulf, Foreign Office, 300.[23]

Saddled with so many other problems, the propaganda value of *al-Haqiqa* was questioned often at the Arab Bureau. Distribution was a headache, encumbered by control of the Foreign Office. Moreover, much effort was wasted when ships laden with thousands of copies were sunk (thirty thousand copies were lost in early 1917 alone). The bureau also expressed doubts as to the effectiveness of the paper's format. *Al-Haqiqa*'s prospective readers, it was felt, were those for whom pictorial representation might have the least meaning. The agency maintained that, as a communications medium, illustrations were unfamiliar to most Egyptians and Arabs. Indeed, the bureau suggested, "to the uneducated the pictures probably convey nothing."[24] Another bureau officer went so far as to suggest the scrapping of *al-Haqiqa* in favor of merger with the French language *La Guerre Illustrée*, which could, he insisted, be adapted with Arabic legends. In this way "it would seem that paper would be saved and the trouble of a special organisation for the production of a separate publication obviated."[25] This suggestion, forwarded to the Foreign Office by Wingate, was subsequently vetoed. But a new distribution scheme was approved to remedy the situation; free distribution of *al-Haqiqa* would be suspended "where it is feared it would injure the paper's status." Bureau officer Lt. H. Fielding assumed a major role in the paper's publication. A former secretary of the Psychological Research Society, he was, in Hogarth's words, an "indefatigable collector of information on all subjects and will do any amount of work. He poses as the complete skeptic . . . always in search of genuine mediums and finding none."[26] What he did find was a distressing indifference to the bureau's publication, which he conveyed to Wingate through an anecdote. "We found, for example, that large quantities were simply sold by weight for wrapping paper. No one is going to buy or be interested in a paper if he finds the latest numbers used for wrapping up bananas."[27] Wingate finally was successful in securing the position of the Arab Bureau as the exclusive office of distribution. As for the suggested merger with *La Guerre Illustrée*, the Foreign Office found numerous objections. This use of a French publication would probably necessitate excision of certain items (such as pictures of ruined churches) that might have been objectionable from an Arab standpoint. Also, it might have proven difficult to develop Arabic legends adequate to underscore the pictorial emphasis on military equipment, which the publication relied on heavily. Such Arabic descriptions, in any case, would be "difficult of comprehension to other than the highly civilised Western mind."[28] One suspects such an arrangement would have required a separate production anyway, so that little increase in efficiency would have resulted. So al-Haqiqa was continued in streamlined form throughout the war and briefly afterward.

The bureau also became involved in the publication of a second so-called newspaper in November 1916. Al-Kawkab was conceived, written, and published in Cairo for distribution in the Persian Gulf, Basra, Zanzibar, Aden, Abyssinia, Somaliland, the Sudan, and northwest Africa. This paper concentrated more on editorial content and political war news than on pictorial representation. Originally the bureau intended to keep al-Kawkab's origin a secret, but this was soon found to be impractical. Rather, it was decided to associate it with the leaders of the Arab movement residing in Cairo who were called upon to contribute. In his report to the Committee on Imperial Defence, Sykes expressed his hopes for the new propaganda organ: "It forms a useful supplement to the Mecca paper the "Kibla" and having at its disposal material which is unknown to the Meccan editors, is able to expose the real aims of Germany and Turkey in a manner which it is hoped, will have a considerable propaganda value."[29] Al-Kawkab was edited by Dr. Shahbandar, a noted Syrian nationalist, and managed by a G. Brackenbery from the Ministry of Public Instruction. But its policy was set by the Arab Bureau through Philip Graves.

The paper enjoyed modest initial success, its excerpts being incorporated into local newspapers in Tunis and Morocco in addition to direct distribution. Published weekly, al-Kawkab was intended for use outside Egypt so as to avoid antagonizing Egyptian nationalists with a paper exhorting the sharif's revolt. There was, however, a high demand for it among Syrians in Egypt and among members of nationalist secret societies with which the Savoy was in contact. As a result, a limited number of issues were circulated in Tanta and Alexandria by means of special agents. The overall scale of distribution, however, was more modest than that of al-Haqiqa, something over one thousand copies dispensed from Algiers to Bushire with the bulk going to newly liberated Baghdad.

The bureau also was responsible for establishment of an official press organ in Mecca. During the summer of 1916, Clayton conferred with Hussein's lieutenant, Fuad al-Khatib, on the specifics, with several objectives in view: (1) to persuade its readers of the "righteousness" of the Arab movement as promoted solely by the Arabs themselves and in the interests of Islam; (2) to explain the evils of rule under the Committee of Union and Progress that necessitated the revolt; (3) to proclaim British intentions throughout the Arabian peninsula; and (4) to persuade the Arab world "that the interest of Islam and allies are coherent and that reciprocal benefits and relations are natural."[30] There is little doubt that, from the beginning, *al-Qibla* (as the new organ was to be called) was meant to be little more than a thinly veiled mouthpiece through which the bureau could increase the effectiveness of its propaganda throughout the Arab world. The Sharifian government, while allied with the British, provided a more detached location than Cairo from which to solicit support. The means to publish, including both equipment and funds, were provided by the Arab Bureau: "We will go through them [*al-Qibla* articles], correcting or adding as necessary. We will give them any stuff which we can't very well publish ourselves and would come better from Mecca e.g. matters concerning religion."[31] In this fashion, the bureau could engage in theological speculation concerning otherwise incendiary topics as the caliphate and the pilgrimage without embroiling Cairo in heated controversy with Indian authorities or weakening the force of Sharifian positions on such questions with the stain of open British support. Moreover, the bureau could use its position to subtly censor the Sharifian press in order to avoid editorial scrutiny of embarrassing British commitments. The subject of Zionism was tagged as one to be particularly discouraged.[32] In addition, lest nationalist elements in Egypt be encouraged, distribution of *al-Qibla* there and in the Sudan was severely restricted and carefully censored by the Arab Bureau.

After Allenby's long-awaited thrust up the Palestine corridor had begun, these propaganda activities were extended northward to the region of impending liberation. Once Jerusalem was captured, a new branch bureau was established by Hogarth and Clayton. The new branch was actually placed under Deedes, who was head of Clayton's political intelligence section. Several officers from the Cairo bureau, including Fielding, were deputed to Palestine. Additional expertise was provided by two journalists for the *Times* who had been claimed by the bureau: Philip Graves, the old Cairo hand, and Harry Pirie-Gordon, dispatched from London early in 1918. In addition to this work, Pirie-Gordon also edited the popular *Palestine Times*, which became the official newspaper of the Egyptian Expeditionary Force.

The propaganda function of the Palestine Arab Bureau had its furtive dimension as well. A suitable home and "Arab Master of Ceremonies" were acquired to help get in touch with and "adequately entertain any Arabs who might come in from the East." Cornwallis, still in Cairo, was optimistic about the new center's contribution, feeling that "no doubt in a short time the Bureau will become a center for the reception of trans-Jordan news and one from which propaganda can conveniently be disseminated."[33] This branch of the Arab Bureau continued clandestine work in the Turkish territories. Various emissaries (including Lawrence) were dispatched to tribes in Palestine and Syria to induce them to abandon the Turk and collaborate with Feisal's bedouin. The Arab Bureau had been thus engaged from the time of Murray's crawl into the Sinai, spreading proclamations and communications from the Sharif of Mecca, assembling tribal durbars, employing native agents, and dropping leaflets from aircraft. Such activities were aimed at both instilling enmity toward Turkish occupiers and eliciting support for an Anglo-Hashemite alliance with which many Arabs (especially Syrians) were not yet entirely comfortable. In at least the first objective, as George Antonius has observed, the efforts of the Arab Bureau and Military Intelligence enjoyed signal success. In a postwar interview with Mehmed Jemal Pasha, who commanded the Ottoman Eighth Army Corps in Syria, that author recorded that "In his view, the disaffection spread in Syria by the Anglo-Arab propaganda turned out to have been more detrimental to the Turkish hold on the country than the military losses caused directly by the entry of the Arabs into the War."[34]

As for the more formal propaganda publications churned out and/or distributed by the Arab Bureau, it remains questionable whether many Arabs were swayed. The more informal techniques, executed by skilled agents and reinforced by the success of the military campaign, certainly bore more fruit. Publications such as *al-Haqiqa* and *al-Kawkab* represented anemic attempts to answer the threat of enemy propaganda and lacked the Islamic credibility inherent in the sultan's position. India, for whose benefit much of this effort was expended, did not allow widespread distribution of Arab Bureau propaganda. Moreover, the Arabs proved not to be the eager sops for Allied cant that many assumed them to be. Observed one bureau officer in 1918: "Propaganda such as the 'kawkab' and the like fail because there is not enthusiasm or faith to preach or the driving force of an ideal behind. The Arabs have been the tools of Turkish intrigue for centuries and are therefore suspicious of all newspapers."[35]

6

A STAKE IN DISORDER

In Pursuit of Arabian Balance

In Arabia the Arab Bureau set out to expedite the war against the Turks while laying the groundwork for indirect postwar British political control. Here again familiar obstacles arose, originating both in Delhi and in the political complexity of the peninsula.

In 1916 Arabia was a region torn by dynastic feuds, a condition aggravated around the turn of the century by the meteoric rise of a young and energetic chieftain to leadership of a renewed Wahhabi revival in southeastern Arabia. Abdul Aziz Ibn Saud assumed the reins of his historically prominent clan in an attempt to restore the vitality of that puritanical sect, which had arisen from the sands of Arabia a century before. In January 1902 he led a small band of followers in the seizure of Riyadh, the former Wahhabi capital, from the Rashidi clan, which had

long held sway over the remote emirate of Nejd. At the head of his bands
of devout Ikhwan (brothers), Ibn Saud continued to expand his power at the
expense of traditional enemies, like the Rashidis and the coastal clans
inhabiting the Arabian rim. By 1915 there were basically three leaders in
the interior who possessed some measure of control over large geographic
areas: Sharif Hussein in the Hejaz, based at Mecca; Ibn Saud in Nejd,
based at Riyadh; and Ibn Rashid in the Jebel Shammar region of northeast
Arabia, based at Hail. While the British ultimately proved successful in
forging alliances with the first two chieftains, Ibn Rashid remained persistently out of the fold, preferring to stay in the pro-Turkish camp. The
history of relations between these three chieftains remains to this day laced
with allegations of jealousy, duplicity, and intrigue.

The lack of enthusiasm with which other prominent leaders in Arabia
reacted to the sharif's uprising was conspicuous and did not escape the
attention of either Sykes or Hogarth. While ostensibly pleased with the
turn of events in Mecca, Ibn Saud regarded Hussein as "essentially
unstable, trivial, and undependable." Further, Clayton was warned that
any pretension to the caliphate on the part of the sharif would be met with
indifference in Riyadh.[1] Although Sykes preferred to remain optimistic as
to the likely behavior of the Emir of Nejd, Hogarth was less sanguine,
believing that self-interest and an aversion to the Turks were the primary
reasons behind Ibn Saud's verbal support. In a contribution to Sykes's
Arabian Report to the CID, Hogarth dubbed the emir "Gallant for an
Arab," a leader who, although nursing a "Teutonic contempt for written
treaties," was not without attributes: "In civil matters he shows unusual
kindness and patience, his internal policy is good and strong."[2]

In his next report Hogarth went farther, recognizing that Ibn Saud's
prejudices against the sharif were "not unnatural" in light of the latter's
opportunistic thrust at Qasim in 1910.[3] It was rather the emir's religious
proclivities that alarmed the bureau's director. Hogarth regarded Wahhabism as a potent, atavistic contagion that threatened to upset Arabian
political equilibrium and, if not extinguish Hussein's revolt, at least divert
it to the point of impotence. Wahhabism, he feared, was too puritanical
and mercurial, and he regarded its resurgence with dread over the long
term. For the moment, however, the ongoing dispute between Nejd and the
Rashidi clan of Jebel Shammar (with whom the Turks were allied) showed
no signs of imminent resolution and served to reduce significantly the
immediate danger that messianic Wahhabism would infect the Hejaz.

The bureau worked tirelessly in these early stages to induce harmony

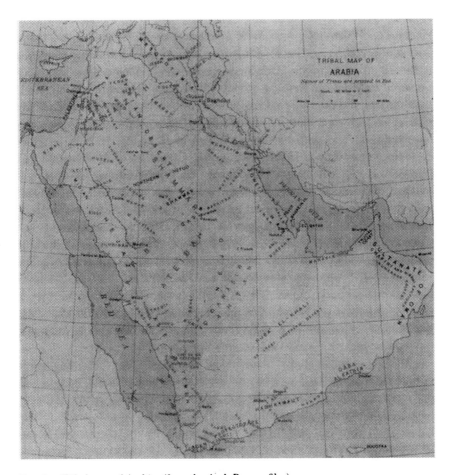

FIG. 5.   Tribal map of Arabia. (from the Arab Bureau files)

between the Sharifian government at Jeddah and Ibn Saud's capital of Riyadh. But despite this preoccupation, the Savoy chafed at the entangling fetters that accompanied involvement of any kind in Arabian politics. For instance, Cornwallis noted the lack of a fixed boundary between the Hejaz and Nejd and posited, "It seems not unlikely that His Britannic Majesty's Government will be called upon to mediate between the Sherif and Ibn Saud in the near future."[4] This seems a curious remark in that the Arab Bureau would later counsel against interference by London in the Khurma dispute, to which we shall turn presently. But it is evident that both Hogarth and Cornwallis recognized a potential source of trouble in Riyadh and were prepared to do everything necessary to make the complex system of British alliances on the Arabian peninsula work. Accordingly, they were prepared to assist the fortunes of Sharif Hussein by neutralizing Ibn Saud, both through the threat posed by Ibn Rashid and leverage provided by the modest subsidy funneled to him by Delhi. One might surmise that the bureau would have enlisted the emir's support against Hail in order to increase pressure upon Fakhri Pasha's Turkish garrison at Medina, but this clearly was not the case. The bureau saw Ibn Saud as an able but inexperienced ruler lacking the sharif's religious importance, beset with excitable subjects, and hampered by poor relations with neighbors in Hail, Kuwait, and the rebellious Ajman of Hasa, which he had recently absorbed. While his star was clearly rising (especially in the wake of Rashidi decline) he simply lacked the sharif's attractiveness as an ally. Hogarth contemplated Britain's relationship to both in the *Arab Bulletin:* "It is in the last degree undesirable that we should be drawn into Central Arabia politics. It should not be forgotten that of the two, the Sharif and Ibn Saud, Ibn Saud is (1) the less powerful potentate and (2) far less able to influence the present general Eastern situation in our favour."[5]

One of Gertrude Bell's biographers has seized on this passage as symptomatic of the malaise with which the writer was afflicted, contending that "some fundamental misconceptions of British policy in Arabia were demonstrated in that paragraph."[6] Such a conclusion is scarcely fair. The Sharif of Mecca was indubitably the paramount chieftain on whom the British could rely. His lineage, titles, and geographic proximity had much to recommend to Cairo's coconspirators. He was the only Arab leader remotely capable of seizing Mecca, thus making a wartime hajj possible. He was for the most part at peace with his neighbors, although old grudges lingered. Bell certainly regarded Hussein's significance as prodigious: "He is the only person who could raise a jehad. . . . The question is whether we can keep him in play. From all the information that comes in he seems to have acquired a very remarkable position in Arabia, but his strength is moral, not military, and if the Turks come down into Syria in force, they might be able to put pressure on him which he could not resist."[7]

Ibn Saud headed a smaller, more fanatical following with far less regional appeal, especially in Syria. Geographically, the Emir of Nejd was isolated and possessed no titular mantle under which a fractured group of Arabian tribes might strike common cause. What seems frequently lost in hindsight is that the Arab Revolt, insofar as many military objectives are concerned, was a notable success. Indeed, it is doubtful that such a project would have fared better under Ibn Saud's leadership. As Gary Troeller has saliently noted, Hussein was, for a host of reasons, the only viable choice as leader. Moreover, "to assert that Britain backed the wrong horse is to view the situation in light of Ibn Saud's subsequent career."[8] Whatever were the causes of the sharif's rapid postwar decline (and they were legion), the conclusion that Britain backed the wrong horse in Arabia remains tenuous.

In fact, Hussein's rather unpopular image with lesser Arabian chieftains served to enhance his attractiveness. Even his possible candidacy for the caliphate was considered innocuous by Wingate because he knew there was scant risk of creating Frankenstein's monster. Such an assumption would have meant little to the likes of Ibn Saud and the Idrisi of Asir. Moreover, inherent political divisions would guarantee British control over the ostensibly autonomous federation of Arab states that he and the Arab Bureau sought to create. The substance could be gained by concession of the shadow. "The Indian fear that the Arab state, thus constituted, might become a menace to British interests," the sirdar wrote, "is sufficiently discounted by the views expressed by these and other Eastern chiefs."[9] In this manner British interests would be preserved, the sharif mollified with grand but vacuous titles, the Turks divested of their empire, and Arabian tribes left to carry on in their insulated, fratricidal continuum. Clayton acknowledged this in a telegram to Wingate, citing "the lack of cohesion which is always quoted as our main safeguard against the establishment of a united Arab Kingdom which might be a threat to British interests."[10] A most necessary qualification for Britain's clients in Arabia was expendability. This outlook was wholly consistent with London's preference that Arabia remain fissiparous. "What we want," Lord Crewe had written earlier in the war, "is not a United Arabia; but a weak and disunited Arabia, split up into little principalities so far as possible under our suzerainty—but incapable of coordinated action against us, forming a buffer against the powers in the west."[11]

The Arab Bureau desired no startling Wahhabi successes against Ibn Rashid, which would have aggravated an already suspicious Hussein. However, limited harassment of Hail by the Wahhabis was desirable, especially if it resulted in interruption of the Rashidi camel trade with the Turks. Wahhabi conquest was unlikely in any case, given the Indian government's parsimony, and such efforts might assist the work of Sharifian forces in the north. Yet every attempt by Cairo to induce military cooperation between Jeddah and Riyadh was stoutly resisted by Hussein. The sharif used his control over the land routes to Nejd, via the Red Sea, to prevent Sir Ronald Storrs from journeying to Riyadh in 1917 and similarly resisted Cairo's attempts to weld its own Wahhabi connection. The king's obstinate refusal to treat with Ibn Saud or the idrisi made the bureau's task of putting the best Islamic face on the revolt much more difficult. "It is bad for propagandist work outside," complained Wingate to Hogarth, "and gives a stick for the anti Arabs to beat the pro-Sherifial and Pro-Arab parties with."[12]

Cornwallis and Clayton grew increasingly disturbed about their failure to sublimate the rivalry between Britain's two allies. Officers at the Arab Bureau, apprised of the potential for discord, went out of their way to explain to Hussein the other treaties by which His Majesty's government was bound. Chief Political Officer Sir Percy Cox wrote anxiously to the Savoy, warning of the increased malignity of the sharif's behavior and of the attempts by his family to discredit Ibn Saud with the British and thereby "make mischief between him and us."[13] The bureau seemed truly puzzled by Hussein's allegations of conspiracy on the part of Ibn Saud with both the Turks and Ibn Rashid. Numerous inquiries to Wilson failed to corroborate the charges that Ibn Saud was "playing us false."[14] Shortly thereafter, Cornwallis informed the residency: "We know from a very good source that this is not the case and also that Ibn Saud has been faithful to his agreement with us."[15]

Cox, now billeted in Baghdad, was determined to bestir Ibn Saud to some martial demonstration. Preoccupied with the Mesopotamian front, Cox wanted badly to neutralize Ibn Rashid either through diplomatic maneuver or military coup de main. His superiors in Delhi, however, were equally resolved that Ibn Saud not be pressured into an imprudent undertaking—one for which India was loath to accept responsibility, financial or otherwise.[16]

Hussein, however, remained chary of any but the most perfunctory gestures of cooperation and alliance. The ingenuous Wilson, worried over the sharif's reaction to Storrs's planned journey to Riyadh, warned that Hussein was not in a conciliatory mood. The British agent was particularly irritated by a note from the bureau highly critical of Hussein's hostility and of his failure to arrive at an amicable arrangement with Nejd and Asir.[17] The note in question was written by Cornwallis while on a mission to Jeddah for the bureau; he characterized Hussein as a truculent, scheming, dim-witted old mountebank, bent on frustrating all attempts to draw Nejd into the fold so as to enhance his own claim to postwar Arabian hegemony. "He is evidently determined," he wrote, "to emerge from this war as the only man who has really fought the Turks," and to whom, he evidently assumed, Great Britain would be most beholden.[18]

The fundamental misconceptions that continue to obscure the Arab Bureau's role simply have no basis in fact. Sharif Hussein was the ally of opportunity, to be exploited and, if necessary, abandoned. Hogarth, Cornwallis, Clayton, and the rest never allowed for the possibility that Hussein's political ambitions would manifest themselves in anything other than the most innocuous forms. To them, such a prospect seemed ludicrous for it would have imperiled the vital interest of the empire.

At the end of 1917, Hogarth composed a revealing note divulging unequivocally what lay behind British support of the Wahhabi emir. First had been the need to counter the power of Ibn Rashid; second, to strengthen Ibn Saud against the money and arms that daily augmented the power of Hussein. Unfortunately, Hogarth now contended, this policy had succeeded too well, leaving open the possibility that Ibn Saud could seize Mecca from the sharif in the absence of Britain's restraining hand. Certainly an offensive by Ibn Saud's Wahhabis against Hail was not to be encouraged lest it succeed and "be a great danger to the peace of Arabia." This represented an abrupt turnaround in the bureau's perspective. "To ensure a balance of power," Hogarth elaborated, "Hail had better remain independent under a Rashid."[19]

This argument for a balance of power in Arabia remained a steady theme. Propounded by the Arab Bureau throughout the war, it was entwined with the acute suspicion of Wahhabism lodged in the highest echelons of British officialdom in Cairo. "Egypt," Hogarth concluded, "does not wish to see Ibn Saud in vassalage to King Hussein, but each to be in such a position as to have a wholesome respect for the other."[20] Wingate's attitude mirrored Hogarth's. Perhaps the lingering memory of Mahdism in the Sudan contributed to the high commissioner's distrust of Ibn Saud and his disciples. More probably it was the stark realization that an Arabia under Wahhabi sway would be much less dependent upon imperial coffers, and therefore less pliant. "I submit," wrote Wingate to Balfour, "that the iconoclastic tendencies of [Wahhabism] would render it a greater potential danger in present circumstances, and less possible to restrain than the King's more secular ambitions."[21] This was but one of many attempts by the high commissioner to discourage London from fulfilling Riyadh's urgent requests for arms.

These demands, all the more strident when contrasted with the emir's earlier timidity, coincided with the arrival of a persistent gadfly on the scene. Harry St. John Bridger Philby's journey to Riyadh as Cox's representative signaled the emergence of a more forward military stance for Nejd. Philby was the long-awaited replacement for the renowned Captain Shakespear, the officer (killed in 1915) who was chiefly responsible for establishing ties with Ibn Saud and for the Anglo-Saudi treaty that emerged from the contact. Philby was destined for fame as a noted traveler in the region, particularly on the Arabian peninsula itself. His later transit of the Great Arabian Desert (from Riyadh to the Red Sea coast) proved a significant geographic achievement. But Philby was not well suited to the role of passive emissary. Ibn Saud's political ambitions soon became his own, casting him frequently in the role of advocate for the Wahhabi point of view and opponent of the political and territorial ambitions of Hussein and his sons. Not surprisingly, Philby's independent spirit frequently brought him into conflict with the Arab Bureau. While he was also somewhat unpopular in Indian circles because of his opposition to the anticipated annexation of Mesopotamia by the Raj, this fact alone was insufficient to endear him to Hogarth. Despite Philby's undeniable talents, the professor regarded him as far too parochial in his perception of the Arabian situation. "He takes a sharply personal view," Hogarth stressed to Wingate,

> and thinks all men must necessarily do likewise. For him Arabia is no part of larger questions, and he is deeply imbued with the idea that Ibn Saud, as his man, is to be championed against a "Cairo Champion." Each of these is just an individual and he does not readily associate them with wider interests e.g. the general war situation or the general Muslim question. He had identified himself entirely with the first before the second became his personal enemy. . . . I find him critical of all his superiors and colleagues e.g. of Sir P. Cox himself, Leachman etc. Ultimately he reckons, I suspect, with himself alone: but, after making his acquaintance, I think you will agree that we all have got to reckon with him.[22]

Philby was later to reciprocate in kind, airing his own complaints about the performance of Hogarth and his bureau: "During my year in Arabia at that time no 'confidential' papers were sent to me in the desert, not even the Bulletin of the Arab Bureau in Cairo, with whose articles I was fundamentally in disagreement. I was backing the other horse."[23] Certainly there was no doubt in his mind as to the bureau's hostility toward Ibn Saud and the Wahhabi phenomenon. He would later elaborate on this in his description of the town of Artawiya, the first Wahhabi settlement to be founded and a symbol of the revival. That oasis was, wrote Philby, "the subject of calumny, misrepresentation and hostile propaganda in the councils of the Hijaz and even in the ante-rooms of the Arab Bureau at Cairo."[24] And quite inauspiciously, Philby's arrival in Nejd coincided with a dangerous buildup of tension between Ibn Saud and Sharif Hussein over another oasis at Wadi Khurma.

Khurma is located in the midst of the Ateibah tribe, which, due chiefly to its border location, contained both pro-Hashemite and pro-Saudi clans. The sharif had gained authority over Khurma from the Turks (following the decline of Rashidi power in the area), which included the authority to levy taxes. But his claim to the oasis (and to the Ateibah) was questionable, for both had traditionally come under the rule of Nejd and its emir, either Rashidi or Wahhabi. Khurma's uncertain status was illustrated by the fact that, although the sharif possessed formal title, the site had not been included in the *Hijaz Handbook* prepared by the Arab Bureau in 1916. This discrepancy was not lost on the government of India, which was quick to relay the fact to the Foreign Office.[25] Director Cornwallis pleaded haste in the handbook's preparation rather than concede deliberate omission and thereby compromise Hussein's claim to Khurma.[26] Philby, however, had made his point.

For Cairo, the row over Khurma was a serious distraction, which was not finally resolved until the Sharifian collapse in 1925. The crisis was sparked by the conversion of Hussein's appointed Emir of Khurma to Wahhabism and the sharif's repeated attempts to remove him. While it is commonly accepted that Ibn Saud's agents had a hand in subverting the authority of the sharif at Khurma, this is by no means an unchallenged fact. The Wahhabi rebels may well have been acting on their own initiative. At any rate, Ibn Saud predictably denied involvement beyond kindred sympathy for his brethren. Indeed it would have been astonishing if he had not, since his subsidy would almost certainly have been withdrawn. The bureau's acknowledgment of Khurma's traditional ties to Nejd was quite beside the point. London had invested lavish sums in Sharif Hussein and was not disposed to permit such an embarrassing setback. Therefore Foreign Secretary Balfour instructed Philby to inform Ibn Saud that while His Majesty's government urged patience and conciliation upon all parties

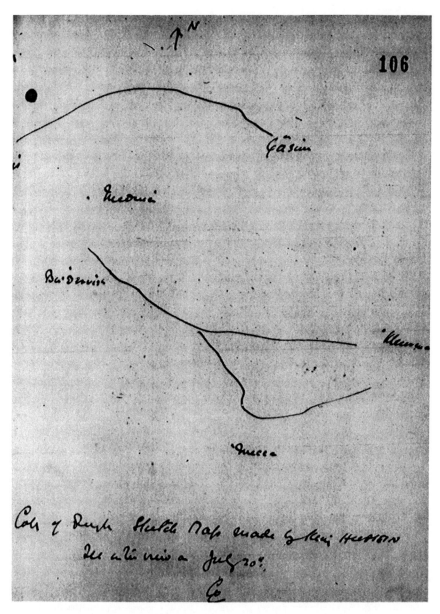

FIG. 6. Sketch made by Sharif Hussein during an interview with officers Bassett and Wilson, demonstrating how easy it would be to "make trouble" for Ibn Saud by dispatching a force to incite a revolt against him at Qasim. (from the Arab Bureau files)

concerned, it could not prevent Hussein from reclaiming land to which he clearly held title and sovereignty.[27]

In this context, the Arab Bureau's notes during the crisis reveal the dual strategy with which it countered Philby's incessant pleas for arms to the Wahhabis. An offensive against Hail was desirable, Philby argued, both to strike a blow against the Turks through their ally and to divert the Wahhabis from the Hejaz and Hussein. But his ploy fell on deaf ears in Cairo, where any suggestion that the sharif's keenest rival be resupplied aroused suspicion. In a communication to Wilson's assistant at Jeddah, the bureau repeated two points: not only had the menace of Hail been considerably reduced since Allenby's advance on Gaza, but the continuance of Ibn Rashid's tribesmen as a viable military force was essential to the maintenance of a balance of power between Mecca and Riyadh. Instead, Cox should tender money and presents in a quantity sufficient to mollify Ibn Saud, but remain sparing enough in the dole of arms to preclude an unsettling military demonstration by the Wahhabis. The objective was to keep Ibn Saud "in play." The bureau insisted that an equilibrium be maintained in order to perpetuate informal British paramountcy in Arabia. From Cairo's perspective, no other choice existed: "Otherwise we seem to risk establishment of two powers in Arabia mutually hostile but to both of whom we have given pledges of support."[28] As for Ibn Rashid, peace overtures from Hail to Abdullah, Hussein's second son, increased speculation at the bureau that he might yet be won over to the revolt without aggrandizing Ibn Saud. This was desirable, since any growth of Wahhabi force at a time when relations between the Hejaz and Nejd were so strained would surely have resulted in the diversion of Sharifian forces to Khurma, either from Abdullah's army around Medina or from Feisal's in the north. As if this were not enough to risk, there was scant guarantee that, once armed, Philby's vaunted offensive would not quickly spend itself, either from irresolution or design. Whatever the outcome, Ibn Saud would be heavily armed at Hussein's expense "in a period of fanatical propaganda." If left unmolested, an anti-Wahhabi regime at Hail might prove "a useful drag on the spread of [the] creed North." Any consequent resentment in Riyadh, while regrettable, would be after all "of more local than imperial importance." With these sentiments, Cox was in substantial agreement.[29]

Late in 1917, Philby journeyed across Arabia to the Red Sea coast en route to a meeting with Hogarth and the sharif in Jeddah. The meeting got off to a bad start, for Hussein was furious that Philby had made the journey without his knowledge, and Hogarth, as the bureau's chief spokesman, was preoccupied with the specter of Ibn Saud's Wahhabi revival and what that portended for Khurma. The professor simply could not shake his philosophical aversion to Wahhabism. The type of penetration that had proven so successful in Khurma was a shadowy thing, impossible to disassociate from Ibn Saud yet difficult to pin on him directly. Personal dislike of Philby and contempt for the views he espoused only served to widen the philosophical chasm between the two men. Philby's arrogant and disrespectful behavior to the sharif—feelings utterly reciprocated by Hussein—made genuine rapprochement even more unlikely. Reporting to Cornwallis of the encounter, J. R. Bassett (C. E. Wilson's assistant) could only conclude that "on the whole, the discussions re Ibn Saud have done more harm than good."[30]

Despite the perfunctory kiss at meeting's end, Philby remained unrepentant and was denied permission by the king to return to Riyadh the way he had come. For his part, Hogarth reassured Hussein that Ibn Saud was not engaged in overt treachery. Failing to convince him, Hogarth detected troubling hints in the monarch's demeanor. The anger that he had shown at Philby's crossing of the Hejaz, while understandable, betrayed a growing insecurity toward his British mentors, his Arabian rivals, and the loyalty of his own subjects. Mounting anxiety over the precariousness of his position, Hogarth thought, militated against provocative action by the sharif. "He is quite firm in his friendship to us," Hogarth concluded, "but none too firm on his throne."[31]

On 21 January, a meeting was held at the residency in Cairo to consider the Arabian situation. Present were Hogarth, Cornwallis, Philby, Symes (Wingate's private secretary), and Wingate. The futility of forging an alliance between the Hejaz and Nejd was formally acknowledged, and a "hands-off" policy resolved (over Philby's objections) as the best method of preventing an open breach over Khurma. While neither ruler would be allowed to open hostilities, this did not preclude reoccupation of the oasis by Hussein's forces. Philby was also ordered to discourage Wahhabi encroachment upon Ibn Rashid's territory. There was nothing else for it but to recognize the muddle and put the best face on it. "There was clearly a conflict of policies and consequently a real alliance between King Hussein and Ibn Saud under existing conditions could not be looked for."[32]

Regrettably for the Arab Bureau's director, options in Arabia were dwindling. Cornwallis knew that the Egyptian treasury was groaning under the strain of the Arabian subsidy while Hussein exploited the military situation to "press recognition [of] grandiose political schemes."[33] Thankfully, Cox was cooperative, limiting the dispatch of military support to Riyadh while counting on Philby to explain things as deftly as possible to Ibn Saud. Indeed, Mesopotamian authorities could hardly have done otherwise, with Allenby warning that dire consequences would result from the untimely diversion of Feisal's bedouin campaigners in Palestine to the remoteness of Khurma. Meanwhile Hogarth's assessment of the sharif's position was grim. In a report entitled, "Position and Prospects of King Hussein," the professor gave the monarch little chance in a military showdown with Ibn Saud's Ikhwan. Hussein's tribesmen were soft in their support and not fired with religious ardor; they likely would "put up very little fight against the fanatical, well-knit force of Wahhabis which Ibn Saud already commands." Elaborating further, Hogarth warned: "Ibn Saud would have something like a walk-over even without the possible coopera- tion of Idrisi, with whom there is reason to think he has some secret agreement. We think him less secure than he thinks himself. On that account among others, we are most unwilling to see Ibn Saud fortified at present with just those sinews of war, money, guns and rifles, by the possession of which Hussein makes a show of equal strength. And at present it is not better than a show."[34]

The attitude of the Arab Bureau toward Philby and his client, Ibn Saud, grew even more contentious throughout the spring and summer of 1918. Bureau officers were leaning to the view that Ibn Saud was engaged in deliberate provocation of the sharif and that Baghdad should send a stern warning to Ibn Saud to yield up Khurma to Hussein. Philby was insubor- dinate, refusing to relay Cox's message and choosing instead to extol the Wahhabi leader's patience in the face of Hussein's persistent goading. Philby's communications struck Hogarth as "not a judge's appreciation of the available evidence, but the ex-parte pleading of an advocate for a client."[35] But Philby chided that, if that were so, London would scarcely allow such a flagrant breach of impartiality. In a note penned to Hogarth in July he once again urged that prudence be impressed on Hussein with respect to Khurma: "The Sharif seems to be bent on provoking a conflict with Ibn Saud but all that so far he has succeeded in doing is to settle the question of the jurisdiction of Khurma finally in favor of Ibn Saud. . . . I sincerely hope that he will definitely be ordered not to return to the charge. Surely he can be firm with him to that extent."[36]

Wingate, prompted by urgings from Cornwallis, dispatched letters to Balfour attempting to sway the Foreign Office in the sharif's direction by hinting that Hussein's allegations of Saudi complicity with Turkish forces in South Arabia were possessed of more truth than originally conceded. The Arab Bureau's director assisted with a flurry of notes to Symes at the residency, urged decisive action by Cairo in the Khurma sector, and painted a gloomy picture of mounting Anglophobia in the Wahhabi camp. He also took exception to Philby's charge that Hussein, not Ibn Saud, was the actual aggressor. Echoing this sentiment, Wingate wired Balfour his opinion that Philby's regrettable assurances to Ibn Saud only served to embolden him. Should he succeed in actually securing a dominant position in Arabian politics, the ramifications would be lamentable for the Muslim world in general—and for "British interests and propaganda" as well. "On the other hand," wired the high commissioner, "the policy advocated from Cairo would be directed to secure the priority of King Hussein without prejudice to the territorial rights of other Arabian chiefs."[37] This direct appeal to Wingate indicated the extent to which pressure could be brought to bear upon Philby through Cox's new replacement in Baghdad, Arnold Talbot Wilson. He doubted whether Ibn Saud would take Cairo's threats seriously, even if Baghdad were sympathetic to Hussein, which, "thanks to their Mr. Philby," they now were not. Pressure was best applied on Philby through London.[38]

Still undaunted, Cornwallis renewed his attack on Ibn Saud, depicting ominous scenarios in which the Wahhabis struck alliances with pro-Turkish elements in Asir. He also complained repeatedly that India was guilty of sanctioning assurances to Ibn Saud that ran counter to Foreign Office directives. But when Philby suggested that London intervene to adjudicate a boundary between the Hejaz and Nejd, Cornwallis declined, deprecating entrance by the British government into the labyrinth of Arabian tribal jurisdiction. Not only did he consider it presumptuous of Philby to propose a boundary without adequate knowledge; the basis of his proposal, he charged, stemmed from "prejudicial sources." Besides, it seemed dubious to Cornwallis whether the conception of boundaries was tenable in nomadic Arabia. Whether or not some readjustment might be necessary later on in recognition of the Ateibah's affiliation with Nejd (a safe assumption), the issue had boiled down to one of face. And in this sense, forcing concessions on Hussein would surely have been risky.[39] Clayton, now assigned with Allenby in Palestine, agreed with the Arab Bureau's director and saw no need to provision Ibn Saud (whose case was, in any event, weak), especially in light of Ibn Rashid's declining military significance and the headaches a fight over Khurma might give to Allenby's plans in the north.[40] As the year wore on, Baghdad came to agree. This failure of Cox to see eye-to-eye with Philby was attributed by the latter to the waxing influence of Gertrude Bell. "I think I am in a minority," Philby complained to Hogarth, "but I believe Sir P.[ercy] would be of the same way of thinking if the elimination [of Ibn Rashid] actually took place. Miss Bell has a soft place in her heart for the Rashids of Hail. You want to preserve Hail's independence to be a source of friction in Arabia."[41] Late in the summer, London responded to Wingate's prodding, instructing Baghdad that "neither party take any action which is likely to lead to an open breach." But in addition, Balfour stressed: "In delivering message to Ibn Saud, Philby should impress upon him the fact that we have a high regard for the King of Hejaz as our ally who has proved his worthiness by his deeds and that we are bound to and intend to protect his legitimate interests as well as those of Ibn Saud himself."[42]

This scarcely veiled warning, while probably not as grave as Cornwallis would have liked, illustrates the respective influence of the director and Philby as communicated through their superiors to London. Cornwallis was also successful in inducing Foreign Secretary Balfour to abandon thoughts of a boundary commission to adjudicate the dispute. Such an attempt, he felt, would not only be futile but could prove counterproductive if Arabs on both sides grew anxious over British motives. To "give colour to such accusations" might prove an added burden that Hussein could scarcely shoulder now.[43] A wiser course, Cornwallis insisted, would be for London to wield the clout with Riyadh that its monthly subsidy (£5,000) earned and hope that some sort of truce would emerge. Bassett, Wilson's assistant at Jeddah, added to the chorus, stressing that he was not convinced that the king's allegations of treachery against Ibn Saud were spurious. On this basis alone, he felt, Khurma should return to the Hashemite fold.[44]

More than any single individual, Director Cornwallis was responsible for London's repudiation of Philby and his point of view. In the late summer of 1918, he peppered Wingate with anxious notes indicting the performance of Philby in Riyadh and Indian officials in Delhi for their handling of the Khurma crisis. His rejection of the idea of direct British arbitration of the dispute was surprisingly effective. He maneuvered successfully to reverse the hands-off policy endorsed in January, gaining in the process a formal statement from London designed to give Ibn Saud pause. In this way, Whitehall acknowledged that the embattled Hussein might justifiably claim some rights under the mantle of Hejaz kingship that London had formally recognized. Cornwallis was adamant that Ibn Saud's denial of guilt for events at Khurma should not be allowed to pass unchallenged, lest a dangerous precedent be set that would hamstring future British relations with him. The government, he argued, should be less subtle in its communications and less insipid in supporting Hussein's right to restore rightful claim. Beyond simple acquiescence to this demand, Ibn Saud should fulfill his obligations as a loyal ally and do his utmost to diminish Wahhabi fervor at the oasis.[45] Clayton was in accord with this view. He stressed that while Hussein's flagging efforts to restore Khurma should not be encouraged, neither should London retreat on its commitment to him. "It would be unfair to Ibn Saud," he wrote, "to allow him to think that our decision is anything but final."[46]

As the crisis wore on into autumn, Delhi and Baghdad grew weary of the constant fencing with Cairo and the verbosity of Philby's dispatches from Riyadh. Cox had long since departed for Persia, leaving in his stead the brusque Arnold Wilson as acting political officer. While there was certainly no love lost between this rather Kiplingesque officer and the "enthusiasts" in Cairo, Wilson soon lost patience with Philby's inability or unwillingness to bring Ibn Saud into line. Believing Philby had outstayed his usefulness in Nejd, Wilson sought his recall, suggesting to Balfour that he had "reached the end of his tether" and should be replaced, preferably by Lieutenant Colonel Gerard E. Leachman of Indian northwest frontier fame.[47] Baghdad's representative in Riyadh, thought Wilson, had only curried Ibn Saud's "exaggerated sense of his own importance." Leachman, on the other hand, "whose virile handling of Arab tribes had been of such value to this force, will probably bring Ibn Saud to his bearings and save much trouble in future."[48] In a lengthy telegram to Wingate, Cox's replacement supported upholding current commitments in Nejd but also expressed a view that might just as easily have come from the Savoy itself: "We have come to a parting of the ways, and I think it is urgent that Ibn Saud should be made to understand that he must come into line and comply with orders of H.M.G. or take the consequences.[49]

As fate would have it, Ibn Saud chose this moment to embark on his long-awaited campaign against Ibn Rashid, and though Hail was still formidable enough to avert collapse to the Wahhabis, the emir's forces enjoyed considerable success and booty. Shortly thereafter, Hussein launched yet another assault upon Khurma and again suffered a reverse. London reacted by canceling a shipment of new Enfield rifles that had been promised Riyadh. Ibn Saud's response to this measure was so menacing, and Philby's protestations so shrill, that the shipment was restored. Ibn Rashid's precipitous military decline notwithstanding, to have restricted the flow of arms to Nejd at the very moment Ibn Saud had acted to fulfill a pledge of assistance long since made would have smacked of blatant prejudice for Hussein, whose own designs on Hail were an open secret. The Arab Bureau, speaking for Wingate, warned Hussein not to overreact. Hail was fair game for all since it remained aligned with the Turks. Cornwallis, however, warned the high commissioner that Wahhabi success against Ibn Rashid would merely whet a fanatical appetite. The message conveyed unease over Hussein's position in the event of a Rashidi collapse, for "the Ikhwan are out for blood" and Arabia was already armed "to a degree hitherto unknown."[50] Wingate accordingly cautioned Balfour that the Foreign Office might yet "have some reason for regarding Nejd as a Bolshevik factor in Arabian politics."[51] Complicating matters, the bureau was clearly apprehensive of Philby's presence in London in early 1919, where his access to the architects of British foreign policy was assured. "Philby has left for England," one of its officers warned Wilson, "where he will doubtless express his views on Arabian politics if he can find an audience."[52]

Hussein's time was swiftly running out; this was clear to all save himself. With the armistice, Cairo's priorities began to shift radically. While the obligatory pledges of support for Hussein would continue, the fiction of his authority over Khurma could now be safely acknowledged as such in Cairo without fear of recrimination. This was now necessary for two reasons. First, too many thorny questions demanded London's attention to permit the comparatively trivial issue of an Arabian border dispute to command much thought. Second, the real threat that the sharif's bitter enemy, Fakhri (commander of Turkish forces besieged in Medina), might seek vengeance by putting his yet-unbowed garrison at Ibn Saud's disposal was not easily dismissed. The residency therefore urged Hussein to accept in lieu of arbitration the very boundary that Cornwallis had rejected only a few months before. This was the Turaba-Marran line, which ran about ten miles west of Khurma; oddly enough, it was Philby's boundary. The emphasis now lay on neutralizing the situation as far as possible while discussions continued as to how best to reinforce the sharif. While not withdrawing support entirely, Cairo was beginning to hedge its commitment in order to preempt civil war in Arabia.

The Savoy, meanwhile, had had enough of this tug-of-war. With the Wahhabis now in unchallenged possession of Khurma, Cairo more frequently saw the dark hand of the India Office, and more particularly Arnold Wilson, at work behind the scenes. Late in 1919 Major Herbert

Garland, who had already established quite a reputation for himself as an adviser to Sharifian forces in the field, arrived in Cairo to replace Cornwallis, who was departing for Beirut. Shortly after settling in at the Arab Bureau, he wrote a scathing report entitled "Lieut.-Col. A. T. Wilson and the Khurma Crisis," which bitterly detailed Baghdad's volte-face in Arabia. Wilson had earlier agreed that the subsidy should have been employed, along with the threat of treaty abrogation, to restrain Ibn Saud, and he had declared as much during a joint meeting in Cairo. But by mid-June his tone had changed to that of an ardent advocate—dismissing Hussein as a venal puppet with little influence, even as he praised Ibn Saud. Garland's sardonic conclusion follows: "From the beginning it is apparent that Col. A. T. Wilson's conversion to our policy of complete support of King Hussein was not long-lived. He appears to have reverted to the original doctrine of the Indian Government which may be expressed—There is no Emir but Ibn Saud and Philby is his proxy."[53]

Nevertheless Hogarth, in his role as Wingate's personal adviser, urged restraint until after Turkish forces had been evacuated from Medina and Asir. In fact, he was the architect of the anti-Wahhabi strategy ultimately arrived at in Cairo and sanctioned in London during spring of 1919. If a retreat from Khurma was not forthcoming, he argued, the subsidy should be discontinued, the 1915 Anglo-Saudi Treaty renounced, and a blockade of Riyadh's gulf ports threatened. Hussein should be restrained from taking any precipitate action on his own, while letting these ultimatums accomplish their purpose: "Hogarth thinks it necessary now to enhance King's prestige in inner Arabia and help him in present difficulties and points out absurdity of our paying Ibn Saud subsidy notoriously used to threaten Hussein in region formerly under the Turks."[54] Garland subsequently submitted a searing report on the Khurma crisis in early summer that both chronicled the bureau's belief in Ibn Saud's guilt and outlined the steps necessary to alter his behavior. First, Garland refused to permit the Wahhabi leader to evade responsibility for the defection of Khurma from the sharif's fold:

> [I]t is now sufficient for our present purposes to know: firstly, that the sect originated close by his own capital and was allowed to flourish there, and its leading missionaries are his own subjects; secondly, that it is merely a desperately fanatical edition of Wahabism of which he is the acknowledged leader; and thirdly, that Ibn Saud has recently put himself at the head of the movement and will certainly not fail to use it for furthering his own ends.

For the purposes of this review, therefore, it is unnecessary to differentiate between Ibn Saud and the Ikhwan or between the latter and the Wahabis.[55]

The British policy of appearing supportive of Hussein over Khurma without firmly backing him up originated, Garland contended, "purely by military expediency and was decided upon in spite of our strong support of King Hussein's claim to Khurma." Nor did the Indian government escape this indictment: "Little was done, however, by India to call off Ibn Saud or to order him to cease his anti-Sherifian propaganda amongst Hejaz tribes."[56] In order to put Ibn Saud in harness, Garland suggested that Whitehall openly threaten his richer districts along the Persian Gulf with the imposition of a blockade or draft other of its treaties on the Arabian peninsula with anti-Wahhabi clauses holding Ibn Saud responsible for the activities of Wahhabi missionaries and empowering other chiefs to expel the more troublesome ones. An obliquely channeled subsidy to Ibn Rashid (through Hussein) was also suggested as a counterpoise to Wahhabi power.[57] Garland became even more aggravated by the subsequent threat of King Hussein to abdicate in protest over British reluctance to back his claim to Khurma. Such a culmination of British relations with the king, he warned, would augur ill for future diplomatic relationships with the Arabs: "How can they trust a power that deals thus with its friends? We should therefore bring about the change [of title] gradually and induce him to accept a pension and honourable treatment so that we may be cleared of any charge of bad faith."[58]

Writing to the residency, Harold Fenton Jacob agreed with the assessment and feared possible damage to British prestige:

> One day we are in favour of making Hussein supreme among the Arab rulers and urging them to acknowledge his suzerainty: the next we allow him to abdicate. None of our Arab friends will repose complete confidence in us thereafter. It matters little what be the reason for allowing the abdication. Arabs are children and must be treated accordingly. That is my experience. It is one thing to blame Hussein for not seeing eye to eye to us in our demands: but it is extremely important not to run the risk of alienating the sympathies of the lot for the contumacy of one. I would strongly urge reconsideration of this policy.[59]

The bureau was groping for a solution in Arabia that might permit a graceful exit without either damaging British prestige or upsetting the delicate political equilibrium that it had striven to achieve. On broad lines, partisanship for Hussein (born of political expediency) had given way to a more general Arabian policy, the parameters of which Garland reiterated to Clayton as: (1) uniformity of treatment, with all relations maintained through Cairo; (2) subsidies conditional on the recipient's acceptance of London's guidance in certain matters; (3) the creation of boundary commissions, where necessary; (4) the conclusion of individual treaties or agreements on which subsidies would be conditional; and (5) strict control by Great Britain of the import of arms and ammunition into Arabia.[60]

The Foreign Office faced a real dilemma here. Certainly Britain was not without obligations regarding its paramount protégé, and it had expended a fortune in his (and its own) behalf. This money had been well spent—the Turks were no longer in Arabia, and the entire region lay prostrate before Britain's imperial might. Hussein's revolt, most assuredly, had hastened that result. Just as surely, the spread of Wahhabism on the peninsula and its threat to the holy cities gave cause for concern. But it was as yet unclear just to what extent this impending civil war had resulted from policy differences between distant loci of British departmental influence—a contrived maelstrom, more a spawn of occidental interference and subterfuge than of indigenous tribal animosity. George Kidston at the Foreign Office, seeing little to choose between Hussein and Ibn Saud, noted that "the whole question is not really a struggle between Bin Saud and Hussain at all, but a conflict of policies between government departments here which could be arranged round a table in London, without the loss of a single life if one or other of the departments concerned can be induced to give way. Each one is cheering its own fighting cock, and the result will evidently be bloodshed."[61]

This view, while accurate on its surface, is inadequate. Hussein was not, at least inasmuch as the Arab Bureau was concerned, Cairo's "fighting cock." As described above, the agency's leaders were far too aware of the sharif's inherent weakness to have adopted him as such. Rather, he was fighting a holding action. The bureau's aim was not to elevate him over the other Arabian chieftains, at least not in any other than a strictly nominal sense. But Hussein's displacement by a more vigorous usurper, particularly a Wahhabi chieftain at the forefront of an energetic movement and capable (by this time) of swift expansion, was a sobering prospect. The bureau continued to view the turmoil in Arabia as it had always viewed it: the best opportunity to exploit native discontent to imperial advantage, through judicious nurturing of the peninsula's chronic political divisions.

With the rout of Abdullah's army by Ibn Saud's Ikhwan at Turaba in May 1919, Hussein's rule teetered at the brink of the abyss. London was compelled to rush to his defense with the same threats Cairo had earlier recommended. The always prudent Ibn Saud, unwilling to risk a rupture with the British just yet, was reined in by an Indian government fretful over the Wahhabi threat to the holy cities (and the possible reaction of its Muslim community). The warnings given early on by Hogarth pertaining to the more unsavory aspects of the Wahhabi phenomenon started to gain credence in Delhi, for it too had always advocated Arab weakness—not strength—as the vehicle by which imperial aims could best be achieved. In that context, India had long regarded the Arab Revolt with suspicion. Now those same tendencies returned to cast a pall over India's relationship with Ibn Saud.

Hussein's arrangement with Cairo, built and maintained on such a porous foundation, was fated to dissolve despite frenetic, last-minute efforts by the Foreign Office to sustain it. The war was over and a new austerity choked the conduits through which British sustenance had once so generously flowed. The Arab Bureau soon lapsed into redundancy, busying itself with monitoring aid to the Hejaz and attempting to assist its fledgling government onto its feet, a thankless task at this stage. But in Arabia at least, the bureau had accomplished its primary purpose: to sustain the Arab Revolt as long as was necessary to defeat the Turks and secure their withdrawal. The bureau's other objective, laying the groundwork for the maintenance of a balance of power on the peninsula, proved more elusive. Perhaps whatever vitality had existed within Hussein's movement spent itself too quickly, or the shadow of British sponsorship was, of itself, politically fatal. Possibly the adhesive provided by Hussein's gold sovereigns was insufficient to triumph over the Wahhabis' spiritual devotion. At any rate, the outcome in Arabia contained, for those working at the Arab Bureau, elements of both astonishing success and profound disappointment.

7

DISCORDANT MOSAIC

The Bureau and Arab Unity

The charge that the Arab Bureau was staffed by dilettantes imprudently swept up in the Arab Revolt, while historically attractive, is inaccurate. Certainly it is true that they shared (with some Arabs) a desire to expel the Turks from the region. It is also correct that the bureau took exception to French territorial ambitions in the Levant. But it is reckless to infer from these positions that Hogarth and company were "enthusiasts" of Arab nationalism, or that simple Fashodist antipathy lay behind their hostility to the infamous Sykes-Picot Agreement.

In Syria as in Arabia and Palestine, the bureau's emphasis, first and last, was on reconciling British diplomatic commitments with strategic requirements. Whenever these two qualifications came into conflict, the Savoy accorded preference to imperial needs. Unfortunately, in much historical writing this preference has been turned on its ear, confusing efforts by the Arab Bureau to further Cairo's conception of Arab "independence" as precedent to those interests rather than in conjunction with them.

Even before the bureau was officially conceived Wingate had set forth his own vision of the future, envisaging a pan-Arab union of federated states preferably linked by a transcendent Arab caliph. An important element of this scheme, however, would be the guiding and paramount hand of Great Britain. The sirdar cloaked his design in altruistic terms, contending that this was "an honest attempt to realise the aspirations, social and spiritual, of an important section of the Moslem World." The qualitative adjective "political," it should be noted, is conspicuously absent. The envisioned federation of semiautonomous states would presumably look to Britain for protection until "some time in the dim future."[1] While Wingate had no desire to impose a particular caliph on the Arab world (a suspicion that nonetheless lingered in the minds of Indian officials), he felt much could be done to kindle such sentiment, especially if Hussein's revolt were successful. The wisest course, the sirdar felt, lay in molding Arab political aspirations to conform with British interests. Clayton saw the best route to this end in separate diplomacy with the various Arab political entities in the manner of the Trucial States. This piecemeal diplomatic approach had much to recommend it, not the least of which was because: "It is in this way that suitable governments could be established in the various districts concerned; furthermore, if the various elements are dealt with separately, there will be no danger of the united and powerful state, which the Indian Government regards with such apprehension."[2]

There is ample indication that Clayton (and later Hogarth) looked upon McMahon's ill-fated pledges to Hussein and Sykes's accord with Picot as unwise. The former, they felt, were far too sweeping in their scope, and the latter too restrictive of future British territorial options. For instance, Clayton had looked askance at French claims in Syria during the negotiations of early 1916, dubbing them "preposterous." But he was astute enough to recognize the direction of currents at Whitehall flowing toward some kind of Anglo-French arrangement. He felt strongly, however, that the French and the Arabs should be encouraged to deal with one another in order to settle the sharp differences that divided them.

Perhaps it seems remarkable that such an important intelligence officer should have been an advocate of frank disclosure. But Clayton was as yet unaware of what the final agreement would contain, since Cairo was not finally apprised until late April.[3] And he was prescient enough to realize the disrepute into which Britain risked falling by her secret dealings with the French. He also recognized, almost prophetically, that concealment of such an understanding would have been difficult in any case, and that "some of our Syrian friends seem to have an inkling that we have handed over Syria to the French, and I foresee trouble." Clayton's recommendation to Wingate was forthright and unequivocal: "The time has nearly arrived when we shall have to tell them so straight out and hand them over to the French to settle with—otherwise we shall risk giving rise to the very friction with France that we have sacrificed so much to avoid. The ways of the F.O. are strange indeed; it seems impossible to get them to face an issue or to decide on any fixed policy—this has cost us many thousands of valuable lives and millions of good money I fear."[4] To contemplate such costly concessions to Paris as then under discussion, unnecessary or not, was hard enough to stomach in Cairo. But Clayton viewed London's behavior as adding fetters to an already entangling situation, thus increasing the risk that those concessions ultimately would be rendered moot. At the very least, he felt, vigorous efforts should have been undertaken to bring the French and Sharifians together; "then if the French and the Arabs absolutely fail to agree, we cannot be blamed by either party."[5]

As far as McMahon's exchange of letters with Hussein was concerned, Clayton saw no great harm in it, especially when ranged alongside the critical need to neutralize what he viewed as the greater threat of an Arabian-augmented jihad. Even if no actual revolt materialized in the Hejaz, the procurement of Arabian neutrality was in itself worth a reply to the sharif sufficient "to put the seal on their friendship." Besides, Cairo's intelligence chief did not regard whatever might emerge between the sharif and the high commissioner as etched in granite. "The influential leaders appear open to reason and ready to accept a considerably less ambitious scheme than that which they have formulated, which the more enlightened allow to be beyond their hopes at present."[6]

Clayton entertained few illusions respecting Arab political aspirations to independent statehood. Nor would he have hesitated to advocate swift suppression of such impulses had he felt otherwise. As established in the precursor to this work, Clayton and his Arab Bureau pursued Wingate's strategy with an eye toward continuing to manage Arab affairs off camera, behind the facade of an independent Arab federation. A more recent chronicler confirms this finding.[7] Yet Clayton, like Wingate, was sensitive to criticism from some (mainly Indian) quarters that Cairo was engaged in a dangerous game of political proselytizing. Officials in Delhi were simply unable to appreciate the atmosphere in which McMahon's commitments were conceived, obsessed as they were with Indian fortunes in Mesopotamia and the subcontinent itself. The viceroy deemed the British war effort in the East a series of "blunders" from which little would be derived in compensation for the high commissioner's careless concessions. Besides, Lord Hardinge pressed, "I fail to see why we should make any sacrifice to the Arabs in that direction in view of the fact that they have been fighting against us the whole time and have no claim whatever upon us."[8]

But in Cairo, the Arabian sideshow was worth the risks it entailed. Clayton and Wingate saw the opportunity to ingratiate Britain with the Arabs, while encouraging a relationship of financial dependence. In this way, Britain might secure primacy over any Arab political entity that might emerge with the peace. Sharif Hussein (McMahon's commitments notwithstanding) had secured for himself little more than rule of the Hejaz. Those areas that managed to elude the grasp of the French and the Zionists would come to terms with London along lines guaranteed to meet the strategic and political requirements of the British. Neither Arab nationalists nor Sharifian partisans would have taken any comfort from the views of Gilbert Clayton: "I think some people have had an idea that we were going to build up a powerful and United Arab state which was going to rob us of all the advantages we might have gained in this part of the world . . . but of course anyone who understands Arabia must fully realise that such a scheme would have been quite impossible even if one had been so foolish as to contemplate it."[9] Wingate's pan-Arab union seemed a useful chimera to Clayton. If a shadowy combination under the spiritual authority of the Sharif of Mecca could be molded, well and good; but the political fabric in the Middle East must remain a patchwork. Storrs, McMahon's oriental secretary, had been warned by Sudanese sources that temporal authority for the sharif over the entire region was utterly impractical, and a British-sponsored claim to the caliphate unthinkable. This appraisal merely reinforced Clayton's belief that Wingate's vision was both useful and innocuous, and "bear out what we have always maintained, that there is no danger of a great, united Arab empire, and that to fall in with the aspirations of the various Arab chiefs to independence can do little more than leave Arabia very much in its present position."[10]

Shortly before departing London for Cairo, Hogarth had reached a similar conclusion. He too looked upon the sharif's ambitions as vain and empty—utterly incompatible with reality yet possessed of considerable opportunity for Britain. The Arab Revolt, however misconceived, would provide needed momentum to the drive against the Committee of Union and Progress in Constantinople. Writing for Sykes's Arabian Report, Hogarth judged Hussein's hopes for leadership of a united Arab empire as "impossible of realisation," but added that "he should be able to rally sufficient of the tribes for a sufficient time to evict the Turks."[11]

Like Clayton, Hogarth did not anticipate a military breakthrough from the sharif's revolt. Neither did he regard the sharif as possessing sufficient regional appeal to act as spokesman for the Arabs in anything other than a vaguely spiritual context. Hussein merely stood out among the many Arabian chieftains as having a wider and therefore more exploitable influence. Like Clayton, Hogarth felt it would be a mistake to equate an agreement with Hussein as a general accord with "the Arabs," for supplemental treaties would be required. "Accordingly," he observed, "the Emir's pretension to be the accepted leader of the tribal population of Hejaz proper may fairly be said to have been justified from the first, and to be so still. We are not here concerned with the means, pecuniary or other, by which its allegiance has been gained or maintained, any more than with its military value. We have merely to record the fact that at present the King of the Hejaz has the political support of these tribes. . . . The King's possible relation to the tribes outside the Hejaz is a matter for separate and subsequent consideration."[12] As long as London remained true to the twin principles of liberation from the Turks and qualitative autonomy suitable to the various districts, such agreements would not conflict with commitments made to Hussein: "But, in the actual default of general organization of those peoples, it would be futile to treat with him alone and to assume that, through him [Hussein] we could influence and bind all the Arabs."[13]

The views of Hogarth are interesting in that he shared the ambiguity that haunted the minds of other Britons struggling in the quagmire of Anglo-Arab relations. While flattering himself as sympathetic to Arab nationalism, he qualified that sympathy to such an extent as to render it meaningless. Overriding considerations intervened that obfuscated whatever vague support for Arab nationalists he might have been willing to tender. Hogarth was an imperial booster and later a member of the Round Table Society. In his earlier writings, he had emphasized the critical position that Middle Eastern lands were bound to play in the future of Western powers. "Every day it becomes less possible," he contended, "for Western Powers, with interests in the Farther East developing till they bid fair to become vital to their own national existence, to leave the Nearer East to its proper devices, and least of all at those points which lie in most intimate geographic relation to the Trunk routes. Neither the shores of the Bosphorus nor Lower Egypt can hope ever hereafter to cease to be objects of the most lively concern to the nations of Europe."[14] Hogarth was disdainful of nationalism among subject peoples from the Dublin slums to the bazaars of Cairo. Correspondingly, he was no less cynical of Hussein's future—"born to rule, but probably not to rule further than his eyes can see."[15] Larger Arab nationalism was a pipe dream rendered insupportable by the divisive nature of regional politics and the decrepit state of Arab civilization in general: "But I have seen too much of the actual country and its peoples and been too much behind its scenes of late years, to be blind to difficulties which beset and impede the realisation of an 'Arab State'."[16] Unity, Hogarth felt, was anathema to Arabs except in an atmosphere of reaction, and even then it was liable to dissipate once the catalyst of an external threat had vanished. Within the bureau, it seemed obvious that the Arabs were far too fractious ever to coalesce into a unified state. George Lloyd echoed Hogarth's disdain for the concept of Arab unity, which "looks all right in artificial light but won't stand close inspection."[17]

To the Arab Bureau's director, Britain's strategic situation was dire enough in 1916 to justify backing Hussein's revolt. Far more than simply neutralizing the bogey of Islamic jihad, the Hejaz rising might accomplish two other important objectives: secure Britain's Red Sea communications and, more urgently, preempt an upsurge of Islamic hostility toward the Entente. The professor maintained that no untoward pledges were made to Hussein in 1915. And while he later expressed remorse that more had not been done to disabuse the sharif of his expectations, it suited Cairo to avoid damaging friction.[18] He preferred indirect influence over annexation, and in this respect he differed most markedly from British officials in Mesopotamia and India. He regarded annexation as both unnecessary and impractical, although he felt the liberated Ottoman territories should, indeed must, be encouraged to look west toward London rather than east toward Delhi. These territories, he believed, possessed neither the inherent wherewithal to strike out on their own with the peace, nor the focus of unity and common purpose that the forging of a unified national state would require. Given these assumptions, Hogarth's conclusion mirrored those of Clayton and Wingate: that the geography of the region and the history of the Arabs must lead inexorably down the path of provincial autonomies united in a "federal" system and "loosely bound together by the influence of blood, language, and to a large extent, Faith."[19] Hogarth later conceded that Britain was honor-bound to give some expression to the "Arab National idea, not only by our explicit pledges, but also by an obligation implicit in the use we made of Arabs to win the war." This federal system would meet his criteria, "but not all at once, or without protection by stronger arms for awhile." Finally, Hogarth added, "the conditions must be fulfilled. The Arabs must really want it, and the foreign powers concerned must want it too. The latter must work not for themselves but for the Arabs—they will be working in their own best interest all the time. The former must work for themselves with the foreigner but not for him. We shall see!"[20]

This passage, included in a text composed after the armistice, highlights the intellectual contradiction that haunted many of those officers intimately connected with the progress and sustenance of the Arab Revolt—knowledgeable of the strategic objectives that underlay its foundation, yet retaining an uncharacteristic impulse to rationalize such exploitation in dulcet tones of benignity. With the proposed federal system, one might have it both ways: the Arabs would be given as much freedom as they could politically handle without compromising British strategic interests. In a letter to Gertrude Bell following the war, Hogarth wrote revealingly, but with characteristic ambiguity, of his intellectual reconciliation between commitments made to the Arab national idea and Britain's need to retain a handle on the future course of events in the Middle East: "we can only hope to make it [the Arab world] any asset for ourselves by guiding it Westward. You see, I still believe in an Arab Nation. I see it as a party enfant, undergoing all the diseases of babyhood, but as born and destined to live and grow, though I do not expect to live to see it a healthy child."[21]

Those who actually ran the Arab Bureau successfully formulated a consensus. Hussein's discontent was Britain's opportunity—both to give desperately needed assistance to Allied fortunes in this theater of war and to lend form to British and Arab political designs in the region. But recognition of the opportunity signified little more. Those with whom Hussein would have to deal regarded him not as a dynamic leader of a messianic movement but as a valuable lever with which to gain strategic advantage. Because of this opportunity and what Cairo regarded as the negligible risk that Hussein's political aspirations would ever come back to haunt them, McMahon's pledges were assessed as useful and innocuous.

The attitudes of Clayton and Hogarth toward Egyptian nationalism offer an interesting perspective from which to begin our examination of the Arab Bureau and Arab nationalism. Both men, it should be noted, were utterly contemptuous of the notion of Egyptians aspiring to the same goals that they were so deftly dangling before the sharif. Early in the war, Clayton actively encouraged British officials to declare a protectorate over Egypt: "if the position of Great Britain in Egypt is to be established on a really firm and lasting basis, both as regards the future welfare and prosperity of Egypt itself."[22] Confiding to Sykes shortly afterward, he was even more blunt in deprecating the liberal line: "I feel somewhat perturbed about Egypt itself. While busy with exterior matters I hope that the keystone of our position in the Near East is not being lost sight of . . . mark my words, I am right. I know I am right. All this claptrap about Sultans and self government is rot. They are not really ready for it and if you have a Palace, every ounce of power and self-government which you think you are giving to the people will go straight to the Sultan . . . and be used against you. Beautiful theories are all very nice, but hard facts remain."[23]

Hogarth was no more generous and, indeed, a trifle more Victorian in his attitudes. He advised Wingate that Egypt was "potentially an enemy country" that begged for annexation and a complete administrative revamping to remedy pervasive corruption and antiquated methods.[24] "Of course Egyptians are not Arabs at all but sons of Ham with a sprinkling of prophet progeny: and all this talk of Arab nationality is fudge. Really they have no interest in anything but the cotton crop . . . and . . . family feuds. What can you do with such but rule them, whether they like it or not."[25] Moreover, Egypt's tepid reception to the news of Hussein's rising surely did little to endear would-be Egyptian leaders to the bureau. The fact that Britain had decided to support the pretensions of an upstart desert chieftain to regional notoriety must have rankled deep. It also made the Egyptian protectorate all the more infuriating.

The debate over deeper Arab Bureau motives resurfaced soon after the armistice. The most virulent criticism came from Anglo-Indian and Mesopotamian quarters, from officials who were quick to blame the bureau for a host of postwar problems in their sphere, particularly the rather ugly revolt that erupted in Mesopotamia in 1920. Anticipating later historians in this connection, the agency was once again depicted as staffed by Arab enthusiasts "fired by the dream of Arab Empire carved from the flanks of Turkey. It was natural, and indeed inevitable, that the Government should make use of those men."[26] These enthusiasts, it was further alleged, encouraged Hussein to aspire to the caliphate and rule over an extended Arab empire encompassing "all Arab lands." The Arab Bureau, the *Times* correspondent in Tehran charged, recklessly "favoured active support of practically all these fantastic claims."[27]

The truth was more prosaic. This perception of the bureau's work arose largely because the flamboyant T. E. Lawrence was linked to it. As has been shown, prominent members of the Arab Bureau were not "fired by the dream of Arab Empire," but were instead sober strategists marching to their own imperial tune. They sought not to foster Arab unity through imperial design, but to incorporate into a loose political network mechanisms of division and dependence with which British influence might be perpetuated. Philip Graves, later a *Times* correspondent in Constantinople, vigorously denied the "enthusiast" label in a rejoinder to the above dispatch from Tehran. This myth of the bureau, he replied, reflected an Anglo-Indian school steeped "in terror of doing anything which might be criticized by Indian Muslims, however fanatical or ignorant." "The Arab Bureau," Graves continued, "never believed in an Arab Empire. It hoped at best for an eventual loose confederation of Arab States, but it fully realized that such a consummation of its policy could not be reached for many years, however desirable it might be."[28] One scholar has recognized that while the Arab Bureau may be said to have preferred, and plumped for, a "Hashemite solution," "As for the ideological subsoil in which these concepts grew— the faith in imperial rejuvenation or, if we prefer, in neoimperialism—the parentage of the Round Table about Curtis and above all, David Hogarth has been recognized since long, with Lawrence as a junior, though the most articulate and versatile member."[29]

As for the caliphate, the Arab Bureau had *initially* hoped to establish Hussein as caliph in order to enhance the international prestige of the hoped-for Arab federation. Critics from Mesopotamia continually fulminated against this policy both during and after the war. The Arab Bureau, they charged, saw great opportunity in this course:

> What more admirable, they reasoned with great plausibility, than to see an Arab empire, whose Sultan should sit in Mecca and be recognized as Caliph and Lord of all the Holy Places, and at the same time be our fast friend enjoying our favour and protection. . . . In support of this brilliant dream they brought forward the most learned and historically correct arguments to show that the Sultan of Turkey had no hereditary title to the Caliphate, and that the Grand Sherif of Mecca had a better family claim. . . . Fortunately, our statesmen remembered the one thing that the

enthusiasts forgot. This was that the Caliphate was no affair of ours and concerned only with Islam itself.[30]

In this way it was hoped the Turkish sultan would be largely divested of his spiritual grip on India's Muslims, and a new Islamic authority allowed to emerge in an Arabia under British influence. Wingate himself was an early advocate of a Sharifian caliphate despite Delhi's sensitivity to the feelings of its Muslim subjects: "I am aware of the close connections in Arabian and other Muslim minds between the cause of Arabia and the institution of the Arab Khalifa, but I feel strongly that to withhold British support of the former in deference to the susceptibilities of certain sections of Indian Muslims with regard to the latter, would be detrimental not only to our immediate interests but to our prestige and reputation among Moslems generally."[31]

While the sirdar was ranged against formidable opposition, this conviction remained integral to his plans for an Arab revolt. The Sudanese noble, Sir Sayyid Ali Morghani, had urged an immediate declaration outlining Britain's policy toward the caliphate, while suggesting that greater Arabia was the logical seat for it and Hussein the "most suitable" candidate. Sufficient support, he suggested, could be surreptitiously garnered through Britain's client chiefs.[32] Storrs expressed similar appreciation of the "obvious advantages, both racial and linguistic, which a Sharifian Caliph might confer."[33] Despite McMahon's hedging on the subject of an Arab caliphate in his correspondence with Hussein, there was indeed support in Cairo for the idea—limited largely to the bureau's warren at the Savoy. McMahon's letters, that agency pointed out, despite conceding only to approve an Arab caliphate if one materialized, had conveyed a misleading impression to Hussein: "But it should be noted that to the Sherif, both temporal and spiritual power are included in the word "Caliphate" and a much wider meaning has therefore been given by him to the extracts . . . than was intended by H.M.G."[34]

However, while Hussein had pushed for return of the caliphate to Arabia in his correspondence with McMahon, he never mentioned himself as a candidate. C. Ernest Dawn has argued persuasively that the sharif "made no use of the question except as a bargaining point" and often expressed support for the Ottoman caliphate.[35] Dawn argues that Hussein was far more interested in the influence he might command as the head of a new Arab state.[36] Notwithstanding this, the Arab Bureau toyed with the intriguing possibilities that Hussein's "ascension" might open up.

Harry Pirie-Gordon, who later joined the bureau in Palestine, coauthored a report on the caliphate in March 1915 that put forth Hussein's case compellingly. The sharif, it noted, headed the tribe from which earlier caliphs had once been drawn; he was (then) under the effective influence of no other power; and he was already in control of the holy city of Mecca, "which in its turn could very well be the spiritual capital of the Moslem world and residence of the Supreme Imam."[37]

Once the bureau began its operation in 1916 plans for the sharif's revolt were carried forward with this principle in mind, but more in the manner of preference than of necessity. Clayton and Hogarth were well aware of the opposition that British backing of Hussein as caliph could ignite. Hogarth tried his best to convince India that this might prove the best means of neutralizing the threat of jihad that a Turkish caliph might perpetually pose, and that "the inauguration of a Khalifa in Arabia challenging the Khalifa in Turkey, will be the best possible safeguard for us in the future particularly if the inauguration be a violent one."[38]

Yet the force of such arguments soon lost their momentum with the outbreak of the revolt in June 1916. Whitehall remained reluctant to antagonize India's Muslims further. Moreover, the mere fact of the revolt itself did much to discredit the notion that the influence of the present caliph was as ubiquitous and commanding as heretofore assumed. Not only had his call to jihad been for the most part ignored by substantial segments of the Arab community, but now the most sacred region of Islam was in open rebellion. Even though London had always taken the line that the caliphate was a matter for Muslims to settle, subsequent events rendered the question academic. Hussein's conspicuous inability to evict the Turks from the Hejaz and the open Wahhabi challenge to his ambitions within Arabia worked to render discussion of his claim to the post of Commander of the Faithful premature at best. Even in the midst of the Rabegh crisis, however, hope lingered within the Arab Bureau. Commenting on the decision concerning the dispatch of British troops to that port, William Ormsby-Gore felt compelled to note that "if Christian troops land in the Hejaz, the revulsion of feeling in India will be really great, and all chance of the Sherif being accepted as Caliph by the Moslem World will be at an end."[39]

Another factor that surely dampened bureau enthusiasm for elevating Hussein's spiritual position was the growing appreciation within the agency of Syrian nationalist hostility to the prospect of Sharifian rule. Little could be gained—indeed, much might be lost—if Britain tied itself to a clearly unrealistic ambition, needlessly antagonizing Arab populations in Syria and predominantly Shia Iraq and risking imperial prestige in the bargain. Even Lawrence had earlier voiced his opposition to a Meccan caliph.[40] Hussein tried repeatedly to gain British acceptance of the title Amir al-Mu'minin (Commander of the Faithful), the proper translation of which caused some confusion. It was determined, however, that such acceptance would have been tantamount to bestowal of the title of caliph on the sharif, so the entreaties were refused.[41]

It is doubtful whether the bureau seriously expected any enlargement of the sharif's title beyond simple kingship of the Hejaz, despite Wingate's conviction that Britain should have sanctioned one. No less a critic than Philby thought the bureau policy duplicitous and claimed to be appalled at "the depths to which British policy can sink!" "I must confess," he continued, "that what ever your view may be, I hold most strongly to the view that our treatment of the King is not only utterly cynical and immoral but inexpedient as being certain to do us incalculable harm in the future. You say you don't care. Perhaps you don't or your career does not lie in the East but there are those that do and its their work you are making more difficult by taking a short cut over difficulties now."[42] Whatever vague suzerain recognition Hussein might eventually earn, the bureau calculated, could be belatedly conferred after the envisioned Arab confederation had become an accomplished fact and favorable sentiment given time to coalesce. If the sharif then attracted a sufficient following, well and good. But the possibility seemed increasingly remote as the war progressed. Late in 1919, with the hopes of Feisal and the Arab Bureau slowly evaporating, the bureau advised Wingate to cut his losses:

> Although it is pretty certain he [King Hussein] does aspire to this position, he knows his influence in the outside Moslem World is so slight that it would be folley [sic] to take any steps towards assuming, or towards getting our help in assuming, this title. There are Arabs in Arabia who would recognise him as Caliph and indeed he may in time be chosen as an Arab Caliph to reign concurrently with the Caliph of Islam, but Indian and other moslems have expressed themselves in no uncertain manner and there is not the slightest chance of Hussein ever being accepted in the Islamic world as Caliph of Islam even if it were necessary for him as King of the Hejaz, which it is not.[43]

In a letter to the *Times* after the war, Philip Graves once again defended his colleagues' conduct in the matter of the caliphate. The Arab Bureau did assist propagandists, he admitted, in pointing out the tenuous nature of the sultan's claim, but he stressed that "it never dreamed of a British choice." The bureau recognized, Graves insisted, that "the choice of a Caliph was an affair of Islam in general, not any section of Islam, still less any foreign non-Islamic State. At the same time, it insisted, and quite rightly, on its point of view—namely, that if Indian Islam accepted the Turkish Caliphate, large sections of Sunni Moslems either did not accept it at all or accepted it under protest and that the unity of Islam was therefore far less real than India prepared to believe."[44] Graves was unmistakably correct in this assertion, for long before war's end the bureau had become disenchanted with the idea of pushing Hussein's candidacy as caliph. Sykes also recognized the futility of such a course, for "the temptation to exploit other folk's gods, has always ended in trouble to those who succumbed. We should only back the Arabs as Arabs not as Moslems."[45]

8

"UN FAIT ACCOMPLI"

The Bureau, the French, and Syria

Unlike the question of the caliphate, territorial concessions to the French aroused considerable passion at the Arab Bureau. Clayton was advised at Cairo in the autumn of 1915 of impending negotiations with the French in London. Once Picot's demands were made known later in the year, he dismissed them as ridiculous and grew impatient with attitudes in Paris that seemed contemptuous of the notion of an Arab revolt. He and Hogarth, already disgusted by the scuttling of a planned Allied landing at Alexandretta (largely at the behest of the Quai d'Orsay), grew more irritated at the latest delays. The French would not accept any British expedition into the region, which they regarded with proprietary interest. Nor were they prepared to renounce the principle of extensive postwar annexation as compensation for ghastly losses along the western front. Clayton complained to his superior in Khartoum that the French did not appreciate the importance of time and cautioned that "if they persist in this attitude they stand to lose everything in Syria. They will lose the substance and be left grasping the shadow."[1]

Convinced of the efficacy of informal control, Clayton found it difficult to understand why Picot insisted upon the principle of formal annexation. He wrote in exasperation to the War Office: "Surely it is better to ensure what would practically be complete control of a native-governed state than to risk losing everything by standing out for the theory of complete annexation. After all, we are in a similar position as regards Baghdad and Basra and possibly portions of southern Palestine."[2] Persisting in his push for an Arab confederation, Wingate pressed for some sort of agreement so that urgent preparations could commence. The sirdar had few qualms about conflicting commitments, feeling that "responsible" Arabs would resign themselves to some measure of direct British control, despite McMahon's carefully chosen language to the sharif. But he was hardly naive enough not to expect some trouble in the future; he predicted, "I think he [Hussein] will smell a rat over the Syrian hinterland."[3] In light of this, Wingate sought (as Clayton had) to encourage a dialogue between Hussein and the French as the best insurance against future misunderstandings. But even in the absence of such a dialogue, the sirdar remained optimistic, his vision seldom reaching beyond the prospects of the Hejaz uprising: "indeed I do not see that even if the French demands are conceded in their entirety, that we can be accused of any serious breach of faith—it is true the Arabs will not get all they wanted, but they will achieve a great deal and in any circumstances, I should think that further discussions will result in a certain modification of the French demand."[4]

Negotiations between Mark Sykes and Monsieur Picot, for all their pitfalls, finally culminated in the infamous agreement in April 1916. Newly arrived in Cairo then, Hogarth was notified of its specific provisions. The intelligence community in Cairo was alarmed that word would leak out, embarrassing all concerned. Wyndham Deedes of Military Intelligence had earlier warned the War Office against divulgence. Commander Hogarth echoed these warnings, afraid His Majesty's government would suffer "grave disadvantage." This was consistent with Hogarth's desire to skirt potentially explosive questions for the sake of short-run strategic objectives. In this vein, the Arab Bureau's director stressed that if London continued to be vague and imprecise in the matter of boundaries with the Arabs, any hasty delineation of this new agreement would clash "with the claims on which he (Hussein) has laid stress." But just as Hogarth had been willing to mislead Hussein in order to expedite the rising, he regarded the Sykes-Picot Agreement as a necessary expedient toward that same end: "I hope, therefore . . . , this Agreement is regarded by our Government now as a purely opportunist measure, with mutual reservation that it cannot but use considerable revision sooner or later for it contains several features which do not promise any final solution of the Near Eastern Question."[5]

Hogarth did not adopt this view because he felt Sykes's crowning achievement threatened Sharifian fortunes in Syria, for he was far too cynical about Hussein's potential for that. But he recognized that French penetration of the Levant could make untold mischief with Anglo-Arab relations. Geographically, for example, concessions to the French in the Lebanon threatened the commercial viability of whatever truncated, autonomous Syrian state might eventually emerge: "As to the ports I have always felt that the exclusion of the Arab independent state or states from the coast is a very doubtful policy. Haifa, Acre and Tyre are all more convenient ports for Damascus than Beyrout."[6] Moreover, the advantages that a British fait accompli in Syria might confer were not to be lightly bartered away. Although that prospect seemed remote in the spring of 1916, Hogarth was adamant that Britain not restrict her future options unnecessarily. Clayton was similarly chary of concessions to the French in Syria and Palestine that "would give her a preponderating voice in those discussions which are bound to arise . . . after the war."[7]

At least temporarily, then, Clayton and the Arab Bureau were willing to live with Sykes's achievement. Hogarth appraised it resignedly as "probably the best we could hope for," but added this caveat: "At the same time the conclusion of this Agreement is of no immediate service to our Arab policy as pursued here, and will only not be a grave disadvantage if, for some time to come, it is kept strictly secret."[8]

Flexibility was the watchword of the Arab Bureau, and the ingredient that it most wished to add to the formulation of Arab policy. In order that Britain might emerge from this conflict better off strategically than when it went in and at the same time retain the good faith of important native elements, policies had to be composed that did not hinder diplomatic adaptation to changing political conditions. Problems arose because neither this practical maxim nor subsequent events squared very well with Anglo-French understandings.

Following Lawrence's meteoric capture of Aqaba in July 1917, Cairo pushed preparations for Feisal's advance northward in tandem with the impending British push at Gaza. Meanwhile the French grew more suspicious that something sinister was afoot in Cairo.

While the parameters for the proposed Arab state had been tentatively outlined, the Hussein-McMahon Correspondence did not specifically name the Hashemite family as beneficiary in terms of political hegemony over that state. Correspondingly, those at the bureau were made increasingly aware, as their colleagues penetrated the Syrian community in Cairo, of the growing opposition of Syrian nationalists to Hashemite suzerainty in Syria. Despite French opposition, Feisal's advance northward represented one means by which Cairo could present Paris with a fait accompli at Damascus. In addition to the advantage of having another British pensioner ensconced in Syria, this campaign also offered an alternative to rule by Hussein in the person of his abler and less doctrinaire son.

The idea to promote Feisal as sovereign for postwar Syria probably originated with Lawrence. In any case, Clayton certainly received the idea favorably. He was well aware of just how unpalatable Hussein would be to most urban Syrians. The sharif's claim to leadership simply would not wash in more modern Syria. "For this reason I incline to the opinion that it is one of the Sharif's sons who we must try to push for Syria."[9] Clayton recognized that any possible Sharifian claim to Mesopotamia likely was dead. Besides, having agreed to consider alterations in the status of the vilayets of Basra and Baghdad, the sharif knew well that his shares were not marketable in Iraq. Moreover, renewed friction between Hussein and Ibn Saud dimmed his prospects for suzerain authority over even the Arabian peninsula. Successful installation of Feisal in Damascus, aside from strengthening Cairo's hand against the French and helping to mollify discontented Syrian nationalists, would provide an opportunity to throw a bone to the sharif in the form of some nominal title.

Hogarth agreed with this objective. While Syria's future inevitably would be complicated by its entanglement with foreign powers, the best chance of achieving political unity "from Taurus to Sinai" lay with the investiture of an emir or prince. Lack of an indigenous political consensus, he felt, dictated this: "No Syrian would be accepted except by his own district or group; nor would any Mesopotamian. If such has to look outside for an Arab, the sons of the Sherif promised they came as Arabs, not as Syrians, and of the only generally acknowledged pre-eminent nobility that exists in Arab lands. . . . Of the rest Feisal is incomparably the most qualified, and the only one in whom I can see the possible unifier of a whole number of provinces such as Syria and Mesopotamia and the promoter of its federation with other provinces."[10] In this way, Feisal might be championed as the ostensible sovereign for the bureau's envisioned federation. In addition, placed as he was to embark on a campaign for the liberation of Syria, he would be in a uniquely advantageous position. Once established at Damascus, Feisal might effectively confront the French and solicit the regional support required to resist their encroachment. For these two reasons, Syria was the linchpin of Cairo's evolving federal design.

Early in 1917, Sykes published a memorandum analyzing the Anglo-French accord reached one year before in which he stressed the need for Britain to pursue the policy previously agreed upon by all concerned in regard to Arab nationalism.[11] In this report, Sykes outlined the measures that would be required to keep the Arab movement from foundering. Military and political officers would have to cooperate forcefully to press Arab national aspirations home. Groundwork would have to be laid: defectors attracted and debriefed, informers recruited for a native intelligence network, Turkish desertion encouraged, and local committees established to step in once the Turks had been driven out. While rhetorically sympathetic toward Arab aspirations, Sykes remained determined to implement the accord reached with Picot in 1916 as the cornerstone of the postwar Middle East.

Neither Clayton nor Hogarth thought much of Sykes, despite his exalted position as special adviser to the Middle East committee in London. To them, he was intellectually shallow and hopelessly verbose, pretending to far more knowledge concerning Middle Eastern affairs than he actually possessed. Hogarth was often irritated by Sykes's tenacious adherence to simplistic and (to some extent) idealistic solutions to complex problems. During a visit to London in 1918, Hogarth, approached to act as his advocate before the Foreign Office, declined with the confession, "I can't be Sykes' devil!"[12] The eminent Oxonian Hogarth could not even let Sykes's 1919 obituary pass unassailed, debunking the claim that he knew Arabic. "The worse of him was," averred the professor, "that he never really worked at anything and remained the superficial amateur to the end."[13] Lawrence agreed, dismissing Sykes as "a bundle of prejudices, intuitions and half-sciences."[14]

Sykes's grand memo did not provide, Hogarth complained, for military developments that might overtake diplomatic protocol (e.g., Feisal before Damascus). In a brief note appended to it, he stressed once again that it was "impossible to have anything but a sliding policy now. There must be room for certain faits accomplis between now and next autumn."[15]

It is interesting to note that George Lloyd praised the memo effusively, lauding the Sykes-Picot Agreement as a good solution in light of the shortage of political acumen and leadership in the region. The agreement, Lloyd argued, "wholly commends itself to those who wish to see one of the great races of the world given scope to develop and use its special capacities in its own way, and to those who hold that civilisation is better served by the amicable cooperation of different racial units than by attempting to ignore or suppress essential divergence."[16]

In May 1917, Sykes and Picot traveled to the East to join Field Marshal Allenby's expeditionary force as their countries' respective political officers. They were instructed to journey to Jeddah on a mission of reassurance to the suspicious Hussein. Included in Clayton's instructions to Wilson (the British agent to the Hejaz) concerning preparation for the encounter is a reference to Lawrence's latest dispatches from Syria, where he was engaged in furtive reconnaissance. These dispatches favorably anticipated the reception Feisal might expect in Syria. Indeed the reports were so encouraging that Clayton was driven to conclude there would be no trouble convincing the French "to accept the 'fait accompli.' "[17]

After conferring earlier with Feisal at Jeddah, Sykes met with the sharif for three and one-half hours on 5 May 1917. At that time, Sykes reportedly "explained the principle of the Agreement as regards an Arab Confederation or State, in accordance with my instructions." In addition, he claimed to have fully informed Hussein of the British position regarding the future of Baghdad vilayet and "the position of military and political predominance which our strategical and commercial interests require."[18] To Picot, Sir Mark wrote of his satisfaction with the proceedings.[19]

Yet the record is mixed as to how forthcoming Sykes actually was in the interview, especially with respect to Baghdad. Elie Kedourie contends that there is reason to believe that "on this occasion, Sykes eschewed precision and plain-speaking."[20]

Lieutenant Colonel Wilson, however, sent his own report on the visit to Clayton, one that renders Sykes's version even more suspect. Professing knowledge (gained from Lloyd) that "Baghdad will almost certainly be practically British," Wilson argued "that we have not played a straight forward game with a courteous old man . . . , for it means that the Sherif verbally agreed to Syria being practically French which I felt sure he never meant to do." It will be remembered that Sykes had likened the postwar French position in Syria to that of the British in Baghdad. The troubled Wilson went to Sykes and inquired, "Does the Sharif etc. know what the situation in Baghdad really is?" Sykes replied, "They have the [Baghdad] proclamation."[21]

The Baghdad Proclamation was written by Sykes and published under authority of the War Cabinet by Major General Stanley Maude after the entrance of Anglo-Indian forces into that city in late 1917. It said in part:

> O people of Baghdad! Remember that for 26 generations you have suffered under strange tyrants who have ever endeavored to set one Arab house against another in order that they might profit by your dissensions. Therefore, I am commanded to invite you, through your Nobles and Elders and Representatives, to participate in the management of your civil affairs, in collaboration with the Political Representatives of Great Britain who accompany the British army, so that you may unite with your kinsmen in the North, East, South and West in realising the aspirations of your race.[22]

Clayton harbored deep reservations about this tactic as well, fearful that the British position in Mesopotamia, heretofore on the back burner, now would be the object of far greater scrutiny and the source of potential conflict and embarrassment.[23] Yet one might wonder at this, for it is not difficult to detect a greater cause for Clayton's concern. To equate French influence in Syria with that of the British in Baghdad connoted de facto annexation of Syria by Paris, thereby seriously damaging whatever authority Feisal might later attempt to assert. While such diplomatic legerdemain proved a sufficient palliative to Hussein, it did nothing but complicate the Arab Bureau's own plans for Damascus and eastern Syria. In June, the Savoy wired the Arab Bureau's sister branch, now based in Baghdad, that agents were busily preparing the ground behind the lines in advance of Allenby's upcoming offensive in Syria.[24] Lawrence, meanwhile, continued to send back optimistic assessments depicting a land eager to welcome its bedouin and Allied liberators.

In that same month, Clayton issued a memo suggesting modifications in the Sykes-Picot Agreement. What he desired, first of all, was the elimination of the southern boundary of Britain's Area B, which would have effectively drawn the Arabian peninsula into the Red Zone. This revision, Clayton maintained, was essential, as "anything less than this jeopardizes our whole position in the East." Even more interesting, however, are his remarks concerning the French. Paris, he argued, had not seen fit to exert itself militarily in the Near East. Britain, on the other hand, had undertaken the Mesopotamian campaign unilaterally and underwritten the Hejaz revolt virtually without French assistance. All initiatives against the Turks had come from British arms: "France, on the contrary, has made no advance towards establishing her claims in Syria, where in any case she has much hostile feeling to contend against which will render the good offices of Great Britain of the utmost value."[25]

Hogarth, on assignment to the Admiralty, also took the offensive, circulating a note denouncing the agreement as fatally imbalanced in favor of the French both "in quantity and quality of territory reserved to occupation or exclusive influence." Continuing on, he questioned whether the compelling reasons that had necessitated the treaty's conclusion in 1916 existed any longer. Hogarth conceded that France's territorial appetite would have to be satisfied on more or less a par with Britain's own. This was inevitable in that no section of the Arab people "is capable . . . of constituting a stable, independent state, or carrying on one when constituted." But this agreement was grievously flawed by its failure to allot primacy in Arabia, in which Britain had "paramount interests." In accord with Clayton's memo, Hogarth suggested an extension of British tutelage over all parts of the Arabian peninsula "in which any Christian Power has a footing," adding parenthetically that he would add Palestine.[26] Speaking in London for Cairo's point of view, the Arab Bureau's guru was throwing down the gauntlet before Mark Sykes. If the situation on the western front was dire enough to demand the continued placating of Paris, so be it. If not, "bear skin agreements" such as the one he had negotiated should be jettisoned, at least until the dust of the war had settled and available options had crystallized. In practical terms, the accord was dead—except in Sykes's fertile imagination.[27]

Reporting back to Clayton from the Admiralty, Hogarth was pessimistic as to the impact of his note on the diplomatic course of events, but he did pass along this tantalizing observation: "The War Office is optimistic about Arabia and Syria, however, and much bucked-up by TEL's [Lawrence's] report and scheme. Tell him to be careful not to justify Mark's idea of him as a Fashoda propagandist. I, too, am credited with a 'fashoda' mind. Only you are uncontaminated in Cairo."[28] This observation was sweeping, lumping the director of Military Intelligence, Curzon, Milner, and the Admiralty into this Fashodist cabal, each one prepared to support scuttling Sykes's agreement with the French. Yet Hogarth, perhaps because of his rather unique position, spoke out most forthrightly in favor of revision. Events were beginning to move too swiftly in Palestine to permit the accord to linger on as the primary basis for a postwar territorial settlement. He recognized that Sykes had become irretrievably alienated from prevailing sentiment. Clayton seized the opportunity, urging Sykes not to bend to the protests of "Bremond and Co." against Feisal's northward advance. The French, he argued, would have to learn to live with the bedouin, especially after their expected entry into Damascus (a reference to Lawrence's report).[29] Shortly afterward, Clayton again wired Sykes a pessimistic assessment of the latter's mission with Picot to Jeddah. Hussein, genuinely or not, professed not to understand the agreement, but this was of little consequence "as I think that events will be too strong for him, and that in the end, he will have to fall into line or out. Feisal will probably be a great deal more amenable than his father."[30]

By this point, Clayton was growing weary of Sykes's posturing and his grand political schemes. In a letter outlining his project for a consolidated Arab-Jew-Armenian combine as the best model for a postwar state, Sykes included a facsimile of an appropriate flag that he had designed.

Sykes was an incurable romantic, smitten with fanciful and often simplistic notions about the nature of civilizations, nations, and races. As a proponent of Tory Democracy, such dated concepts as benevolent aristocracy, an iron sense of social position, and noblesse oblige figured prominently in his perspectives on the East. Although still largely untainted by the materialism and merciless utilitarianism that he felt were by-products of Western industrial progress, the East faced tough challenges that threatened the very existence both of Ottoman culture and Eastern "character": "The East preserved, then, all the qualities which the West had lost: a social order compounded of small, intimate communities; authority hallowed by mercy, descending by small degrees from governor to governed; lord and serf, rich man and poor man rooted in the indignities and obligations of their station, owing respect to each other, and moved neither by fear nor contempt; all doing homage in their lives and thoughts to the divine eternal order of which their society on earth was but the mirror."[31] This purity of social spirit, Sykes felt, was under assault from foreign influences spearheaded by his culturally hybrid Levantine, who insidiously introduced Western evils while owing no allegiance to the nation or culture that he undermined. Sykes's grand vision, therefore, was to erect a confederation or "combine" of nations that would provide a tutelary, agrarian environment, purged of Western crassness, in which disenfranchised Arabs, Jews, and Armenians might be delivered from limbo and become "genuine" people armed with national consciousness and reawakened to more honorable traditions long since abandoned. His contempt for Levantine Jews, Arabs, and Armenians is unmistakable, yet he sought redemption through national regeneration, agrarian in nature and almost medieval in structure; he dreamed of a society where squires, lords, and peasants might live in a reconstituted amity, without the intrusion of Western capitalistic acquisitiveness and cultural sterility. Where "Levantinism" had not yet insinuated itself, uncorrupted representatives of the old order might take up the reins and begin anew. Thus might the Jews have their nation in Palestine, the Armenians theirs in Armenia, and the Arabs theirs in Arabia.[32]

Of course, Sykes must have known that he was implicitly sabotaging the Sykes-Picot Agreement with such notions. Whether he was actually intent on this strategy is impossible to conclude definitively, because he died in 1919. What is clear is that his colleagues in the Middle East took him far less seriously than those in London. While idealistic, his combine scheme defied conventional logic, as "the three peoples had far too few interests in common to fall in with his dream."[33]

Clayton's response was to dissemble. "I quite see your arguments," he wrote to Sykes, "regarding an Arab, Jew, Armenian combine and the advantages that would accrue if it could be brought off. We will try it, but it must be done very cautiously and, honestly, I see no great chance of success."[34] Yet just one week earlier he wrote revealingly to Gertrude Bell of the project and its expositor: "Mark Sykes talks eloquently of a Jewish-Armenian-Arab combine, but the Arab of Syria and Palestine sees the Jew with a free hand and the backing of H.M.G. and interprets it as meaning the eventual loss of his heritage. Jacob and Esau once more. The Arab is right and no amount of specious oratory will humbug him in a matter which affects him so vitally."[35]

Clearly, Clayton thought such trifles as Sykes's combine project premature in light of the extensive political and diplomatic groundwork that had yet to be laid. He was also wary of doing anything to encourage further participation by Sykes in the preparation of postwar arrangements. Clayton knew from Hogarth's notes that Sykes was in ill health and, if not aroused, might well leave the conduct of affairs to those on the spot in Cairo. As for the Sykes-Picot Agreement, it was "as old and out of date as the Battle of Waterloo and the death of Queen Anne." Far better to ignore it, he wrote to Lawrence, and "let it die of inanition" than to argue with Sykes and risk "raising him to activity." As for the French: "we cannot expect [the French] to see this yet and we must therefore play up to it as loyally as possible

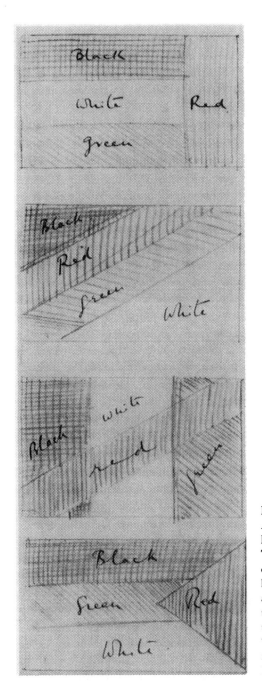

FIG. 7. Flag facsimiles for a new Arab state, designed by Sykes in a letter to Wingate in February 1917. The suggested colors were symbolic of the Arab dynasties: Abbassid, black; Omayad, white; Alid, green and red for the sharif and "most of the trucial chiefs." Sykes suggested that the ensign should be flown "whenever the French flag is flown" in areas A and B. (from the Arab Bureau files)

until force of circumstance brings it home to them."[36] The author's original conclusion with respect to the bureau's efforts to undermine the Sykes-Picot Agreement is confirmed by David Fromkin's recent work, in which he notes the irony that "the Arab Bureau which he [Sykes] had created became the center of the plot to destroy it."[37]

Clayton anticipated Arab success along the Jordanian flank that would sweep Feisal into Damascus under the protective wing of Allenby's expeditionary force. Faced with such an overwhelming preemption, Paris would be compelled to come to terms with territorial revisions. France would accept this arrangement because it simply would have no other choice. Its military options in the Levant were nonexistent and her prospective subjects (if the Arab Bureau was correct) implacably hostile to French penetration. For these reasons, Sykes was informed from Cairo, "it becomes more and more evident that the French will never make good their aspirations in Syria unless they take some more active military part in this theatre." Forswearing unseemly Fashodist skepticism, Clayton resorted to unalloyed prevarication: "I do not speak in any Anti-French spirit. As you know, I am doing my utmost to help them to act in the spirit of our agreement, but it is impossible to get round solid facts."[38] Such cant is vintage Clayton. He was fond of parrying Sykes's intrusions through complimentary reassurances from Cairo, intended at once to soothe and to manipulate. His correspondence is laced with the same disdain felt for Sir Mark in many Eastern quarters. However, Sykes's influential position in London's higher circles necessitated Clayton's ingratiating letters in the fall of 1917.

Cairo's appreciation of the pivotal position Syria might command in the direction of the postwar Arab world also militated against territorial generosity toward the French. Several reports from inside the Arab Bureau stressed the critical role that Syria was destined to play in the fortunes of Arab national development. Geographically, Syria was the Arab world's traditional link with the West as well as its economic clearinghouse. Bell labeled it "the head and brains of the Arab movement." Historically, Syria was "the well from which United Arabia springs and by which it is nourished."[39] William Ormsby-Gore echoed these sentiments in a note to the War Cabinet, noting that if "an Arab Nation is to be born at the end of this war it is round Damascus that it must naturally gravitate."[40]

Early in 1918, Lawrence submitted a report entitled "Syrian Cross-Currents," which reduced British alternatives to starkly imperialistic terms. In this report, he dismissed the opposition of native Syrians to Hashemite rule as "obscurantist" and recapitulated the chief contribution of Hussein's revolt: dividing Islam against itself to Britain's inestimable advantage. To Lawrence, Syrian expatriates abroad (especially in Cairo) were pawns, to be easily and readily sacrificed: "They have a pathetic belief in the idiot altruism of Britain and France. Themselves hardly capable of courage and unselfishness, they credit us with little else."[41] Moreover, he regarded the stakes in Syria in very Europocentric terms. The Sharifian invasion of Syria, Lawrence posited, "is going to affect the other phase of European rivalry in the Levant, by determining whose candidate is going to gain control of the trade routes and commercial centres of Western Asia."[42]

Early in 1917, Lawrence wrote another disparaging assessment in the *Arab Bulletin* regarding the likelihood of a distinctly Syrian development of "national feeling." The Turks had been far too successful in "sedulously fostering" jealousy and division to allow for the slightest possibility of "spontaneous union." Yet young Lawrence did see one remedy for Syria's divisive malaise: "only by the intrusion of a new factor founded on some outward power or non-Syrian basis, can the dissident tendencies of the sects and peoples of Syria be reined in sufficiently to prevent destructive anarchy . . . not an efficient administration but the minimum of central power to ensure peace and permit the unchecked development of customary law."[43] This is merely a thinly veiled version of Cairo's position, for even if France had been willing to exercise "the minimum of central power" in the Syrian hinterland, Lawrence would certainly have been the last person to suggest it. That role he had clearly reserved for Britain. He was later to expand further on his vision for a "Brown Dominion." The Arab idea of national union was nothing more, insisted Lawrence to his superiors, than "episodic combined resistance to an intruder." The impulse for unity, he felt, was anathema to the Arabs except in an environment of reaction and liable to rapid dissipation once that external threat had vanished. The credibility of that impulse was therefore dependent upon the extent to which it was forced upon them by foreign influence, and "Unless we or our allies, make an efficient Arab empire, there will never be more than a discordant mosaic of provincial administrations."[44] Hogarth clearly regarded such tutelary measures as unlikely to meet with insurmountable objections from Hussein, because of the opposition among many urban Syrians to the prospect of Hashemite rule. "He shows himself so openeyed," he wrote in the *Arab Bulletin*, "about the capacity of his race, and the level of political sense to which it has fallen that, undoubtedly, he will accept for it, when the time comes, a measure of tutelage and protection far more drastic than the Syrian intellectuals will hear of. . . . So he half shuts his eyes to much he knows, as well as we, is amiss."[45]

The Arab Bureau, working closely with the Palestinian branch under Clayton, extended the contacts with Syrians in Cairo made initially by one of its officers, Osmond Walrond, who took grave exception to Lawrence's appraisal of the exiled Syrians. Walrond, protégé and private secretary to Viscount Milner while in South Africa, joined the Arab Bureau in the fall of 1917. His task was to penetrate Syrian nationalist societies in Cairo. In this he was successful, being initiated into al-Qahtaniyya as its only European member. Al-Qahtaniyya subsequently merged with the national-ist al-Ahd, which Clayton had found too emasculated by the Turks in 1916 to investigate. Walrond detailed the depth of anti-Hashemite feeling in this group as well as their intense suspicion of the French. Doubtless a typical Cairene disdain for the Arabian bedouin played a part in this; it also reflected a clear rift between Walrond and Lawrence, who persistently downplayed the practical importance of communications with such exiles. Walrond felt that divisions between the Syrian and Sharifian elements had to be meaningfully addressed for Feisal to stand any chance in Damascene politics. As for Lawrence, Walrond sneered that "I think he is a little too fond of the Bedouin and their rags."[46]

But Walrond also noted that the Syrians with whom he was in contact would probably not react favorably to British overtures as long as Allied policy remained "undecided and obscure."[47] In his reports, suspicion repeatedly surfaced as he stressed the risks of attempting to keep the Arabs in play while the aspirations of the French were entertained in London: "While we on our side and the King may be said to be flogging a horse whose legs we have hobbled and identifying ourselves with a cause whose case will not bear the strict examination of equity and common sense, our allies openly proclaim their intention of looking after Arab interests in Syria, or part of it, and providing the inhabitants with counsellors whether they will them or no."[48]

Hogarth was also busily canvassing Syrian opinion. In February, he conducted an interview with Dr. Faris Nimr, a noted Syrian expatriate in Cairo who had a history of cooperation with the Arab Bureau. Nimr's party desired a free, integral, self-governing Syria (inclusive of Palestine) with its own king or prince as a constitutional monarch within a larger federated Arab union. Hogarth was given to understand that Feisal would be accept-able, but not his father. Yet, while specifically rejecting participation by either the French or Hussein in the new state, Nimr did not rule out some

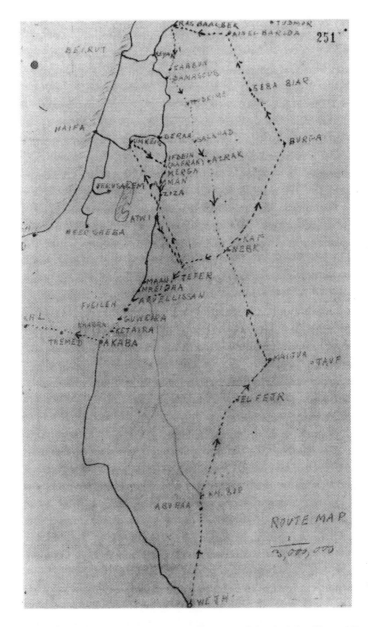

FIG. 8. Sketch map sent by Lawrence to Clayton in July 1917 detailing raiding
and reconnaissance mission designed to open Aqaba for use as an extra supply
base for Arab forces and to sound the possibilities of Sharifian action in eastern
and southern Syria. (from the Arab Bureau files)

sort of nominal overlordship for the king. "He fully agrees with King Hussein," reported Hogarth, "that no Arab unity, however shadowy, can come about till we recognise the title. The name will then gradually create a reality."[49] Hogarth's "reality" was the larger federation which he, Clayton, and the Arab Bureau hoped to forge. Nimr's comments kindled optimism because he seemed amenable to some role for Feisal and favored Britain as tutelary power. Most importantly, his testimony provided further evidence that nationalist Syrians were serious in their opposition to French encroachment. If popular acceptance could be gained for Hussein's claim to kingship of the Arabs, the facade over which Cairo sought to preside would be complete. The prospect of a similar arrangement in Mesopotamia, once Indian objections were overridden, gave rise to optimistic speculation at the residency: "Thus might we secure the substance whilst formally renouncing the shadow of ownership or sovereignty of Arab lands: and, by this renunciation, strengthen our hands against political penetration in Syria, and allow Syrian prejudice, Moslem partiality, and Zionist opportunism to combine and operate on behalf of pro-British and Anti-Hun influences throughout the Arab countries." This scenario could only be realized, however, if London agreed to ditch the Sykes-Picot Agreement and abandon the Palestinian Arabs.[50]

This brings us to the next point of controversy in Anglo-Arab relations. A deputation of seven Syrians residing in Cairo sent a message to Hogarth through Walrond requesting clarification of British policy toward Syria. Hogarth's reply subsequently became known, in historical diplomatic parlance, as the Declaration to the Seven. The intent of this statement has been interpreted in many different ways. The gist of the message was that Britain recognized the "complete and sovereign independence of the Arabs" in territories that were either independent prior to the war or liberated by the Arabs themselves in the course of it. Those areas occupied by the Allies or remaining under Turkish control at the end of hostilities would be dealt with in conformity with the "principle of the consent of the governed."[51] The Syrians then proceeded to cross-examine Hogarth. When asked what was meant by "political principles," the professor replied that he could not go beyond the words. Asked whether such governments as the Arabs established would be recognized by His Majesty's government, he answered affirmatively, provided they were properly established and effective.[52]

To George Antonius, this pledge provided confirmation of earlier promises, yet in more unequivocal and unambiguous terms than before: "an

authoritative enunciation of the principles on which those pledges rested."
At a stroke, Hogarth's declaration to the seven Syrians both sanctified
Britain's commitment and consummated its perfidy. For this reason alone,
Antonius contended, it stands as "by far the most important statement of
policy publicly made by Great Britain in connexion with the Arab Revolt;
and yet strangely enough, it has remained one of the least known outside
the Arab World."[53]

Another work dealing with this period suggests that the declaration was
symptomatic of the confusion that characterized the British government's
attitude toward Arab nationalism—an ambiguous, tentative reflection of
Britain's schizophrenic stance. This author dubs the declaration a "marked
British espousal of Arab sovereignty," adding: "It clearly showed that the
British, far from wishing to acquire territory in the Middle East, invited
the Arabs to participate on the basis of military and political equality in
the new structuring of the Middle East."[54]

But the actual truth seems to lie somewhere between machination and
muddle. Clearly, Hogarth's response flowed naturally from Cairo's pursuit
of an alternative to the Sykes-Picot Agreement. Forewarned of the considerable opposition that would follow any attempt by Feisal to extend
Hashemite control over Damascus, the bureau took measures to ascertain
the extent and nature of that opposition (hence Walrond's penetration of al-
Qahtaniyya). Hogarth's declaration was merely the logical culmination of
the bureau's labor and an expression of sentiment that had surfaced on
several occasions over the previous year. Clayton told Sykes that "for the
moment it is intended to let the agreements die gradually until the time
comes to administer the 'coup de grace' . . . it is my own personal opinion
that the agreements are out of date, reactionary, and only fit for the scrap
heap. It is absolutely clear that the times have so changed that agreements
of that nature, however liberally conceived, at the time, will not hold a
drop of water at any conceivable peace conference."[55]

Shortly after Walrond's meeting with the Syrians, Wingate wired an
alternative program to Sykes that reflected the bureau's vision as well as
his own. It suggested (1) outright opposition to the administrative separation
of Syria and Palestine; (2) acceptance of Feisal or another son of Hussein
as constitutional ruler of Syria; (3) complete disassociation, in secular
matters, of the Sharifian government from Syrian affairs; (4) assumption of
the caliphate by Hussein.[56]

Hogarth's message was not an outstretched hand but the proffered
crutch. This is partly verified by the Syrians' tepid reaction to it. Nor was

it another rung in the ladder of calculated deception of the Arabs, designed to relax their vigilance toward the French. Rather, Hogarth was laying the plough to the furrow, preparing the ground for Feisal's installation in Damascus with the ultimate view of realizing pan-Arab union with which he, Clayton, Cornwallis, and Lawrence hoped to win the peace for Great Britain. The medium through which this effort was conducted was the Cairo Arab Bureau. One noted Syrian author has succinctly observed that the Declaration to the Seven canceled neither the Sykes-Picot Agreement of 1916 nor the Balfour Declaration of 1917: "But if the principle of the 'consent of the governed' was to be applied the validity of both would be undermined if not completely annulled."[57]

The major roadblock to Cairo's forward policy, of course, was the reluctance on the part of Whitehall to scrap their treaty with Paris, despite the swiftly moving pace of events in Palestine. Clearly Balfour and Lloyd George, at the end of 1917, harbored deep reservations about the accord, especially its provisions dealing with the Mesopotamian vilayet of Mosul and the dispensation of Palestine. But the critical state of the war effort, especially in the wake of Russia's withdrawal from the Entente, argued against risk of an Anglo-French rupture. Neither could London attempt to attenuate Feisal's advance northward (as the French would have liked), as recently discovered peace feelers from the Turks to Sharifians and Syrian exiles were worrisome. Perceived duplicity now could sunder the Arab movement entirely, and imperil Allenby's Transjordanian flank.

Visiting London in the summer of 1918, Hogarth was appalled by the lack of policy and direction at the top. He could not let the opportunity pass to inject some substance into the leadership vacuum. While drawing attention to the many systemic flaws that continued to hamstring political consistency, Hogarth described what Feisal would minimally accept. His recommendation conformed with the view prevailing at the Cairo residency, including establishment of self-governing states—federated or otherwise— in Syria (except Palestine), upper Iraq and Mesopotamia (except Basra), and throughout the Arabian peninsula. Anything less, he warned, "will be considered a breach of faith and damaging to British prestige."[58] So it appears Hogarth viewed the moment right to up the ante. Rather than insist on major revisions in the Sykes-Picot Agreement to secure British interests in Arabia and Palestine, he now played the trump card dealt him by Feisal's presence in Syria to press for complete abandonment of the accord. Clayton's hopes for a British-dominated confederation were utterly dependent upon Feisal's "making good" in Syria, a task for which Allenby's cooperation was essential. Yet for all the calming effect that an official acknowledgment of support for this policy might have had on the Arab movement's discontented elements, the opportunity remained unexploited. Time was of critical importance: "I think it is in any case desirable, however, that H.M.G. should decide on the policy, if only to ensure that our own administrators lose no chance of impressing it on those Arab chiefs with whom they are in contact. In this way an atmosphere will be created and the way made easier for development of the policy when the favourable time comes."[59]

This sense of urgency underscored the need for some sort of pronouncement that would defuse Turkish overtures and reassure the Arabs as to Anglo-French intent. Moreover, this seemed to be the time for grand pronouncements. In the wake of President Wilson's January announcement of his twelfth point, respecting the self-determination of peoples, Britain felt pressured to conform, at least rhetorically, to the prevailing sentiment.

This was the genesis of the ill-fated Anglo-French Declaration, which has been cited as another element in the diplomatic smokescreen that London sought to place between its commitments to France and the restive suspicion of its Arab allies. Hogarth contributed to the draft after numerous revisions and deletions that are themselves interesting to note (for instance, the word *independent* was replaced by *native*). In this draft, Britain and France pledged their good faith to establish such "native" governments in all "Arabic-speaking areas." A codicil excluding upper Iraq and Palestine was deleted. The two powers likewise denied intent to occupy, annex, or protect those liberated areas unless their native governments proved unable or unwilling to do so or to prevent another power from doing so.[60] Writing from Oxford, Hogarth regarded the proposed declaration as a necessary evil, to reassure the Arabs until such time as London officially recognized the Sykes-Picot Agreement as moribund. He felt that such a proclamation effectively "amounted to little," but if the above agreement lingered on "it can hardly go farther, and it would, I feel, ease the situation for a time."[61] The text of the declaration read in part: "France and Great Britain are at one in encouraging and assisting the establishment of indigenous Governments and administrations in Syria and Mesopotamia . . . and recognizing these as soon as they are established."[62] Still, Hogarth was unable to suppress the bitterness he felt at having to resort to such deception. In a note to Robert Cecil at the Foreign Office, he vented frustration over what he perceived as the source of this hypocrisy: "As for my supposed anti-French sentiment, it is confined to colonial matters. Three years have taught me that in these, without trace or exception, the French work against us, their interests being contrary to ours everywhere except in Europe, and ready to offer active opposition as soon as the War is over. Picot works underground through his agents, just as hostilely as DeFrance or Bremond or any other Frenchman. It is knowledge of the travail which creates and maintains the 'Fashoda' attitude as Mark Sykes calls it."[63]

The Anglo-French Declaration provided a valuable breathing space within which to fend off both Arab and French importunities while allowing events to run their course. Paris deemed it necessary to allay Arab suspicion, while the Arabs welcomed it as yet another confirmation of Allied commitment to their national aspirations. To Clayton and Hogarth this measure was yet another step toward renunciation and displacement of the much-maligned Sykes-Picot Agreement. The Anglo-French Declaration, urged George Lloyd, should be in substitution of, and not incident to, the Sykes-Picot Agreement. That accord, he conceded, was "a source of embarrassment of the moment [and] should make us hesitate before pledging ourselves once again to a specific policy—even negative—for adoption in hypothetical circumstances."[64] Coincident to this, Hussein should be fed whatever platitudes and gestures might be required. These tactics, Lloyd suggested, "will procure us that delay which is valuable in all negotiations, but doubly valuable in the East." Meanwhile, Britain's bargaining position must inevitably improve, he insisted, once Allenby's offensive had reached fruition.[65]

Given Hussein's repeated threats of resignation, such palliatives were unavoidable if the Arab movement was to be spared a crippling blow. The revolt was splitting along many seams just now. Syrian exiles eyed Feisal's fitful advance up the Jordan with rising apprehension. Turkish overtures, made in the wake of Bolshevik disclosure of the secret treaties, severely strained the Anglo-Arab alliance. Also, a serious rift had developed between Feisal and his father over the former's reliance on "outsiders" such as Nuri as-Said and Ja'afar Pasha al-Askari in his officer corps. Cornwallis warned from the bureau that Hussein was becoming increasingly unpredictable and cautioned that unless effective remedial actions were taken the success of the revolt would be placed at risk.

But clearly, Clayton was playing for larger stakes. It was not just the loss of Arab military support the bureau feared. Loss of the symbolic value embodied in Feisal's army, which would be of such great political use in Syria, might now be lost even before it could be exploited to imperial advantage. As Allenby's new chief political officer (and now a brigadier general), Clayton recommended to London that Hussein be informed that Whitehall would support the union of independent states in central and southern Arabia and "welcome the Sharif as suzerain." As for Syria and Mesopotamia, Clayton suggested the assurance that "the Allies will uphold the principles of freedom and self-determination of peoples as the basis of settlement."[66] Such vacuous pronouncements were designed to do little more than shore up Hussein's sagging morale while redirecting his personal ambition towards Arabia proper and saving Syria and Mesopotamia for future accommodation.

Once Allenby's final offensive got underway, the end came swiftly. Damascus was entered on 1 October in what some historians charge was a staged affair, designed to cast Feisal in the role of Damascene liberator. Some evidence does suggest that British units were restrained to this end. Moreover, Allenby's swift recognition of the Arab provisional government on the heels of Damascus's fall certainly suggests that this policy had official sanction.[67]

Allenby's advance continued inexorably northward, culminating finally in the Mudros Armistice of October, which effectively ended hostilities. Cairo's fait accompli finally seemed within sight, and the field marshal's grip was total. Allenby's vice-consuls ensconced themselves in every major Levantine city (even those in the French sphere) and were backed up by a military colossus of over two hundred thousand men.

The scope of Britain's advantageous position was not lost on policymakers in London. In December, Lloyd George seized the opportunity to demand cession of the Mosul vilayet in Mesopotamia, and Palestine "from Dan to Beersheba." Clemenceau, perhaps sensing his relative weakness, acquiesced at once. But the French premier was not prepared to extend such generosity to Feisal; and it became increasingly clear that something more than an advisory role was contemplated in Paris for the Syrian hinterland. As foreign dignitaries flocked to that city to debate the peace, Feisal's future seemed daily less secure.

Against these demands, Lloyd George at first held firm. Such French claims seemed in contravention of both the Sykes-Picot Agreement and McMahon's pledges to Hussein. Besides, while Paris might blithely dismiss the contribution of the Arabs to Allenby's success, French noninvolvement in the war against Turkey was conspicuous.

The campaign that subsequently developed to resist further French encroachment into Syria clearly enjoyed wide support among British officials in that theater. In April the Arab Bureau submitted a report on the many Syrian nationalist cells that had, by this time, flocked to Feisal's ranks. While the extreme nationalists remained a worry, the Savoy was confident: "in their sober moments they realize that the Syrians are quite unable to govern themselves and must depend on outside assistance. This assistance they would prefer to be given by England: they are strongly anti-French and declare that the majority of Syrian Arabs are bitterly opposed to any form of French protectorate or guidance."[68] The actions of Allenby and Wingate gave substance to this preference. The field marshal frequently obstructed French attempts to assert their authority in the Lebanon and encouraged anti-French demonstrations by Feisal and his minions, or at least such was the suspicion of both Foreign Minister Balfour and the prime minister. Allenby even went so far as to lobby openly for a British mandate in Syria, although Lord Curzon, chairman of the Middle East committee, rejected this idea out of hand.[69] It is probable that his close relationship with Clayton, Hogarth, Lawrence, and their circle was partly responsible for this. While the conduct of military affairs remained Allenby's province, political direction continued to come from Wingate and the Cairo Arab Bureau. Viewed in this light, the fact that the field marshal came to adopt similar opinions to those long propounded at the Savoy seems hardly a revelation.

As for the Arab Bureau and the Paris peace conference, suffice it to say that its influence was extant but hardly so pervasive as often assumed. Lawrence acted as the bureau's spokesman, not its leader. His notoriety and panache, however, made him the logical choice to fight the war of words on behalf of Clayton, Cornwallis, and the rest. While Hogarth also journeyed to France, he left it to Lawrence to strike the pose and draw the unfriendly fire.

As French pressure for a quid pro quo increased on Lloyd George, Clayton dispatched a flurry of telegrams to the Foreign Office urging abandonment of earlier agreements as untenable in light of developments. Of these commitments, Clayton pleaded: "these . . . policies are incompatible the one with the other, and that no compromise is possible which will be satisfactory to all three [Arab, French, and Zionist] parties."[70] As to whether and how agreements should be revised, Clayton's suggestions were predictable. France should be induced to renounce all her Syrian claims in favor of Britain "with due regard to Arab aspirations and Zionist aims." Paris, he suggested, could be mollified with control of Constantinople and the thankless task of reorganizing and reconstructing the Turkish state. In this way the "Sick Man of Europe" might finally find solace in French arms, while Cairo held sway over those vital land routes to India. A British mandate "would put the seal on British predominance throughout the Arab countries; would render Great Britain paramount in Islam; and would safeguard the Eastern Mediterranean and routes to Mesopotamia and India by securing control of the Aleppo-Mosul line."[71]

Indeed, many officials in Syria were already behaving as if dispensation of the mandate were a foregone conclusion. In a report entitled "Syria in October" written from impressions gleaned from her transit of the region en route to Paris from Baghdad in 1919, Gertrude Bell claimed that Colonel Cornwallis (now British consul in Beirut) and other officers with whom he served "assumed the acceptance of the Mandate by ourselves as a possibility. With whatever sincerity they and those under them may have played the guise of temporary neutrality, it was inevitable that their attitude to the Arab administration should have been influenced by the uncertainty which they shared with the Arabs, as to what the final status of the country could be. All uncertainty helped to strengthen Arab hopes."[72] Clayton was optimistic that the mandates commission being planned in Paris, ostensibly to ascertain the drift of Syrian opinion, would find in favor of Britain and thereby expedite this solution. Apparently, however, the French had few illusions as to their own popularity in Syria or the wisdom of their participation on such a commission. For this reason Hogarth, in attendance at the peace conference, knew the mandates commission was dead in the water: "And I'm bound to say, if we are determined d'avance not to act on its finding, should this be in favor of a British Syria, it is little use its going."[73] Hogarth had been skeptical of the commission's proposed work since it had first been suggested, figuring realistically that the deck would probably be stacked in favor of the French. Delay in its dispatch, he felt, was clearly designed to await the substitution of French for British troops in Lebanon. Sympathetic toward Clayton's great hopes for and sponsorship of the commission in Syria, Hogarth commiserated: "I keep everyone reminded of what its collapse may mean to you but we are powerless before French passive resistance."[74]

Despite the departure in April of the much ballyhooed King-Crane commission, few doubts remained as to the ultimate dispensation of the mandates.[75] Hogarth, disgusted and frustrated that the bureau's work had come to this sorry pass, unburdened himself to Clayton: "Failing that, I must resign and go back to Oxford sick at heart at all this fiasco and the melancholy consummation of four years work. To think that we are to hand over Faisal and Syria to Senegalese troops. . . . I won't blame the Arabs . . . if they get out their rifles."[76]

The fate of Syria, oddly enough, rested ultimately not with the War Office or the Foreign Office but with the Exchequer, groaning under the accumulated exactions of World War I and postwar territorial occupation. Grown weary of trying to wear down Clemenceau and beset with more pressing difficulties in Ireland, Egypt, Mesopotamia, and India, Lloyd George came increasingly to view Syria as expendable. The prime minister handed the problem over to Lord Curzon, for whose knowledge of Eastern questions Hogarth maintained a hearty disdain. Curzon was also tired of wrangling with the French over Syria at a time when so many other pressing problems begged for attention. Balfour shared this fatigue. The issue had been debated for too long, hamstringing the conclusion of Anglo-French settlements in other areas. Lawrence's grandstanding in Paris and London also had the unfortunate effect of alienating would-be supporters and drawing international attention to a most embarrassing diplomatic muddle. Far better to bite the bullet and leave Feisal to his wits. On 13 September 1919 Lloyd George and Clemenceau met to formalize their agreement, guaranteeing the evacuation of British troops from Syria by 1 November. Clayton had already been informed by Picot of the impending agreement and of France's intention to gut the mandates commission. "If this is true," he wired bitterly to Curzon, "I would suggest that I ought to have been informed by you."[77]

The Arab Bureau's grand design for Syria, for all its imperial promise, foundered on the shoals of European diplomacy. While arguments advanced by the residency and the bureau for continued British presence in Syria were compelling, larger considerations irresistibly intruded. Syria was the cornerstone of the hoped-for Arab federal union. Without Damascus, the reality would be a truncated version, shorn of its head. British credibility suffered accordingly with the loss of Syria, delivering a fatal blow to the emergence of a viable political strategy with which to guide nascent Arab political growth. Worse, a powerful and potentially dangerous European competitor was now entrenched bestride the strategic land routes of empire. Finally, with the collapse of the bureau's dream of an ersatz confederation, the pervasive influence with which Britain (and more particularly Cairo) had hoped to dominate the region was now forfeit, leaving the Middle East dangerously vulnerable to the twin demons of political instability and foreign intrigue.

9

UNEASE IN A PROMISED LAND

The Arab Bureau and Palestine

In Palestine, as in Syria and Arabia, the Arab Bureau sensed an opportunity that might be turned to imperial advantage. But the agency recognized, early on, inherent limitations within Zionism that conflicted directly with its own postwar objectives.

Certainly, by 1916 Zionist proponents had won powerful friends within the British government. Chaim Weizmann's scientific contributions to the war effort were partially responsible, as was the desire of British propagandists to unite worldwide Jewry around the Allied cause. Moreover, British intellectuals long had flirted with the prospect of prophetic fulfillment in Palestine. But inside the British government, that proposal also bespoke important strategic and imperial motivations. As early as 1845, E. L. Mitford of the Ceylon Civil Service had suggested the "reestablishment of the Jewish nation in Palestine as a protected state under the guardianship of Great Britain [that would] place the management of our steam communication entirely in our hands . . . and . . . place us in a commanding position [in the Levant] from whence to check the process of encroachment, to overawe open enemies and, if necessary, to repel their advance."[1] Construction of the Suez Canal bolstered advocates of such views. Herbert Sidebotham, on the staff of the *Manchester Guardian* and an ardent "student of war," parlayed such geopolitical considerations among many men of government. Along with colleague W. P. Crozier and editor C. P. Scott, Sidebotham effected an interesting (and persuasive) conjunction of Zionist goals with British strategic objectives. On 22 November 1915 an article appeared in the *Guardian* entitled "The Defense of Egypt," in which Sidebotham expounded on the logical fusion of Zionist and British interests:

> The main line of supply for the Turkish armies now in Palestine runs east of the Jordan, and if this line were to remain in the possession of a possibly hostile Power, it would outflank the natural line of defence for Egypt. Moreover, we are in Mesopotamia engaged in operations which seem likely to give us a new province, which ought not to be separated from Egypt by hostile territory. If Palestine were now a buffer state between Egypt and the north, inhabited as it used to be by an intensely patriotic race, friendly as it was in the past to Egypt because that Power was less aggressive as a rule than the great military Empires of the north, the problem of Egypt in this war would be a very light one. It is to this condition that we ought to work.[2]

To other observers, however, the risks entailed in the Zionist program must have seemed daunting. Surely the Turkish rulers of Palestine wanted no part of the scheme. And while Sultan Abdul Hamid was willing to permit very limited, unorganized immigration of Jews to the Holy Land, indigenous resistance in Palestine was evident by century's turn.

However aggrieved, local inhabitants were slow to erupt. Their reticence, coupled with circumvention of official proscriptions on various settlement organizations, allowed pressure to subtly but inexorably build. Jewish settlers might enter as religious pilgrims en route to holy shrines and therefore under the protection of foreign consuls. Many entered Palestine via Egypt, then under British control. Ottoman Jews, friendly Arabs, foreign consuls, or consular agents were occasionally employed as buyers of land for various Zionist front groups. And judicious bribery sometimes proved useful in diverting the gaze of Turkish officials assigned to oversee matters of immigration and land purchase. Finally, to the dismay of many Palestinian peasants, some Arab landlords were not above profiting from the speculative sale of their land, even to Jews.

The Young Turk revolution of 1908, while initially raising Zionist hopes, ultimately worked against any liberalization of the immigration law. Widespread celebration after that event was followed by scattered attacks on Jewish settlements throughout Palestine. An aggravating factor was the "nationality" problem accentuated by the Balkan wars, which strengthened those in the Turkish government who opposed relaxation of immigration restrictions. Both Turkish nationalists and anti-Zionist Arabs demonstrated vehemently against any contrary consideration. On the basis of local patriotism, dedication to Islam, and nascent Arabism, opposition to the Zionist movement coalesced. Fears raised by the Balkan wars over manifest Ottoman weakness, however, prompted the Committee of Union and Progress to briefly reconsider its Palestine policy in order to curry favor among international financiers and attract foreign capital. That idea ran afoul of thunderous opposition from Arabs throughout the region. By 1914 Arab anti-Zionism had become formidable. The Jews, it was now alleged by some, had exploited their guise as freemasons to gain control of the CUP. Rashid Rida charged that Zionist conspirators hungered after a superstate extending from Palestine to Iraq, which they hoped to extort through control of European banks and (by extension) the Ottoman debt. Initiatives that had been passed in the hope of encouraging Jewish assimilation, such as one promoting the acquisition of Ottoman citizenship, were forced back onto the shelf. The opposition, by 1914, had opened anti-Zionist societies in many cities of the region. The forces opposing accommodation with Zionist settlement groups simply proved too compelling by the summer of that year to allow change in official Turkish policy.

Some Palestinian Arabs too had been touched by the writings of Arabist and pan-Islamic thinkers and, while not yet devoted to the concept of distinctly Arab nationhood, were groping for a change away from ancient patterns of loyalty and affiliation. Though such notions were still new and somewhat alien to most Palestinians, an emerging consciousness was palpable, attributable partly to the fears aroused by the Zionist phenomenon. A. H. Hourani has offered this summation of the difficulty:

The conflict between Arabs and Jews in Palestine was not dissimilar. On the one hand, the Arab people were just in the process of passing into conscious nationhood, and thus of formulating the desire to include in a single political structure all those territories where the population was predominantly Arab. On the other hand, there was a group of Jewish thinkers who wished to fit the complex reality of Jewish history within the framework of the Western concepts of "race" and "nation." . . . Thus there arose an irreconcilable conflict. The Jews claimed Palestine, both on grounds of need and because of their traditional connection with it; the Arabs could not abandon it, both because by any ordinary political criterion it was theirs and because its geographical position made it essential for the unity of Arab peoples.[3]

Although Jewish settlers in Palestine numbered only about 85,000 in 1914, scattered among approximately forty colonies in the midst of some 600,000 Arabs, their influence in the game of imperial politics would prove immeasurably greater. Notwithstanding future events, resistance to the Zionist idea had greatly intensified. World War I, which was about to assume center stage in the region's geopolitical drama, was an interruption and not the genesis of well-rooted communal problems. "It may be argued," Neville Mandel has asserted, "that the Balfour Declaration was not so much the starting point of the conflict as a turning point which greatly aggravated an existing trend."[4]

The traditional image of the Arab Bureau as an anti-Zionist cabal, while seductive, remains inadequate.[5] Its reservations over Whitehall's embrace of Zionist principles stemmed from anxiety over British fortunes in Palestine rather than from shared indignation with an aroused Arab community.

A notable exception to this trend was William Ormsby-Gore (fourth baron of Harlech), who served on the bureau's staff in late 1916 and was conspicuously pro-Zionist. During his stint at the Savoy, Captain Ormsby-Gore wrote an optimistic report for his superiors entitled "The Politics of Jerusalem." In this report, he suggested that the postwar government of that city would be afflicted with substantial difficulties under any other than a British regime. Moreover, he stressed that the prospects favorable to a British occupation were not confined to that holy city: "In spite of the rarity of Britishers, English prestige is very strong and the desire for England to take over the country was widespread. Even the moslems of every class would not be adverse to British rule once they see its benefits and privileges. It is the universal belief of all prominent Syrians both in Egypt and in America that England would be received with open arms not only in Palestine, but also in Syria and by the Druses of the Lebanon."[6]

Upon his return to London and the War Office, Ormsby-Gore's belief in the prospects of a British Palestine was reinforced by Chaim Weizmann, who was persuasively lobbying for Zionist goals at Whitehall. Before long he became an enthusiastic advocate, involved in planning for departure of the Zionist Commission and actually accompanying Weizmann to Palestine in 1918. Unfortunately, Ormsby-Gore's eagerness to promote Zionist aims often transcended the bounds of taste. In the spring of 1917, he wrote to Sykes: "I think we ought to use pogroms in Palestine as propaganda. A few spicy tales of atrocity would be eagerly welcomed by the propaganda people here—and Aaron Aaronsohn [head of the NILI Jewish spy network] could send some lurid stories to the Jewish papers."[7] There was, of course, nothing revolutionary in this suggestion. The British government had certainly employed shameless atrocity propaganda in the past (e.g., Belgium). But Ormsby-Gore's embrace of this tactic to promote a policy still under review would certainly have raised some eyebrows at the Savoy. While the Arab Bureau and Military Intelligence had benefited handsomely from their connections with Aaronsohn's Palestine organization centered at Athlit, and those cooperative Zionists were becoming more eager for some sort of positive pronouncement from London, Clayton was not convinced that such a course would be wise:

> Indeed, I am not sure that it is not as well to refrain from any definite pronouncement just at present. It will not help matters if the Arabs—already somewhat distracted between pro-Sherifians and those who fear Meccan domination, as also between pro-French and anti-French are given yet another bone of contention in the shape of Zionism in Palestine as against the interests of the Moslem residents there. The more politics can be kept in the background, the more likely are the Arabs to concentrate on the expulsion of the Turks from Syria, which, if successful, will do more than anything to promote Arab unity and national feeling.[8]

Clayton's apprehension was certainly understandable. With Allenby about to commence his northward advance, Feisal's continued diversion of Turkish strength east of the Jordan was more important than ever. Even more critically, such imprudence could well have placed the bureau's anticipated Arab confederation at risk. Zionist contributions notwithstanding, it seemed impolitic to raise such thorny issues now. Moreover Clayton, unlike Balfour, was unmoved by Zionist arguments for a "national home" in Palestine. Of Sykes's support for the scheme, Cairo's intelligence chief was critical; of the philosophical principles that underlay Zionist logic, he was contemptuous, as earlier demonstrated in his reaction to Sykes's Jewish-Armenian-Arab combine scheme (see page 157 above).

Moreover, while the prospect of a stable European community settled in the Palestinian corridor was a comforting thought at Suez, British sponsorship of a Zionist homeland in Palestine would certainly draw the blackest outcries from the Arabs and, worse, provide the catalyst for an Arab unity that everyone was anxious to prevent. The Arab was well aware, Clayton insisted, that he would fare poorly in a commercial joust with the Jew who was "a far better businessman than himself and prone to exact his pound of flesh." To treat with Zionism courted disaster, he felt, and warned Sykes that "by pushing them [the Arabs] as hard as we appear to be doing we are risking the possibility of Arab unity becoming something like an accomplished fact and being ranged against us."[9]

On 2 November 1917 the War Cabinet approved the pro-Zionist pronouncement afterward included in a letter from Balfour to Lord Rothschild, president of the British Zionist Federation. The letter read in part:

> I have the pleasure of conveying to you, on behalf of His Majesty's Government, the following declaration of sympathy with Jewish Zionist aspirations which has been submitted to, and approved by, the Cabinet: "His Majesty's Government view with favor the establishment in Palestine of a national home for the Jewish people and will use their best endeavors to facilitate the achievement of this object, it being clearly understood that nothing shall be done which may prejudice the civil and religious rights of existing non-Jewish communities in Palestine, or the rights and political status enjoyed by Jews in any other country." I should be grateful if you would bring this declaration to the knowledge of the Zionist Federation.[10]

Clayton had steeled himself against, but was resigned to live with, this ambiguous "declaration." He was willing to accept Sykes's reassurances that further concessions from the Zionists would render it a more flexible pronouncement, possessing some basis upon which negotiation with the Arabs might be possible. Without this modification, however, Clayton saw little chance that the considerable apprehension felt by most Arabs toward the Zionists could be allayed.[11]

Many of Clayton's and Hogarth's written thoughts cannot be entirely acquitted of the charge of anti-Semitism. The *Arab Bulletin* was occasionally punctuated by oblique allusions to the supposed ubiquity of Jewish influence, especially in the higher circles of the Young Turks in Constantinople.[12] The Arab Bureau, however, was opposed to the declaration more from fear that the Arab Revolt had been needlessly jeopardized. Surely anti-Semitism was rife throughout the ranks of British officialdom in Cairo. But so was a hearty contempt for the Arab. Viewed through a prism of strategic imperatives, the question of Palestine was simply one facet of the overall imperial strategy that Cairo was looking to implement. Yet as the basis of that plan rested upon maintenance of a politically anemic Arab world, the Palestine problem was potentially catastrophic. Feisal and Hussein were allied with and financially dependent on Great Britain. Feisal's stock in Syria, already questionable among Arab intellectuals, would have been totally bankrupt had his mentors bartered away Palestine. Aside from dashing Cairo's hopes for a pan-Arab confederation, the resulting backlash might have drastic repercussions in Mesopotamia as well. The Arab Bureau, already faced with the complexities of the impending peace, was not in a position to receive Balfour's ill-timed pronouncements very warmly: "there is no doubt nothing that hampers so greatly our local relations with the existing non-Jewish inhabitants of Palestine, as the vagueness of our declaration in favour of Zionism. It is idle to suppose that any one in possession can feel at his ease in a Promised Land."[13]

Thus far, Hogarth had succeeded in double-talking Sharif Hussein into quiescence. His explanation of the Balfour Declaration, conveyed during a visit to Jeddah in January 1918, was as ambiguous as the foreign secretary's original pledge and stressed that "no people shall be subjected to another." Reminding Hussein that worldwide Jewish influence was prodigious and that any opportunity to appease that influence was not to be lightly cast aside, Hogarth concluded his explanation thusly: "Since Jews return to Palestine favoured by Jewish opinion of [the] world and inasmuch as this opinion must remain a constant factor, and further as H.M.G. view realization of this aspiration with favour, H.M.G. are determined that in so far as is compatible with freedom of existing population, both economic and political, no obstacle should be put in the way of realisation of this ideal."[14]

This ambiguous rhetoric, though sufficient to mollify the sharif for the moment, left serious questions unresolved concerning whether or not Palestine was included in the independent area promised by McMahon in 1915. This question has since spawned voluminous and often heated debate and need not detain us here. But there is little doubt that, whether or not Palestine was a twice-promised land, its perception as such by many Arabs seemed ominous to the Arab Bureau. Clayton and Hogarth were not blind to the strategic advantages that a British Palestine might afford, and favored the required revisions in the Sykes-Picot Agreement necessary to bring it about. Nor were they unconscious of the benefits that London felt Jewish settlement might bring. Those at the Arab Bureau did not deny the strategic principles that underlay Balfour's move, and they were not averse to pursuing them if such pursuit did not offend the Arabs. Awaiting the arrival of Weizmann's Zionist Commission in the spring of 1918, Clayton (now posted with Allenby) expressed to his Foreign Office superiors his hope that things might yet be put right "by impressing upon local Jews the real sense of the British Government's declaration and the necessity for taking up a reasonable and conciliatory attitude which will calm fears of local Arabs and lead to sympathetic cooperation of the two communities."[15]

Had Clayton really come to believe in the likelihood of harmonious coexistence? This is doubtful in light of his suspicion toward ultimate Zionist political aims. But it is possible, indeed probable, that he hoped to salvage a binational compromise sufficient to satisfy Zionists' cravings for identification with their ancient homeland while remaining under the aegis of Great Britain and linked with the Arab community under the rubric of some larger confederacy. Such a scheme had much to recommend it, in his view. From an imperial standpoint, a strong, pro-British buffer might be secured to the north of Egypt and the Suez Canal. Moreover, Clayton believed in the formidable influence of worldwide Zionism, and the opportunity to garner that influence behind support at the peace conference for a British Palestine was not to be lightly squandered.[16] Clayton even mused that the Palestinian peasant would benefit by an infusion of Jewish capital and enterprise into his land.[17] He seemed to envision a role for Jews in Palestine not dissimilar from that of Armenians in Turkey during less dreadful times, undertaking many of the financial and commercial services that the native population was simply unwilling or unable to provide and "by which alone an Arab state can maintain itself."[18]

This sanguine outlook rested, however, on Clayton's hope that Weizmann's mission would demonstrate to the Arabs a flexibility hitherto imperceptible. At least his own sense of Britain's Zionist policy could accommodate such a vision. "You may not perhaps be aware," he wrote confidently to Gertrude Bell, "that the Zionist policy is not that of the establishment of a Jewish state, . . . but aims at the institution of a Jewish home or centre of Hebrew culture in Palestine."[19] One suspects the chief political officer was stricken here with a spasm of wishful thinking. Clayton had largely engineered Weizmann's impending visit and may well have hoped that, once the Zionist leader had engaged in face-to-face talks with Feisal, a reasonable modus vivendi would be struck between them.[20] There is further evidence, however, that those attached to the Arab Bureau may have been misled as to the real intentions of Weizmann and his colleagues. Hogarth, for one, sensed trouble on the horizon. Citing the acute Arab apprehension that would most certainly attend the commission's arrival, Hogarth advised: "it is hoped that no time will be lost in making known as widely as possible the real policy of the Commission, which is understood to be opposed both to expropriation or exploitation of existing land-owners, and also to any Jewish political control of Palestine. For the very moderate number of Jews expected to settle there, it is considered that the almost derelict lands, and unappropriated marshy and sandy areas will provide ample scope."[21]

Indeed, in his subsequent 4 June meeting with Feisal, Weizmann was conciliatory to the point of outright duplicity, denying intent to seek an independent Jewish state: "Dr. Weizmann pointed out that the Jews do not propose setting up a Jewish government but would like to work under British protection with a view to colonising and developing the country without in any way encroaching on anybody's legitimate interests."[22] This masterful performance followed Clayton's script perfectly, prompting renewed optimism among his colleagues that affairs in Palestine might be put right. The Zionist Commission had proved less obnoxious to the Arabs than had been feared, with Weizmann rehearsing his later assurances to Feisal with Syrians and Palestinians with whom he came in contact. The message was basically the same—that no Jewish government was contemplated. All that the commission was seeking, he insisted, was "a home for the Jews in the Holy Land where they live their own national life, sharing equal rights with other inhabitants."[23] The commission's conduct, insofar as the bureau appraised it, might have been moderately successful in soothing Arab anxiety about the Balfour Declaration and eliciting a grudging acceptance of these modest aims. Cornwallis, summing up his Arab Bureau report on the commission's visit, was cautiously optimistic:

There is no doubt that this frank avowal of Zionist aims produced a considerable revulsion of feeling amongst the Palestinians, who have for the first time come in contact with European Jews of good standing. They have had the conviction forced on them that Zionism has come to stay, that it is far more moderate in its aims than they had anticipated, and that by meeting it in a conciliatory spirit they are likely to reap substantial benefits in the future. Suspicion still remains in the minds of some, but it is tempered by the above considerations and there is little doubt that it will gradually disappear if the commission continues its present attitude of conciliation.[24]

Other officers connected with the bureau were not as sanguine, especially those in direct contact with the Arabs and the Syrians. Perhaps more than anyone else, Hogarth rejected Zionist arguments for Palestine. He regarded the intellectual case for a Jewish homeland as specious. Taking the antiquarian perspective, he saw the Jews as simply one of many peoples whose fortunes had led to Palestine and felt that this fact alone was scant basis for territorial claims millennia hence. Tiberius's expulsion of the Jews he blithely construed as "voluntary abandonment" to till "more profitable fields" elsewhere. Hogarth's intellectual disdain for Zionism was rooted in a measure of anti-Semitism, it might seem, but also in what he perceived as the fundamental inequity inherent in Zionist employment of ancient claims that, aside from their contemporary irrelevance to Palestinians, were historically insupportable in light of the Arabs' long presence in the area. On this basis alone they possessed a "prescriptive right" to their land: "As for the Jewish claim to Palestine, it is based of course, on well known beliefs about ancient history, in which such an element of the supernatural is involved, that it is futile to submit it to any process of argument or discussion."[25]

Yet Hogarth saw no future in Zionism unless it was accompanied by Jewish political dominion in Palestine. Consequently, he dismissed the assurances of the Zionist Commission as disingenuous, calculated to lull the Arabs. While disclaiming any overt imperialist sympathies, Hogarth simply sought an alternative in Palestine to enlarging an "already overgrown Empire." This he found difficult, for he too was aware of the need to preempt occupation by another power "that we do not, and they do not want!"[26] He also knew the benefits that might accrue from modest Jewish settlement and so was willing to back Weizmann as long as his program remained moderate. But to Hogarth, Zionism made no sense intellectually without the corollary of a Jewish political entity. For this reason, he could not purge himself of nagging doubts about the direction that Balfour had chosen. Also irritating to him were the hollow disavowals (which Clayton had so welcomed) respecting Zionist political ambitions. But Clayton's view was prevalent at the Foreign Office—especially in the mind of his former colleague Ormsby-Gore, who wrote a minute critical of Hogarth's grim predictions for Palestine, riposting: "I disagree entirely that Zionism will require a *main forte*. The Zionists seek no political domination, only peaceful penetration and will succeed or not in accordance with whether they prove themselves the best cultivators of the soil and the most efficient people."[27] To this, an exasperated Hogarth replied:

> I can't agree that we should, or can, shape our private policy (whatever we say in public) on an assumption that "Zionists seek no political domination etc.," what Sakalow says and Weizmann, if pressed, admits (he has so admitted to me) and the logic of facts all forbid! There will be no effective force behind Zionism unless the Jewish Home in Palestine means Palestine for the Jews as a nation politically dominant there under whatever protection be eventually imposed. This will and can only come about by pressure on the existing population, not by its free or even peaceable consent.[28]

Osmond Walrond, the bureau officer in close touch with Syrian nationalists, also found Britain's Zionist policy difficult to defend. Complaining that it had greatly compounded already pressing difficulties, he claimed little could be done beyond reassuring the Arabs that Allied "good sense" would ensure fair play for both communities in Palestine.[29]

Once appointed chief political officer in Palestine, Clayton was starkly disabused of earlier hopes that a general settlement might be amicably concluded. His skepticism grew particularly after the armistice had been declared and preparations for the Paris peace conference had commenced. In Clayton's view, pervasive fear and anxiety had not abated among Palestine's Arabs; on the contrary, it was building daily, due partly to the imprudent tone of Jewish propaganda. He objected to several points in the new Zionist program that had been advanced by Weizmann, points that effectively sounded the death knell to "moderation." These points were: (1) that Palestine's first governor-general be a Jew; (2) that the governor-general's executive council be at least 50 percent Jewish; (3) that the legislative assembly be at least 50 percent Jewish; (4) that the future Jewish state comprise a "Greater Palestine," with enlarged boundaries; and (5) that a land law be enacted proscribing ownership in excess of a fixed amount of land, with any extra land expropriated at fixed prices by the government and devoted to the development of Jewish colonization. Clayton had already suggested that Britain should receive mandates for both Syria and Palestine in which to erect an autonomous government "with due regard to Arab aspirations and Zionist aims." Between the Zionists and him there was simply no middle ground.[30] Whitehall, weary of backing Feisal's effort to resist the acquisitive designs of France, was anxious to secure Palestine at all costs; if this should mean ditching Feisal, so be it. Both the Zionists and the French had to be appeased, even if this had to be done at the expense of Palestinian fortunes. Even warnings from the Arab Bureau that support of Zionism in Palestine would necessitate a burdensome military occupation fell upon deaf ears in London and profoundly irritated Balfour, Curzon, and Palestine's new governor, Sir Herbert Samuel. Given the Exchequer's austerity campaign, such warnings were far from welcome, for the last thing these men desired was a fiscal attack upon Zionist policy. Shortly thereafter, Clayton was relieved by the pro-Zionist Col. Richard Meinertzhagen.

One can only speculate as to the divisions spawned within the British intelligence community in this region by the Balfour Declaration and its aftermath. Wyndham Deedes, Allenby's political intelligence chief, was sympathetic to the Zionist project and after his return to England worked tirelessly in its behalf. Hogarth, however, had grown even more disgruntled by the spring of 1919. While appreciating Weizmann's moderate attitude, he felt forces were at work that endeavored to reach far beyond the pale of compromise and conciliation: "I am personally backing him [Weizmann] wholeheartedly so long as he is moderate, but I fear things have gone too far in Palestine for us to take cover, with that Jew council in evidence, without trouble. Still there stands H.M.G.'s Declaration about the National Home! It must mean something and this is the least it could mean!"[31]

Philip Graves, former *Times* correspondent in Constantinople who was later transferred from the Cairo Bureau to duty with the political mission under Clayton, was tepidly sympathetic to Zionist aims. He regarded the proposed settlement of Palestine as potentially beneficial to the region and its inhabitants. Following the war, Graves was instrumental in exposing as forgeries "The Protocols of the Learned Elders of Zion," which had been widely exploited as anti-Semitic propaganda. His subsequent work, *The Land of Three Faiths*, was likewise hailed as pro-Zionist because of several references to the praiseworthy activities of colonists in Palestine. This reaction, however, was bitterly resented by Graves, "who, as an honest and very well-informed observer resented any suggestion that he might have strayed from the straight and narrow path of impartiality prescribed for a correspondent in the Near East into the specious meadows of propaganda on behalf of any nation, creed, party or interest in his quarrelsome and suspicious bailiwick."[32]

Graves was clearly enamored of neither Jew nor Arab. Rather, he viewed Palestine as a strategic opportunity for Britain, provided the region's destructive forces could be harnessed. Religious and ethnic ardor had to be dampened, at least on the surface. He was later critical of the British administration in Palestine in this connection, feeling that it was too pliant and yielding at times to both communities; and he had no qualms about calling on British muscle, if needed, to maintain order: "These people all want the hard hand but it's we that should apply it, not the Z.C. [Zionist Commission] or the Arabs. The Black and Tans . . . are coming out. . . . At last the right men are coming to the right place."[33] He was contemptuous about the Zionist Commission committing "gaffe after gaffe."[34] Graves characterized the Jews as "white people with a kink in them . . . intense, energetic, jesuitical and utterly tactless." Still it was for the Arabs that he reserved most of his criticism, depicting them as ill led, ignorant, excitable, and mendacious—"picturesque niggers." His equivocal attitudes toward the Palestine question probably came closest to typifying the perspective of the Arab Bureau. "I don't know," he confessed to his superiors at the *Times*, "who I want to win. On the whole I think the poor devil of a British official is the man to back against both."[35]

To Graves, Palestine was a poor candidate for statehood, with the Arabs "ill-led ignoramuses only good for parish politics" and the Zionists of "no use in politics at all." British suzerainty over the affairs of both provided the only possible solution, and "[t]here can be no question that its possession gives us great prestige in the world. This may be mere *panache* but to those who are religiously minded or whom the romance of history attracts, the moral advantages of our hold on Palestine outweigh many other considerations."[36]

The Balfour Declaration had come as a rather unwelcome surprise to the officers of the Arab Bureau. But its attitude toward both Jew and Arab in this regard remained cynically (but logically) pragmatic to the end. Its officers did not actively lobby against the establishment of a Jewish political entity in Palestine. One of Lawrence's biographers, having little save the *Arab Bulletin* and Lawrence himself to go by, was unable to discern any "collective view" within the agency on the Zionist question.[37] Ultimately the bureau came to hope that the Zionist homeland, if it had to be given form, might be kept amorphous enough to reap for Britain the strategic benefits that increased Jewish settlement might confer without inflaming Arab sentiment. On this question perhaps more than any other, the Savoy's optimism bordered on naïveté. But most important decisions and negotiations pertaining to Palestine took place in faraway London and conformed to demands very different from those prevailing at the bureau. Denied the essential advantage of close proximity to these, the Arab Bureau had little choice but to ride the prevailing wave.

10

DEMISE AND ECLIPSE

With Wingate's arrival in Cairo in early 1917 the stage was set for a major redrawing of spheres of political and military responsibility. Although the new high commissioner retained his preeminent position in dealings with the Hejaz government, he was also assured full authority over the conduct of military operations in the Hejaz. Wingate got on well with Edmund Allenby, Murray's replacement as commander of the Egyptian Expeditionary Force, and the two took little time to reach a general understanding on the delimitation of their respective spheres of authority. That boundary ran roughly along a line from Aqaba (Feisal's eventual base) to Maan. Allenby would be responsible for military operations to the west of that line and Wingate to the east, although the two men agreed that the high commissioner would be in charge of Arab relations on both sides of the line.

Other changes were also in the offing, most significantly a redefinition of the relationship between the various intelligence organizations. Collaboration and cooperation were now demanded. Weekly meetings were convened at the residency, with representatives from the Arab Bureau (Hogarth and Cornwallis were usually present), GHQ Intelligence, and the Press Bureau in joint consultation. "The whole organization," reported Cornwallis, "is in closest touch with the Military Intelligence Dept. EEF."[1] In November, an additional streamlining innovation was introduced with the creation of the Hejaz Operations Staff (HOS). This unit, placed under the command of Maj. Alan Dawnay (whom Clayton wanted badly to deny the Arab Bureau directorship), was constituted to deal solely with the military exigencies of the Arab Revolt, thereby relieving both Allenby and the Arab Bureau of this burden. Code-named "Hedgehog," the HOS worked closely with and often at the direction of the bureau in the manner of a military arm. Their work was so close, in fact, that the two units were often indistinguishable, with officers used almost interchangeably between the HOS and the two bureau locations in Cairo and Palestine. The new staff also absorbed many and sundry administrative functions with which Hogarth and Cornwallis had long been saddled, besides absorbing the Hejaz mission of Wilson and his small cadre of advisers. Although Wilson, as British agent, remained in command of British advisers on the peninsula, overall command stayed with Wingate in Cairo rather than in Khartoum.

The Hejaz Operations Staff was also responsible for coordinating Arab military activity with that of the Egyptian Expeditionary Force, once Feisal had placed himself under Allenby's command. A new line of authority was arrived at distinguishing Wingate's from Allenby's sphere, this time drawn laterally between Aqaba and Tebuk to correspond more closely with the British advance. Initially, the HOS maintained three bases (at Jeddah, Wejh, and Yenbo) from which its officers sortied on countless intelligence expeditions and raids against the Hejaz railway.

Much confusion has been wrought in histories of this period by the shadowy and imprecise nature of departmental divisions that prevailed in this theater. Many of the British heroes of the Arab Revolt were not attached to the Arab Bureau directly but were, in effect, its eyes and ears in Arabia and Palestine, submitting the vital intelligence reports without which proper functions would have been impossible. This situation was made murkier by the fact that bureau members such as Hogarth, Cornwallis, Parker, and Lloyd made infrequent inspection excursions to the Hejaz when warranted. Of that magnificent group of advisers, only one was a long-standing officer of the Arab Bureau—and that was T. E. Lawrence.

A major transfer followed closely on the heels of the creation of the HOS. Clayton, for so long the architect of Cairo's political intelligence network, was tapped in February 1918 to join Allenby as chief political officer, a position of potentially enormous influence. It was a sensible decision in light of the many changes then being made, which delegated more departmental authority while concurrently centralizing overall control. As a result, the manifold duties for which Clayton had assumed responsibility devolved upon lesser lights. While Cornwallis now took charge in Cairo, Clayton remained in close contact via two staff captains from the bureau, one to serve with Deedes in the EEF's political intelligence department and another directly under him to act as a liaison with Cairo.

Hogarth accompanied Clayton to Palestine but was in far too great demand to remain. He darted frequently between the front and Cairo, and more infrequently to the Hejaz or London. Perhaps not surprisingly, he found scant comfort in returning to the Savoy: "I find the Arab Bureau rather gone to seed—it always does when Clayton . . . leaves it. This sounds preposterous but is so. This is a boat which won't row between the strokes. It's most disappointing that it should depend so much on persons. Lawrence can keep it alive . . . but not the permanent staff—confound 'em!"[2]

Certainly part of this plaint is attributable to Hogarth's unfailing immodesty. He was prone to regard himself as the indispensable man—a sort of peripatetic guru in whom the most authoritative knowledge and wisdom concerning the Middle East resided. "You ask about my position in the Arab Bureau," confided Hogarth in a letter home: "Well—in a sense I *am* the Arab Bureau. Cornwallis is its official chief. The position is, in fact, awkward, especially now with this [Zionist] Commission coming to me for every need, without reference to him. . . . I have never formally described that arrangement or I should have deprived him of his salary but practically, the situation is much as we were at first."[3]

By the spring of 1918 much of the dynamism had indeed evaporated from the bureau's activities. Palestine, not Egypt, was now the center of action, and many of the old officers had by this time been plucked out for service elsewhere. Those who remained had little to do save for the recondite digging for the completion of charts, area handbooks, personality profiles, and the like. The bureau no longer played much of a role in military matters. Hussein was no longer fighting for the survival of his rebellion, and defeat of the Turks awaited Allenby's final thrust. The bureau's early hopes for a role as an overall coordinating body had long since ceased to have meaning. In fact, the war in the Hejaz had become something of a backwater. The bedouin armies there had lost the initiative and seemed a bottomless drain on the Egyptian treasury. Its commanders bickered and intrigued against the Wahhabis and among themselves. The sharif himself had grown increasingly suspicious and quarrelsome, prompting nervous letters to the residency to which the bureau responded soothingly in order to allay Hussein's "dangerous state of mind."[4] The war in Arabia languished around the siege of Medina and sporadic attacks along the Hejaz railway. What martial vitality remained in the revolt had gone north with Feisal—to Aqaba and then on toward Syria. Clayton was gone with Allenby; Lloyd was in London; Ormsby-Gore was also there, preparing the departure of the Zionist Commission; Philip Graves had advanced to Palestine; and Lawrence (aside from an occasional dash back to Cairo) was in the wilds. Only Cornwallis remained out of the original group, and Hogarth did not relish the prospect of his own return: "The old Arab Bureau at Cairo has got rather dispersed and probably, as long as the war lasts, it will never be again what it was."[5]

By this time, Hogarth was deeply depressed over Britain's policy malaise. It was little use enhancing the logistical efficiency of British military campaigns without political decisiveness and resolution from the top, preferably along lines submitted by the Arab Bureau. While the agency's hopes to provide that desired consistency were now stillborn, its access to the powerful in Cairo and in Palestine was not to be denied. But the bureau's local clout proved insufficient to its needs. Potentially conflicting commitments had been made to the French, the Arabs, and the Zionists. With the end of Turkish resistance in sight, the day of reckoning was near in Syria and Palestine. Even if London should bestir itself and take the steps that the Savoy desired, critical groundwork was lacking. A spate of crises loomed on the horizon: a critical shortage of bullion for the subsidy, the Wahhabi threat, potential conflict between Feisal's bedouin and Syrian nationalists, the age and infirmities of Sharif Hussein. Moreover, many administrative woes persistently defied solution, including communication breakdowns between London and Cairo and generally inconsistent treatment of the same question by different departments. Such problems troubled Hogarth: "But I think you agree that someone should go to learn the true attitude of Whitehall to our problems here, what is still considered possible and desirable, and how our policy here is to be oriented. At present it looks like sheer drift, so far as London is concerned."[6] Not one to underestimate either his own influence or his persuasiveness, Hogarth was off to London to set things right. Scarcely a month later he submitted a memo from the Admiralty to the War Cabinet entitled "Memo on the Arab Question," in which he outlined remedial steps which he felt should be taken:

1. That a fully manned and responsible Arab Bureau or Near East Ministry in London be maintained
2. That Clayton be returned to his supervisory position over the Arab Bureau (assisted by Cornwallis) as part of a dual role with that of CPO [Chief Political Officer]/EEF
3. That direct communication between the Cairo Arab Bureau and London be maintained
4. That the establishment of the Arab Bureau in Cairo be increased "to enable it to deal with all the western area of the Near East"

The third recommendation also contained the tantalizing parenthetical afterthought, "This is most important for reasons which I could explain privately."[7] It is quite possible that Hogarth was alluding to Wingate's almost parental interference, for it was the high commissioner through whom he would have normally communicated with the Foreign Office, and Hogarth had been working at the residency as a personal adviser. Under McMahon, Arab Bureau circumvention of the residency to the Admiralty or the War Office had been routine, and Wingate had taken it upon himself to bring it back under control. Clayton's suggested reassumption of authority in Cairo is also interesting and seems to suggest Hogarth's dissatisfaction with both Wingate and Cornwallis. The professor clearly seems to have been pushing for a more independent and politically viable Arab Bureau, one more faithful to the original design.

However, Hogarth would leave London rather disillusioned. The indecision and vacillation he found at the top confirmed his worst fears. There was "no one taking hold of the Near Eastern question at present here and no one looking ahead. Generally people are optimistic and vague."[8] What policy directives did filter down from London, Hogarth complained, seemed to come from an informal subcommittee consisting of Sykes, Lieutenant Colonel W. H. Gribbon (War Office), and John Shuckburgh (assistant secretary in the India Office Political Department). Indeed, the creation and life of the Arab Bureau, for all its bygone influence, now seemed only to accentuate its own irrelevance insofar as London was concerned.

By the time of the armistice in October 1918 the Cairo Arab Bureau had undergone a notable transformation in both its composition and its function. And by the time of Wingate's replacement as high commissioner by Allenby in March 1919, the bureau had become almost a branch of the residency. Shorn of most of its more illustrious members, the agency came under the directorship of Herbert Garland, who had distinguished himself as an adviser to Sharifian forces in the Hejaz. With the conclusion of hostilities it was left to Garland and his assistant, Capt. C.A.G. Mackintosh, to wind up affairs on the peninsula as soon as possible. While mundane, this was no easy task. Hashemite and Wahhabi tribesmen were still eyeball-to-eyeball over the Khurma oasis, the Hejaz government flirted with financial insolvency, and the truculent Fakhri Pasha still refused to surrender Medina to Abdullah's bedouin. A great deal of time was absorbed simply in conducting many of those daily financial and diplomatic operations that Hussein's government was not yet mature enough to assume. Even more pressing, perhaps, was the necessity of weaning Hussein from the lavish subsidy he had enjoyed since the tumultuous summer of 1916, a problem made even more pressing by the building tension between the king and Ibn Saud.

The controversial subsidy had long proven a thorn in the side of the British. The Sharif of Mecca received his first shipment of gold sovereigns in March 1916, in the amount of £53,000. Commencing 8 August 1916, the official subsidy figure was set at £125,000 per month, a sum that was to be frequently exceeded on Wingate's authorization. In November 1916, for example, £375,000 was dispatched (mostly to cover pilgrimage expenses). This money was to have been used by the sharif to pay his armies and to bribe sheikhs and tribes into joining his revolt. Theoretically, payments were broken down into five categories representing the four armies under the command of Hussein's sons and an allotment for the upkeep of the shrines and pilgrimage facilities as well as the operation of the Sharifian government at Jeddah and Mecca: £40,000 for Feisal, £30,000 for Abdullah, £20,000 for Ali, £20,000 for Zeid, and £15,000 for expenses at Mecca and Jeddah.[9]

As receipt of funds from London was often irregular or entirely delinquent, Wingate found himself in the position of having to draw upon a rapidly diminishing Egyptian treasury to meet British obligations. By the spring of 1917 the situation had become serious. Hussein insisted that he needed an additional £75,000 monthly to meet his bloated payroll. Cairo was simply not in a position to comply with this request on its own. By June 1917 the Egyptian treasury had only £200,000 in gold available for the Hejaz.[10] Various alternative schemes were explored to combat the problem such as substitution of rupee notes, silver, or agricultural commodities for a portion of the subsidy. But India was uncooperative, silver was scarce, and agricultural goods too dear in wartime Egypt to permit their dispatch to Arabia; and Hussein was adamant that the entire payment be continued in gold, although he was eventually forced to accept modest shipments of rupees and goods in lieu of that precious metal. Wingate had no choice but to badger London until relief was finally dispatched, mostly from War Office funds.

One particularly galling aspect of the subsidy to those at the Arab Bureau was its flagrant misuse by the Sharifian commanders. For instance, British officials were aware that much gold had simply vanished, leaving discontented tribesmen months in arrears. This was sometimes due to ineptitude on the part of bureau officers placed in charge of piloting that money to its proper destination. For example, in late 1917 the bureau was apprised of the fact that friendly tribesmen around the port of Wejh had not been paid in several months. After several inquiries concerning the matter, Wilson advised the bureau from Jeddah that Lawrence was at fault for the foul-up. In September, Wilson noted, Lawrence had without authorization removed £25,000 from Aqaba that had been earmarked for the Wejh September subsidy. The next month, the £25,000 payment was sent to Wejh—but mistakenly addressed to Emir Ali instead of Sharif Sharraf, commander of the Wejh garrison. Ali lost little time in dispensing the bulk of the shipment (all but £1,500) to his own men at Wadi Ais and forwarding the meager remainder on to Wejh. The result was that the garrison had received just £1,500 for the first three months of autumn, leaving Cairo with a £65,000 void to fill.[11]

Such incidents were all too common during the war and constitute probably the most justifiable criticism of the Arab Bureau's performance. But it is facile to make such judgments in hindsight without regard to certain extenuating facts. For a great deal of its information on actual conditions on the Arabian peninsula, the bureau was compelled to rely heavily upon the Jeddah Agency and the reports submitted by Agent Wilson and his cadre of advisers. This group had an enormous task before them, was ludicrously undermanned, and, understandably, was more concerned with the conduct of military operations than with fiscal vigilance. Moreover, the bedouin commanders, whom the bureau strongly suspected of squandering the sharif's treasure, were extremely secretive about their financial affairs. Finally, there was no one leader whom the British could hold responsible for proper use of the subsidy, for each of the king's sons was a power unto himself. In March 1918 W. A. Davenport was sent to Abdullah's camp to report on the urgency of the latter's appeals for more gold. He found urgency aplenty: the bedouin force consisted of only seven thousand men despite a subsidy allotment for ten thousand, and most of those tribesmen were in arrears.[12] Hussein's intercession was tactfully sought, but to no avail. None of this, however, dissuaded Wilson from peppering the bureau and the residency with desperate telegrams asserting: "I personally consider that we have got more than full value for our expenditure up to date and am of the opinion that the increase now applied for, . . . is far from being in any way excessive payment for the great advantages we have received and can legitimately expect to receive later on if we take proper advantage now of the cards in our hands."[13] Wilson continued to be a strong advocate for increases in subsidy payments, despite the undeniable waste attending them. He conceded that £200,000 a month was a tidy sum but was quick to reiterate the benefits that had accrued from the Arab Revolt, which he characterized as "a running sore in the Turkish side . . . apart from the very valuable material and political advantages which the British Empire may reasonably expect to reap." "Personally," he added, "I should be much surprised if any military and political 'firm of brokers' did not repeat that the investment was eminently sound and dirt cheap at the price."[14]

Faced with such reports from the man on the spot, the bureau was simply in no position (logistically or otherwise) to keep the close tabs on imperial funds that the Exchequer would have liked; their only effective agent on the Arabian peninsula for most of the war was Lawrence, an officer from whom little frugality might have been expected. It was not until after the war that the bureau, in an effort to soften the blow that a diminution in the subsidy would certainly inflict, became involved in evaluating and monitoring Hussein's expenses as prelude to a more austere dole.

The Arab Bureau had also undergone substantial organizational growth as a result of the extension of its activities into Palestine and Syria. The significance of its growth, however, remained confined to western Arabia and the sphere of Allenby's military operations. Its influence in Mesopotamia had long since lapsed. Shortly after the replacement of Sir Percy Cox (who went trouble-shooting in Persia), Arnold Wilson abolished the bureau's Basra branch—the last vestige of Sykes's eclectic vision. Those bureau officers left in Cairo were essentially holding the fort in lieu of those who had left for service under Allenby, either with frontline units or support garrisons in the (now) occupied territories. They were left, in Gertrude Bell's words, with "nothing to do" except attend to the more mundane circumlocutions of Arabian finances and do their best to act as liaison between Jeddah and the residency.[15]

Following the war, however, the debate on the Arab Bureau's future was renewed afresh. In the absence of wartime justification, the agency's champions contrived a worldwide reorganization of Near Eastern intelligence within which the Arab Bureau would play a greatly expanded role. The first blueprint for this scheme was submitted in January 1918 by two bureau officers: Lieutenant Colonel Pirie-Gordon (lately of the *Times*) and Captain Mackintosh. This program envisioned an agency that would: (1) collect information on all Muslim populations; (2) advise on policy toward these peoples; (3) control all such political affairs in Arabia, Persia, Turkey, and Muslim Africa hitherto under the control of consular services or the government of India; (4) help to set subsidies; (5) facilitate joint Foreign Office–India Office policy formulation; (6) study the question of Muslim education with due regard to local requirements; and (7) examine the political effects of missionary activity. The new bureau, they suggested, should be staffed by civil, not military, personnel so as to avoid the stigma often associated with an espionage network and be as inconspicuous as possible. Duplication of or rivalry with imperial organs might be avoided by the creation of a twin bureau in London that would collate, publish, and distribute intelligence from all sources.[16]

The political essence of this plan was further refined in a booklet written by Harold Fenton Jacob (who had transferred to Cairo from Aden) entitled "A Plea for a Moslem Bureau." In this controversial tract, stress was laid on the importance of preparing for whatever sort of temporal authority might ultimately emerge in the Islamic world in the place of the moribund caliphate and, where practicable, influencing the direction of that force: "All we can do is to foster the several Arab states within our Empire, and to aim at their future confederation, in the hope that one day there shall emerge the strong man who shall weld them together."[17] This had always been the aim of the bureau, provided a sufficiently pliant leader could be found and sold to the rest of the Islamic world. The Arab Bureau, Jacob thought, was the obvious medium through which an effective union of Egyptian and Indian perspectives might be at long last realized, and British influence over a newly liberated Islamic world consolidated. The mood of Egyptian and Indian Muslims was, Jacob argued, of mutual interest to both Cairo and Delhi and had to be molded in concert with, rather than in contravention of, one another. The Arab Bureau, as it then stood, was simply unequal to the achievement of these wider objectives:

> This Bureau has outgrown its swaddling clothes and should give place to something more imperial. We want a Moslem Bureau, with a widely reaching interchange of ideas and aims. It is not enough to say that India's views are widely divergent from Egypt's. This may be so, but our aim should be a frank interchange of views, and the desideratum is coordination of aim. If we think differently we shall act differently, and this spells confusion. We require one common policy in dealing with Islamic questions within the Empire.
>
> While we have no one dominant principle, India is cogitating a scheme of her own. Moslems want to unite. Let us be sure they unite with our approval and under the auspices of our King.[18]

Such pleas harken back to late 1915 when a similar unity of purpose was so frantically sought. The plea had simply been updated. Where before Cairo laid emphasis on the need to neutralize the sultan's appeal within the Islamic world, the stress was now laid on the best route by which Britain might sustain wartime gains in that same arena.

Jacob's proposal was more grandiose than any of Sykes's and proposed in a manner guaranteed to alarm Indian officials. Its design was simple and straightforward. An expanded (and much more formidable) Arab Bureau was to be established in London as a central registry responsible for the distillation and dissemination of all intelligence relative to the Islamic world received from the bureau's branches. These branch bureaus were to act as intelligence sensors, geographically situated to accommodate clusters of ministries, agencies, and consulates of a particular region (e.g., Gibraltar, Malta, Egypt, Constantinople, Mesopotamia, Aden, India, and Singapore). Each of these geographical designations included a group of local agencies. For instance, the area designated for India also included the administrations of Ceylon, British East Africa, and the Indian Ocean fleet anchored at Trincomalee. All of these branches were to receive intelligence reports from these administrative arms, reports that would then be collated, distilled, and passed on to the central Arab Bureau in

London. The central registry would in turn report to the Colonial Office, the Admiralty, the War Office, the India Office, and finally the Foreign Office, which would report to the Eastern Committee, the seat of ultimate authority over the entire system (in theory). Freedom of correspondence between all internal organizations was to be maintained, and personnel for the Arab Bureau branches were to be drawn from the ranks of the Foreign Office, the Colonial Office, and various naval and military staffs (including MI5) as required.[19]

This plan was not without its champions. Foremost among these was Allenby himself. The field marshal (now Egyptian high commissioner) dispatched a lengthy endorsement of the scheme to the War Office in May 1919, along with a lengthy explanation as to why the new concept merited immediate adoption:

> The peculiar opportunities which now offer of obtaining all kinds of information regarding the countries of the Near East will not recur after peace conditions obtain, whilst trained intelligence personnel who might now readily consent to continue intelligence duties in a Near Eastern Organization . . . will soon be lost to this form of Government Service by demobilization and dispersal to private employment in civil life. . . . It is certain that if a decision be long delayed the Bureau will not be so efficient an organisation as would be the case if continuity of touch and personnel were maintained.[20]

Allenby insisted that this reorganization should occur as soon as possible, despite the turbulent political atmosphere prevailing over yet-unsettled territorial questions. Indeed, that very uncertainty seemed to argue for implementation at the earliest opportunity. But the high commissioner's position was complicated by his insistence that the Cairo Arab Bureau continue to play a dominant role among the various branches being contemplated. This insistence stemmed from the growing concern aroused by the agitation of Zaghlul and other Egyptian nationalists. The bureau's potential value to the Egyptian government in a surveillance capacity had been hinted at by its proponents during the war. The reorganized Cairo bureau, Allenby suggested, should comprise four departments: (1) military and political intelligence; (2) commercial and economic intelligence; (3) historical, ethnographic, and geographic research; and (4) a record office designed for the compilation of personality profiles, details of suspects, and monitoring of propagandists' activities. For best results, Allenby contended that intelligence activities throughout the region come under his direct supervision. "In this way," he added, "it will be assisted materially in appreciating the political situation in Egypt."[21] His assistant, Rennell Rodd, agreed that Cairo remained "on the whole the most appropriate center to collect and collate the information of the Islamic world."[22]

However, this bold attempt to reorganize Near Eastern intelligence was fated to come to grief over the same obstacles that had so crippled the original bureau in the East. The attempt to retain such a prominent position for the Cairo organization aroused even more opposition now than it had in early 1916. Besides the more predictable opposition from India, many officials in London were chary of repeating past mistakes or reopening old wounds. Suspicion ran rampant that Cairo's bureaucracy hankered after a preeminent position in Britain's dealings with the Arab world. Such apprehension was not completely unwarranted, as neither the residency nor the Arab Bureau had ever been discreet about this ambition. Just days after the latter's inception was approved in London in early 1916, McMahon gushed to Grey at the Foreign Office: "It is badly wanted not only to build up knowledge of a little known country and people which must *henceforth* grow into greater prominence and importance, but to counteract propaganda which, now and hereafter, threaten to injure our position in the Eastern World" (emphasis added).[23]

While this permanent status had never been officially confirmed by their superiors at the Foreign Office, most officials staffing the bureau and the residency regarded the agency's continuance as a sine qua non of Arab policy for the remainder of the war and thereafter. Even before the armistice, Wingate foreshadowed a vision not unlike the intelligence schemes concocted shortly afterward. "We have the nucleus," insisted Wingate, "of a satisfactory control organization in the Arab Bureau, which I sincerely trust will be maintained and even enlarged after the war . . . [cites branches in Iraq and Palestine]. The corresponding work of these branches should be continued after the war and direct interchange of information arranged with Eastern and Western African Moslem countries e.g. it will be well worth while, in my opinion, to start a special branch of the Bureau in Zanzibar."[24]

But London remained skeptical. Opinion was not openly hostile to the concept of an expanded intelligence network per se, but rather taken aback by Cairo's enthusiasm for it. Deedes, now a general at the War Office, supported an expanded and more centralized system but opposed any enhancement of Cairo's role in the new bureaucracy. Egypt, he maintained, was already sufficiently monitored by the intelligence services of its military establishment. Deedes had learned well the lessons of bureaucratic weakness that emerged from the Arab Bureau's wartime experience: "As long as we are to remain an Eastern Empire, there is only one place where we can afford to centralize and that is London . . . (as the . . . most complete centre of communication). . . . And it would be a mistake to suppose that because Egypt is a great British centre in the Mohammedan world, it is necessarily the most important centre of Mohammedan intrigue."[25]

India's theoretical objections were much as they had been in 1916, when the India Office insisted on changing the bureau's title from "Islamic" to "Arab." Aside from the legacy of embittered relations between Delhi and Cairo left from the war, India utterly rejected the idea of dealing with the Islamic world as a conceptual whole, fearing perhaps that to do so would somehow hasten its transformation into political reality. Such notions would, Shuckburgh minuted, "have the effect of formally recognizing—and to that extent promoting—the solidarity of Islam."[26] Arnold Wilson reminded superiors in Delhi that the bureau had been primarily a war measure, the peacetime utility of which "appears to have ceased," and forwarded his understanding that the Cairo bureau had been virtually relegated to a residency branch.[27] The most strident condemnation of Jacob's program came, however, from Hirtzel at the India Office:

> I am strongly opposed to this proposal and to the theory that underlies it. . . . The underlying theory is to be found in . . . Colonel Jacob's note or in Lieut. Commander H. Pirie Gordon's Memo viz. that we ought to have an "Islamic policy." . . . If we want Christianity and Islam permanently ranged in hostile camps, let us by all means have an "Islamic policy." It is moreover just what the Panislamist wants—to have his pretensions taken at face value and his bogey made into something that will really make the flesh creep. . . . By all means let our intelligence officers everywhere collect all the information they can. But if we set up a special mechanism to collect Islamic information, we shall inevitably begin to see everything through Islamic spectacles and shall become suitable subjects for that kind of "suggestion" which the Panislamist has so successfully practised in the past.[28]

Such apprehension, alarmist as it may appear in hindsight, must be viewed in the context of the time. At that moment, the Raj was being rocked by the incendiary alliance struck by Gandhi with leaders of the Khalifat movement to protest Britain's supposed complicity in abolition of the Turkish caliphate. In such a volatile atmosphere, Indian officials shrank from aggrandizing an Arab Bureau that preferred to deal with Islamic peoples as an aggregate community rather than as a "discordant mosaic."

For similar reasons, the scheme met with opposition at the Foreign Office. Foremost among opponents was Hubert Young of the Middle East department and lately of both Mesopotamia and Arabia. His reaction echoed Hirtzel's: "I have always opposed this idea as tending to lay stress on religious rather than political movements. On the contrary, it was a suggestion that Arab Bureau was already forming itself into such an organization and that Cairo was not the place for it."29 But perhaps most significantly, the hostility of Lord Curzon, acting foreign secretary and chairman of the Middle East committee, doomed the project. His lordship deemed the plan ill-timed and "intended to deal with areas of which the political future is at present uncertain."30

A slightly modified version of Jacob's blueprint was drawn up by Maj. Gen. William Thwaites of the War Office in the summer of 1920, following an inspection tour of the Near East the preceding spring. His report, like many preceding it, attacked the multiplicity of organizations with a hand in Middle Eastern intelligence while urging the Foreign Office to seize the moment. "We should lose no time," he warned, "in setting up this organization, for we shall never have so favourable an opportunity as the present, when we have troops, Missions, and High Commissioners in many places where, under pre-war conditions, we only had diplomatic or consular representatives."31 But aside from the addition of two European branches of the Arab Bureau in Rome and Switzerland, this plan differed little from the earlier one in either content or popularity in London. While no mention was made in it of a conspicuous role for the Cairo bureau, the climate for a scheme pervaded with "Arbur" branches was inauspicious. "It is not perhaps surprising," Young remarked, "that Cairo should plump for the 'larger Cairo' alternative. I have little doubt that Baghdad would plump for the 'larger Baghdad.' Not as a visitor to London, but because I am convinced it is the right solution, I plump for a larger London."32

Austerity finally intervened to scale down the bureau's activities. In the first few years following the armistice, cutbacks in the British military presence were mandated by the Exchequer, already struggling with a potentially ruinous accumulation of debt. Press revelations respecting the bureau's 1920 expenditures were, therefore, particularly untimely.

In June 1916, the treasury had limited the bureau's annual staff expenditures to a niggardly £3,000. Two years later, following up a bureau request for an increase in that allotment, the treasury "discovered" that the Arab Bureau was spending over £14,000 annually, including £2,000 on native papers and almost £10,000 in additional subsidies, bribes, and the like in what was referred to as "Clayton's secret account." "We cannot," the treasury lords concluded, "regard that state of things as satisfactory. The control by the Foreign Office was palpably insufficient."[33] Surely, the essence of such understatement might have been more profitably recognized in 1916.

The bureau's opponents had won. The Indian government, the India Office, and the Exchequer successfully persuaded the Foreign Office that the possible benefits of a permanent agency were outweighed by the anticipated disruption within the imperial bureaucracy. Arnold Talbot Wilson, Cornwallis's old nemesis, delivered this final calumny after the war: "The Arab Bureau in Cairo died unregretted in 1920, having helped to induce His Majesty's Government to adopt a policy which brought disaster to the people of Syria, disillusionment to the Arabs of Palestine and ruin to the Hijaz"[34]—a partisan verdict, to be sure.

CONCLUSION

Triumph of Perversity

What might be concluded about the Arab Bureau and its performance? Had it ultimately proven itself an asset or a liability in the formulation and execution of British policy toward the Arabs? Had it arrogated unto itself a role quite beyond the framework of its original sponsors? If the latter is true, then to what extent did it, as yet another source of political input, influence the direction or color the tone of British diplomacy in the war-torn Middle East?

Certainly the bureau's mandate to streamline the machinery from which Arab policy was generated was a nebulous one. Support for this new concept was never championed with any sustained resolution from the top and thus was consigned early on to be a "castle in the air." Indian hostility, while not formidable enough to scuttle the launch of the Arab Bureau in early 1916, was effective in neutralizing the wider expectations that early supporters of the agency had entertained. The significance of Delhi's success here is difficult to overstate, for it effectively deprived the bureau of its catholic foundation, restricting its room for maneuver and ensuring the triumph of the very parochialism it had been created to suppress. It also stamped the Arab Bureau with the perspective of officials in Cairo, and more specifically that of the burgeoning group of Sudan service officers who rose to prominence there.

This failure to gain the acceptance necessary to induce departmental cooperation precluded the exorcism of damaging political hobgoblins. This problem, of course, was most glaring in Britain's Arabian policy. The Foreign Office was often forced to respond fitfully to exigencies as they developed, in a reactive, piecemeal fashion. Examples of this can be found in the extension of Cairo's political authority over the southern Red Sea littoral in early 1917 and in the warnings from London to Ibn Saud that undoubtedly prolonged but failed to salvage Sharif Hussein's political fortunes. These were steps that would not have been necessary had the Arab Bureau been allowed to function along its original lines. Instead, its role was to remain more adversarial than reconciling, ultimately resulting in a polarization between Cairo and Delhi that was even worse than when the bureau had begun its work. In this sense the Arab Bureau proved a failure, less a result of improper or inadequate performance than because of Foreign Office unwillingness to actively prosecute the Arab policy it had so tentatively initiated. Systemically, as Lawrence himself later pointed out, imperial diplomacy would remain as diffuse and convoluted as ever it had been:

> The affairs of the Middle East are . . . the joint concern of the Foreign Office, the India Office, and the War Office; three of the strongest departments, each with a tradition.
>
> In each are officials with experience and knowledge, who write admirable minutes in criticism of the others' recommendations. It is natural that three such offices should be hostile and fond of scoring off one another. It is less natural that their hands, who are not civil servants, would work on the same lines. . . .
>
> The war has had the effect on the offices of making the young men younger and the old men older. The blood-thirstiness of the old men—who did not fight—towards our late enemies is sometimes curiously relieved against the tolerance of those who have fought and wish to avoid making others fight again tomorrow.[1]

In other respects the bureau acquitted itself admirably, especially in its logistical handling of the Arab Revolt's first tenuous months, when it was the departmental orphan-child. Even long after that role had been relinquished, its officers constituted the key personnel and intelligence liaison with the Sharifian government. This was delicate work, sustaining the sharif's often flagging morale while taking great care to avoid provoking India and attempting to lay the political groundwork necessary to the bureau's conception of postwar imperial objectives. Given the enormous obstacles of inertia and departmental animus placed in the way of these goals, it does not now seem surprising that the success of the Arab Bureau in achieving them was disappointingly alloyed.

The officers of the Arab Bureau were Arab enthusiasts only in the sense that, where India saw looming catastrophe, they saw opportunity. It has been amply demonstrated that they were *not* the starry-eyed romantics so often depicted in the secondary literature, especially respecting the political pretensions of the Arabs themselves. In lieu of substantive work about the Arab Bureau, however, this erroneous impression persists. The bureau's differences with officials in London and Delhi regarding Arab policy were rooted not in any spiritual compulsion to see Hussein's revolt carried through to its logical conclusion, but in a fundamentally different imperial concept. Its officers viewed the Arab Revolt as the vehicle by which both to hasten the eviction of the Turks and to provide Britain with a relationship to the Arabs that would ensure its postwar dominance. This design was calculated to enhance Britain's influence in this vital region, in order to fill the void left by the Turks' departure. Theirs was a more modern, and somehow more insidious, stratagem incorporating mechanisms of artifice and manipulation that would bestow the necessary flexibility to confront the rising tide of Arab nationalism and extend Britain's stay in both India and Egypt.

The Arab Bureau viewed Arab divisiveness as the cornerstone on which an innocuous confederation (preferably under Hashemite aegis) might be based. It was for this reason that they schemed to prevent any of the major Arabian chieftains—supposed allies included—from gaining destabilizing strength and threatening the delicate balance of power on the Arabian peninsula. The timeworn imperial dictum of *divide et impera* had proven effective in the past and could be counted upon once again to ensure continued British paramountcy. To the Arab Bureau, subtle devices such as puppet rulers and well-placed subsidies might prove more useful, and markedly less abrasive, than viceregal edicts. If properly implemented, such a scheme would, they were confident, provide the best of both worlds; British influence might be secured without resort to burdensome (and possibly provocative) occupation. Such a confederation would remain innocuous and useful as long as native trust in Britain and the word of its administrators survived the war. Moreover, since the inclusion of Syria was a sine qua non of this strategy, the bureau would oppose sharing the spoils of war with France and provoking Arab wrath by sponsoring a Zionist homeland. As it happened, the requisite Arab trust was lost by the surrender of Syria to the Quai d'Orsay, and Palestine to the Zionists. Whether or not these concessions were allowable under McMahon's pledges actually matters little, for the ambiguity of their wording was sufficient for the Arabs to look upon them henceforth as perfidious capitulations. Clayton, Hogarth, Lawrence, and others anticipated quite accurately the rumblings of Arab discontent that resulted. Consequently, the bureau remained tentative in its initial support for the Sykes-Picot Agreement, predicating tepid acceptance on the understanding that substantial revision would be forthcoming.

Throughout its brief administrative existence, the Arab Bureau strove to exploit those aspects of Arab and Islamic culture that might be turned to British advantage. The pilgrimage, the caliphate, and intertribal hostility were all viewed from the perspective of the anticipated confederation and the installation of informal measures of control. In the assumption of this role, the bureau had crossed its own Rubicon—evolving from a rather obscure advisory agency into a persuasive advocate of a strategy espoused by its progenitors in Khartoum and Cairo. While his notions concerning bureau intent are inaccurate, in my view, Elie Kedourie is indisputably correct in his observation that "[i]t is clear that both Clayton and Cornwallis were . . . acting not as advisors, putting forward various alternatives for the consideration of their superiors, but as advocates pushing a particular policy with whatever arguments seemed most convincing."[2] In this sense, the Arab Bureau obviously exceeded its mandate from the Foreign Office. But deprived of the fundamental assumptions from which that mandate had sprung, it had little choice.

The road down which the Arab Bureau marched could only have been paved in London, not in Cairo. Following their formula, and assisted by the irresistible tide of military and political events, the bureau hoped to reverse Syria's fate by driving home the strategic advantage of Allenby's fait accompli in the Levant. As for McMahon's pledges, the bureau had always felt they could be circumvented without seriously injuring Britain's reputation in the Middle East. That same confederation within which Arab "nationalism" might find limited expression would not be permitted to outgrow its political swaddling clothes. Success in the installation of Feisal on the Syrian throne, coupled with some grand but innocuous title for his father, would be palliative aplenty. In this manner lip service could be given to President Wilson's twelfth point and British interests in this vital region protected at one and the same time. If India would not look to her strategic viscera, then Cairo would—thereby securing the safety of both bastions of British power in the East. Having cited the multifarious complexity of this task, one writer succinctly observed:

> One's surprise is not that the men who had to deal with these complexities made mistakes, but that they did not make more; not that the vexed question of the undertakings to the Arabs were in terms so general as to have given rise to bitter controversy, but that the men on the spot were, even at the time, so aware of the inherent difficulties that they withstood the pressure put on them to make more explicit promises which they might not be in a position to implement . . . even without it [the question of a Jewish national home] there was a maze of diverse and distracting demands through which the Arab Bureau honestly tried to steer a course. And only too often the simile of the juggler reverts to mind—with one hand tied behind their backs by the necessity of allowing for French and Russian interests; by the weighty objections of the Indian Government; by decrees of their own Government to whom the problems of the Near and Middle East were but one movement in the mighty symphony of world war.[3]

While this evaluation is dated by several decades and seems substantially intuitive, it comes perhaps much closer to the mark inasmuch as the enormous complications of the war are more fully appreciated.

Of course, the Arab Bureau's opponents ultimately proved too powerful to overcome. It unquestionably had overestimated the political impact of Allenby's expeditionary force in Syria, arrayed against the complex and variegated issues of the peace. Similarly, it had failed to accurately discern the depth of Zionist intent and Whitehall's commitment to a Jewish homeland in Palestine. Moreover, the Arab Bureau had made many enemies during its short life: in the Indian government, the military administration in Mesopotamia, the Egyptian high command, and the India Office in

London. Nor had what some regarded as its profligate way with the public purse endeared the bureau to the Exchequer. Finally, there is a momentum attending a concatenation of historical events that is difficult to reverse. Given the political situation prevailing in Europe at the time of the armistice, the outcome in Syria, for instance, seems now to have been inevitable.

Whatever the single or collective reasons for the bureau's failure (and ultimately its demise), a glimmer of intellectual triumph is perceptible even today. Despite the moral ambiguity of bureau motives, hindsight must flatter voices that counseled against furtive partitions of the Levant or religious entanglement in Palestine. As disciples of an alternative to native confrontation and burdensome overcommitment they remained imperialists, but more sober and less bombastic (although, in their own way, just as arrogant) as those who had gone before. In this novel pragmatism, the officers of the Arab Bureau were ahead of many of their contemporaries, and the empire was the worse for not having listened.

NOTES

Introduction

1. Norman N. E. Bray, *Shifting Sands* (London: Unicorn Press, 1934), 71.
2. Arnold Talbot Wilson, *Mesopotamia: A Clash of Loyalties*, vol. 2 (London: Oxford University Press, 1931), 109–10.
3. Elizabeth Monroe, *Britain's Moment in the Middle East, 1914–1956* (Baltimore: Johns Hopkins Press, 1956), 36.
4. William J. Olson, *Britain's Elusive Empire in the Middle East: An Annotated Bibliography* (New York: Garland, 1982), 53–54.
5. David Howarth, *The Desert King: Ibn Sa'ud and His Arabia* (New York: McGraw-Hill, 1964), 122.
6. Ernest Main, *Iraq from Mandate to Independence* (London: George Allen and Unwin, 1935), 52.
7. Monroe, *Britain's Moment*, 36.
8. Sari J. Nasir, *The Arabs and the English* (London: Longman Group, 1976), 125.

9. Richard Aldington, *Lawrence of Arabia: A Biographical Enquiry* (Chicago: Henry Regnery, 1955), 134.

10. T. E. Lawrence, *Seven Pillars of Wisdom* (Garden City, N.Y.: Doubleday, 1935), 58–59.

11. Howard M. Sachar, *The Emergence of the Middle East, 1914–1925* (New York: Alfred A. Knopf, 1969), 151.

12. Bruce Westrate, "Imperialists All: The Arab Bureau and the Evolution of British Policy in the Middle East, 1916–1920 (Ph.D. diss., University of Michigan, 1982), 298–99; David Fromkin, *A Peace to End All Peace: Creating the Modern Middle East, 1914–1922* (New York: Henry Holt, 1989), 171.

13. Edouard Bremond, *Le Hedjaz dans la Guerre Mondiale*, "a'lequelle il se conformait comme il en avait l'ordre" (Paris: Payat, 1931), 98.

14. Gilbert Falkingham Clayton, *An Arabian Diary*, ed. and intro. by Robert O. Collins (Berkeley and Los Angeles: University of California Press, 1969), 25.

15. James Morris, *Farewell the Trumpets: An Imperial Retreat* (New York: Harcourt Brace Jovanovich, 1978), 251.

16. Clayton, *Arabian Diary*, 64.

17. Zeine N. Zeine, *The Struggle for Arab Independence* (Beirut: Khayats, 1960), 9–10.

18. Elie Kedourie, *In the Anglo-Arab Labyrinth* (Cambridge: Cambridge University Press, 1976), 136.

19. Elie Kedourie, *England and the Middle East: The Destruction of the Ottoman Empire, 1914–1921* (London: Bowes and Bowes, 1956), 109–10.

20. H.V.F. Winstone, *Gertrude Bell* (London: Jonathan Cape, 1978), 185.

21. Briton C. Busch, *Britain, India and the Arabs* (Berkeley and Los Angeles: University of California Press, 1971), 202.

22. Linda Carol Rose, "Britain in the Middle East, 1914–1918: Design or Accident?" (Ph.D. diss., Columbia University, 1969).

Chapter 1

1. Henry Foster, *The Making of Modern Iraq: A Product of World Forces* (Norman: University of Oklahoma Press, 1935), 129.

2. Letter from Capt. W.H.I. Shakespear, 19 January 1915, cited in Arab Bureau Summary of Historical Documents, PRO, F.O. 882/5, 149.

3. George Antonius, *The Arab Awakening* (New York: J. B. Lippincott, 1939), 149.

4. C. Ernest Dawn, *From Ottomanism to Arabism: Essays on the Origins of Arab Nationalism* (Urbana: University of Illinois Press, 1973), 27.

5. Ibid., 149–50. See also Ronald Sanders, *The High Walls of Jerusalem* (New York: Holt, Rinehart and Winston, 1983), 231.

6. Dawn, *Ottomanism to Arabism*, 155, 157, 86.

7. J. C. Hurewitz, *Diplomacy in the Near and Middle East: A Documentary Record*, vol. 2 (Princeton: Princeton University Press, 1956), 13–17.

8. PRO, F.O. 371/2768, file 938, no. 69301.

9. PRO, F.O. 371/2786, file 34982, no. 155203.

10. Rose, "Britain in the Middle East," 130–31.

11. PRO, F.O. 371/2768, file 938, no. 69301.

12. Ronald Storrs, *The Memoirs of Sir Ronald Storrs* (New York: G. P. Putnam's Sons, 1937), 168.

13. Dawn, *Ottomanism to Arabism*, 115.

14. Zeine, *Struggle for Arab Independence*, 9–10.

15. Suleiman Mousa, " 'A Matter of Principle': King Hussein of the Hijaz and the Arabs of Palestine," *International Journal of Middle East Studies* 9 (1978): 194.

16. Kedourie, *Anglo-Arab Labyrinth*, 126.

17. Wingate to Clayton, 11 May 1916, SAD C.P. 47012.

18. Barbara Tuchman, *Bible and Sword* (New York: Funk and Wagnalls, 1956), 327.

19. Kedourie, *England and the Middle East*, 67.

20. Storrs, *Memoirs*, 168.

21. Sykes minute, PRO, F.O. 371/2781, file 201201, no. 304720.

22. Ronald Storrs, *Orientations* (London: Nicolson and Watson, 1945), 196.

23. Sykes minute on Arabian Report, n.s., vol. 14, 15 October 1916, I.O.L., L/P&S/10/586, file 705/1916.

24. Lady Francis Bell, *The Letters of Gertrude Bell*, vol. 2 (New York: Boni and Liveright, 1927), 374–75.

25. *Parliamentary Report of the Mesopotamian Commission*, cmnd. 8610 (London: His Majesty's Stationery Office, 1923).

26. David G. Hogarth, "Present Discontents in the Near and Middle East," *Quarterly Review* 234 no. 464 (October 1920): 411.

27. Sykes appreciation of Arabian Report, no. 14, 106 (2), pt. 1, I.O.L., L/P&S/10/586, file 705/1916.

28. Clayton note (undated), SAD W.P. 135/7.

29. Phillip Knightley and Colin Simpson, *The Secret Lives of Lawrence of Arabia* (London: Thomas Nelson and Sons, 1969), 48n.

30. Herbert to Clayton, 7 November 1915, PRO, F.O. 882/2, AP 15/7.

31. Sykes to Clayton, 28 December 1915, PRO, F.O. 882/2, ARB 15/4.

32. Admiralty Intelligence to Clayton, 20 December 1915, PRO, F.O. 882/2, ARB 15/3.

33. Sykes to Clayton, 28 December 1915, PRO, F.O. 882/2, ARB 15/4.

34. Ibid.

35. Clayton to Hall, 13 January 1916, PRO, F.O. 882/2, ARB 16/5.

36. Ibid.

37. Ibid.

38. Hall to Clayton, 20 December 1915, PRO, F.O. 882/2, ARB 15/2.

39. Grey to McMahon, 1 January 1916; McMahon to Grey, PRO, F.O. 882/2, ARB 16/1.

40. Deedes Papers, box 2 (DS 125), DR 588.4, 15 January 1916.

41. McMahon minute, 20 January 1916, PRO, F.O. 371/2670, file 5057, no. 12391.

42. Report of Committee of Imperial Defence, 7 January 1916, PRO, F.O. 882/2, ARB 16/4.

43. Oliphant minute on above CID report on the Arab Bureau, 20 January 1916, PRO, F.O. 371/2670, file 5057.

44. W. Langley to McMahon, 17 February 1916, PRO, F.O. 882/2, ARB 16/9.

45. Clayton to Wingate, 14 February 1916, SAD W.P. 136/2.

46. Wingate to Clayton, 19 February 1916, PRO, F.O. 882/2, ARB 16/10.

47. Clayton to Parker, 10 December 1915, PRO, F.O. 882/2, AP 15/4.

48. French to Clayton, 13 July 1916; Clayton to French, 27 July 1916, PRO, F.O. 882/2, ARB 16/16.

49. McMahon to Nicolson, 2 February 1916; Nicolson to McMahon, 19 February 1916, PRO, F.O. 882/2, ARB 16/10.

50. Clayton letter to Wingate, 14 February 1916, SAD W.P. 136/2.

51. Deedes Papers, box 2 (DS 125), DR 588.4, to Mother from Shepheard's Hotel, Cairo, 15 January 1916.

52. Arab Bureau Report, May 1916, PRO, F.O. 371/2771, file 18845, no. 95497.

53. Arab Bureau Report for September 1916, PRO, F.O. 371/2781, F188311.

54. James Aldridge, *Cairo* (Boston: Little, Brown, 1969), 198, 213, 232.

55. Cornwallis to Hogarth, 21 June 1916, PRO, F.O. 882/5, HR6 16/18.

56. Deedes Papers, box 2 (DS 125), DR 588.4, 9 February 1916.

57. Wingate to Clayton, 13 September 1916, SAD C.P. 470/3.

58. Parker to Wingate, 6 July 1916, SAD W.P. 137/3.

59. Arab Bureau Report, May 1916, PRO, F.O. 371/2771, file 18845.

Chapter 2

1. Clayton, *Arabian Diary*, 54.

2. Wingate to Clayton, 9 April 1916, SAD C.P. 470/2.

3. T. E. Lawrence, *Seven Pillars*, 57.

4. H.V.F. Winstone, *The Illicit Adventure* (London: Jonathan Cape, 1982), 41–42.

5. Jeremy Wilson, *Lawrence of Arabia: The Authorized Biography of T. E. Lawrence* (New York: Atheneum, 1990), 1009 n. 96.

6. Desmond Stewart, *T. E. Lawrence* (New York: Harper and Row, 1977), 127.

7. Wingate to Hardinge, 16 June 1917, SAD W.P. 145/8.

8. T. E. Lawrence, *Seven Pillars*, 58.

9. Winstone, *Illicit Adventure*, 78–79; Cairo Intelligence Bulletin, 23 May 1915, W. O. 157/691, cited in Jeremy Wilson, *Lawrence of Arabia*, 189.

10. See Knightley and Simpson, *Secret Lives*, 35ff.; M. R. Lawrence, *Home Letters of T. E. Lawrence* (Oxford: Blackwell, 1954), 280.

11. Aldington, *Lawrence of Arabia*, 128.

12. David Garnett, ed., *The Letters of T. E. Lawrence* (London: Jonathan Cape, 1938), 192.

13. David G. Hogarth, entry on Lawrence in the *Encyclopedia Britannica*, 14th ed., cited in John E. Mack, *A Prince of Our Disorder: The Life of T. E. Lawrence* (Boston: Little, Brown, 1976), 146.

14. David G. Hogarth, "Mecca's Revolt against the Turk," *Century Magazine* 100 (1920): 409.

15. T. E. Lawrence, *Seven Pillars*, 63.

16. Aldington, *Lawrence of Arabia*, 191–92.

17. Robert Graves, *Lawrence and the Arabs* (London: Jonathan Cape, 1935), 140.

18. Wilson to Clayton, 22 November 1916, SAD C.P. 470/4.

19. Elizabeth Monroe has informed the author that Cornwallis took special measures not to leave private papers behind.

20. Wingate telegram, 9 October 1918, SAD W.P. 150/4.

21. T. E. Lawrence, *Seven Pillars*, 58.

22. Storrs, *Memoirs*, 54.

23. Clayton, *Arabian Diary*, 59.

24. Wingate to Wilson, 17 November 1916, SAD W.P. 143/1.

25. Clayton to Symes, 24 December 1914, SAD W.P. 134/8.

26. Colin Forbes-Adam, *The Life of Lord Lloyd* (London: Macmillan, 1948), 66 (letter to Blanche, January 1915).

27. Fforde to Hirtzel, 20 March 1916, I.O.L., L/P&S/10/576/F4744.

28. Fforde to Hirtzel, 30 March 1916, ibid.

29. Hirtzel note, 20 April 1916, ibid.

30. Holderness note to Hirtzel, 25 April 1916, ibid.

31. Grant to Hogarth, 24 June 1916, I.O.L., L/P&S/10/576/F4744; Hirtzel minute, 1 August 1916, ibid.

32. McMahon to Balfour, 20 December 1916, ibid.

33. Winstone, *Illicit Adventure*, 81.

34. Ibid., 181.

35. Ibid.

36. Lady Francis Bell, *Letters*, 2:519.

37. Storrs, *Memoirs*, 169n.

Chapter 3

1. Bray, *Shifting Sands*, 75.

2. Arabian Report, no. 3, 31 July 1916, I.O.L., L/P&S/10/586/F705.

3. Hogarth memo, 10 June 1916, PRO, F.O. 882/5, HRG 16/11.

4. Arab Bureau Memo, 25 June 1916, PRO, F.O. 882/5, HRG 16/20.

5. Arabian Report, no. 3, 31 July 1916, I.O.L., L/P&S/10/586/F705.

6. Arab Bureau to Wingate, 10 July 1916, SAD W.P. 138/7.

7. Maj. Gen. Walter Campbell to I.G.O. Savoy, 29 June 1916, PRO, F.O. 141/736, F2475.

8. Hogarth to Wingate, 29 June 1916, SAD W.P. 137/6.

9. Wingate to Robertson, 9 July 1916, SAD W.P. 138/5.

10. Wingate to Clayton, 24 April 1916, SAD W.P. 136/5.

11. Wingate to Clayton, 15 June 1916, SAD W.P. 137/4.

12. Wingate to Stack, 29 June 1916, SAD W.P. 137/6.

13. Clayton to Wingate, 7 September 1916, SAD W.P. 140/3.

14. Hogarth Papers, folder 1 16(1), DR 588.25.

15. Hogarth to Wingate, 29 June 1916, SAD W.P. 137/6.

16. Wilson to Wingate, 14 September 1916, SAD W.P. 140/4.

17. Clayton to Wingate, 14 September 1916, ibid.

18. Ibid.

19. Hogarth letter from Cairo, 9 November 1916, Hogarth Papers 16(1).

20. Lawrence memo, July 1916, PRO, F.O. 882/5, HRG 16/30.

21. Wingate to McMahon, 28 September 1916, SAD W.P. 140/8.

22. Hogarth to Clayton, 17 August 1916, Hogarth Papers.

23. Wingate to Wilson, 21 August 1916, SAD W.P. 139/4.

24. Clayton to Wingate, 24 September 1916, SAD W.P. 140/6.

25. Parker to Wilson, 8 October 1916, Parker Papers.

26. Parker to Arab Bureau, 23 October 1916, ibid.

27. Lloyd note, 27 December 1916, PRO, F.O. 882/6, HRG 16/85.

28. Ormsby-Gore, "Note on the Arabian Situation," 10 December 1916, PRO, F.O. 882/6.

29. T. E. Lawrence, *Seven Pillars*, 111.

30. *Arab Bulletin*, no. 32.

31. Arab Bureau Report, "The Rabegh Question," 10 January 1917, PRO, F.O. 882/6, HR6 17/4.

32. Fforde note, 17 November 1916, PRO, F.O. 882/12.

33. Parker to GHQ, 10 September 1916, Parker Papers.

34. Parker to Arab Bureau, 10 December 1916, ibid.

35. Parker to Cornwallis, 26 October 1916, ibid.

36. Wingate to Arab Bureau, 21 December 1916, PRO, F.O. 141/825, no. 11981771.

37. Wingate to Foreign Office, 8 January 1917, PRO, F.O. 141/825, no. 11981794.

38. Wilson to Wingate, 26 October 1916, SAD W.P. 141/2.

39. Sykes appreciation of Arabian Report, no. 16, I.O.L., L/P&S/10/586/F705.

40. Janet Courtney, *An Oxford Portrait Gallery* (London: Chapman and Hall, 1931), 43, cited in Mack, *Prince of Our Disorder*, 148.

41. Viceroy to Chamberlain, 27 July 1916, PRO, F.O. 882/12, IND 16/3.

42. Arabian Report, no. 3, 31 July 1916, I.O.L., L/P&S/10/586/F705.

43. Cornwallis to Clayton, 9 August 1916, PRO, F.O. 882/15, PIL/16/4.

44. R. Graham to Residency, 12 August 1916, PRO, F.O. 882/15, PIL/16/6.

45. Political Department Simla to Chamberlain, repeated Cairo, 4 September 1916; McMahon to F.O., 5 September 1916, SAD W.P. 140/3.

46. Clayton to Wingate, 7 September 1916, SAD W.P. 140/3.

47. Arab Bureau to Wingate, 19 October 1916, SAD W.P. 141/5.

48. Draft communique, "The Pilgrimage of 1916," PRO, F.O. 882/15.

49. Arabian Report, no. 24, 3 January 1917, I.O.L., L/P&S/10/586/F705.

50. Sykes appreciation of the above, ibid.

51. Hogarth report, March 1916, I.O.L., L/P&S/10/586/F705; Clayton to Wingate, 7 September 1916, SAD W.P. 140/3.

52. F.O. to McMahon, 13 September 1916, PRO, F.O. 141/426, F1198.

53. Sykes appreciation of Arabian Report, November 1916, I.O.L., L/P&S/10/586/F705.

54. Hirtzel minute on the above, 6 November 1916, ibid.

55. Report by Ruhi on Mecca, November 1916, PRO, F.O. 371/2783, F2233112.

56. Arab Bureau Report on Ottoman Bank, 31 October 1916, PRO, F.O. 371/2781, F199283.

57. Wingate to Grey, 16 November 1916, SAD W.P. 143/5.

58. Cornwallis to Sykes, 17 November 1916, PRO, F.O. 141/738/3884.

59. Wilson to Wingate, 24 November 1916, SAD W.P. 143/7.

60. Sykes minute, 21 November 1916, PRO, F.O. 371/2781, F119283.

61. Note by George Lloyd, 27 December 1916, PRO, F.O. 882/6, HRG 16/85.

62. Ibid.

63. Pearson to Cornwallis, 27 February 1917, PRO, F.O. 882/15, PIL 17/1; Cornwallis to Clayton, 1 April 1917, PRO, F.O. 882/12, KH 17/10.

64. Secret report by T. E. Lawrence to Wilson, 16 April 1917, PRO, F.O. 141/456, F559.

65. Wilson to Clayton, 21 May 1917, SAD W.P. 145/6.

66. Sykes to Graham, 8 May 1917, PRO, F.O. 882/16, SP 17/25; Graham to Wingate, 8 May 1917, SAD W.P. 145/7.

67. Clayton to Joyce, 30 October 1917, PRO, F.O. 882/17, HRG 17/91.

68. Clayton note on Arab Legion, May 1917, PRO, F.O. 882/2, AL 17/8.
69. Lloyd note to Wingate, 8 June 1917, PRO, F.O. 141/746, F4833.
70. Sykes to Clayton, 13 July 1917, PRO, F.O. 882/2, AL 17/11.
71. Clayton to F.O., 30 September 1917, SAD W.P. 146/4; Clayton to Sykes, 15 December, SAD C.P. GS 513/1.
72. Busch, *Britain, India and the Arabs*, 177.
73. Jukka Nevakivi, *Britain, France and the Arab Middle East, 1914–1920* (London: Athlone Press, 1969), 66.
74. Ormsby-Gore note, 13 January 1918, PRO, F.O. 371/3381, F207.

Chapter 4

1. Hirtzel minute, 9 December 1915, I.O.L., L/P&S/10/576/F4744.
2. Hirtzel note to Oliphant, 17 January 1916, PRO, F.O. 371/2670, F5057.
3. See Busch, *Britain, India and the Arabs*, 100.
4. Elizabeth Monroe cites the examples of Capts. G. Leachman and Hubert Young, both of whom possessed extensive knowledge of the Near and Middle East. They were, however, conspicuously underutilized by the Indian government. See Monroe, *Philby of Arabia* (London: Pitman Publishing, 1973), 47.
5. Clayton to Wingate, SAD W.P. 135/5.
6. Wingate to Callwell, 23 December 1915, SAD W.P. 135/7.
7. Hirtzel minute, 23 February 1916, I.O.L., L/P&S/10/586/F705/1916.
8. I.O. to Viceroy, 16 April 1916, PRO, F.O. 381/2771/F18845, no. 79197.
9. Hirtzel minute, 10 April 1916, I.O.L., L/P&S/10/576/F4744.
10. Lake to Foreign Department, Simla, 11 June 1916, I.O.L., L/P&S/10/576/F4744.
11. Foreign Department, Delhi, to F.O., 20 June 1916, PRO, F.O. 887/2, ARB 16/4.
12. Ibid.
13. Chamberlain to Viceroy, 27 May 1916, I.O.L., L/P&S/10/576/F4744.
14. Viceroy to Foreign Department, Simla, ibid.
15. Hirtzel minute, 18 May 1916, ibid.
16. Hogarth note to McMahon, 28 June 1916, PRO, F.O. 141/735/3894.
17. Viceroy to Foreign Department, Simla, I.O.L., L/P&S/10/576/F4744.
18. Letter by G. Bell to her father, 11 February 1916, cited in Elizabeth Burgoyne, *Gertrude Bell: From Her Personal Papers* (London: Alfred A. Knopf, 1961), 35.
19. Letter by G. Bell to her father, 14 May 1916, ibid., 375.
20. Bell to T. E. Lawrence, 18 March 1916, SAD W.P. 136/4.
21. Bell to Hogarth, 20 May 1916, PRO, F.O. 882/13, MES 16/6.
22. India Office commendation of G. Bell, 20 January 1917, I.O.L., L/P&S/10/576/F4744.
23. Hogarth letter to Mary, 8 March 1917, Hogarth Papers, file 2.
24. Report by George Lloyd, PRO, F.O. 882/6, HRG 16/8.
25. Ibid.
26. Winstone, *Illicit Adventure*, 210; Arab Bureau Report for November 1916, 1 December 1916, PRO, F.O. 371/2781, F188311.
27. John Presland, *Deedes Bey: A Study of Sir Wyndham Deedes, 1883–1923* (London: Macmillan, 1942), 251.
28. Hubert Young, *The Independent Arab* (London: John Murray, 1933), 72.

29. W. F. Stirling, *Safety Last* (London: Hollis and Carter, 1953), 67–68.
30. Lawrence to Intrusive, Cairo, 8 April 1916, PRO, F.O. 882/15, PNA 16/2.
31. Ibid.
32. Arnold Talbot Wilson, *Mesopotamia*, 304–5.
33. Viceroy telegram, 15 May 1916, PRO, F.O. 371/2771, F18845.
34. Viceroy to Wingate, 17 June 1916, SAD W.P. 137/3.
35. Sykes appreciation of Arabian Report, no. 20A, 27 June 1916, I.O.L., L/P&S/10/586/F705/1916.
36. Parker report, 6 December 1916, PRO, F.O. 371/3043, F903.
37. Delhi, Foreign and Political Department, Secret Report no. 18, 23 February 1917, ibid.
38. Sykes minute, 1 January 1917, ibid.
39. McMahon to F.O., 8 January 1916, PRO, F.O. 371/2670, F5057; Wingate to F.O., 1 January 1917, I.O.L., L/P&S/10/576/F4744; Clayton to Sykes, 14 January 1916, PRO, F.O. 371/2771, F18845.
40. Intrusive to Nicolson, PRO, F.O. 882.
41. Hirtzel minute, 3 August 1916, I.O.L., L/P&S/10/576/F4744.
42. Holderness minute, August 1916, ibid.
43. Cox memo, 17 July 1916, I.O.L., L/P&S/10/576/F4744.
44. Hirtzel note, ibid.
45. W. Langley to Treasury, 28 August 1916, ibid.
46. G. Bell letter to her father, 24 January 1916, Burgoyne, *Gertrude Bell*, 34.
47. Arab Bureau Summary of Historical Documents Pertaining to Arabia, 29 November 1916, PRO, F.O. 882/5, HRG 16/65.
48. Nalder to Turton (Red Sea Patrol), 12 June 1916, PRO, F.O. 882/10, ID 16/10.
49. Arab Bureau Report, "Hedjaz and Yemen Politics," 28 March 1916, PRO, F.O. 882/10, ID 16/5.
50. Delhi Political Department to Resident, Aden, 22 June 1916, PRO, F.O. 882/10, ID 16/14.
51. Turton to Resident, Aden, 29 June 1916, PRO, F.O. 882/10, ID 16/15.
52. O'Sullivan to R.N.O., Port Sudan, 30 June 1916, PRO, F.O. 741/36, F2475.
53. Wilson to Wingate, 5 August 1916, SAD W.P. 139/5; Wingate to Clayton, 3 August 1916, SAD C.P. 470/3.
54. Arab Bureau Summary of Historical Documents, 29 November 1916, PRO, F.O. 882/4, HRB 16/65.
55. Cornwallis note, 6 July 1917, PRO, F.O. 832/11, ID 17/10.
56. Jacob report, November 1916, PRO, F.O. 371/2783, F236300.
57. Lloyd report, June 1917, PRO, F.O. 882/14, MIS 17/9.
58. Viceroy to Balfour, 7 August 1917, PRO, F.O. 882/18, YE 17/21.
59. George Lloyd, "Note in the Arabian Confederation," June 1917, PRO, F.O. 882/18, YE 17/18.
60. Ibid.
61. Cornwallis to Clayton, 20 August 1917, PRO, F.O. 882/18, YE 17/27.
62. Jacob note on positions of South Arabian personalities, 25 October 1917, PRO, F.O. 882/18, YE 17/32.
63. Garland note, PRO, F.O. 882/20, AP/19/2.

Chapter 5

1. Phillip Knightley, *The First Casualty* (New York: Harcourt Brace Jovanovich, 1975), 84.

2. *Arab Bulletin*, vol. 2, no. 42, 15 February 1917.

3. Note by Major Hennessy on pan-Islamism, 14 February 1916, SAD W.P. 136/2.

4. Clayton to Parker, 3 December 1915, SAD W.P. 135/7.

5. McMahon to Grey, 25 January 1916, PRO, F.O. 371/2771, F18845.

6. Wingate letter to Murray, 4 July 1916, SAD W.P. 138/1.

7. Wingate to Clayton, December 1916, Clayton Papers, cited by Robert O. Collins in intro. to Clayton, *Arabian Diary*, 66.

8. Hogarth to Clayton, 17 August 1916, Hogarth Papers, 13(1), DR 588.25.

9. Sykes to Clayton, 17 December 1917, SAD W.P. 147/5.

10. Clayton to Sykes, 15 December 1917, PRO, F.O. 371/3043, F903, no. 237729.

11. Hogarth to McMahon, 19 July 1916, PRO, F.O. 141/461, F1198.

12. Minute by A. H. Wiggin, 10 September 1919, PRO, F.O. 371/4208, F17610, no. 127072.

13. Minute by H. Young, 10 October 1919, PRO, F.O. 371/4208, F17610.

14. Wingate to Clayton, 17 April 1916, SAD W.P. 136/5.

15. Wingate to Clayton, 24 February 1916, SAD W.P. 470/1.

16. Montgomery to Cheetham, 21 January 1916, PRO, F.O. 141/475, F2047.

17. McMahon to Montgomery, 28 February 1916, ibid.

18. Lawrence to Montgomery, 16 June 1916, ibid.

19. Storrs, *Memoirs*, 212.

20. Foreign Department, Simla, to McMahon, 20 June 1916, PRO, F.O. 141/710, F3156.

21. Clayton to War Office, 18 August 1916, PRO, F.O. 141/475, F2047.

22. Philip Graves to Storrs, 4 November 1916, ibid.

23. De Bunsen (F.O.) to Wingate, 12 June 1917, PRO, F.O. 141/375, F2047.

24. Arab Bureau Report on Muslim Propaganda, 11 February 1917, PRO, F.O. 141/776, F787.

25. Fielding to Cornwallis, 28 February 1917, PRO, F.O. 141/375, F2047.

26. Hogarth Papers 2(11), from Cairo, 19 January 1917.

27. Fielding to Residency, 21 March 1917, ibid.

28. De Bunsen to Wingate, 23 July 1917, ibid.

29. Sykes, Arabian Report, 24 January 1917, I.O.L., L/P&S/10/586/F705/1916.

30. Note by Fuad al-Khatib, 19 July 1916, PRO, F.O. 882/14, MIS/16/8.

31. Clayton to Symes, 25 July 1916, PRO, F.O. 882/14, MIS 16/9.

32. Arab Bureau to Khartoum, 1 September 1916, SAD W.P. 140/2.

33. Arab Bureau Report, June 1918, PRO, F.O. 371/3397, F19579.

34. Antonius, *Arab Awakening*, 227–28.

35. Osmond Walrond, "Note on the Arab Movement," July 1918, PRO, F.O. 882/14, PA/18/11.

Chapter 6

1. Basrah to Intrusive Cairo, 5 January 1916, SAD W.P. 136/1.

2. Arabian Report, 1 March 1916, I.O.L., L/P&S/10/586/F705.

3. Arabian Report, 12 March 1916, ibid.

4. Cornwallis note to Residency, 11 September 1916, PRO, F.O. 882/8, IS/16/7.

5. *Arab Bulletin;* see Winstone, *Gertrude Bell*, 181.

6. Ibid.

7. Bell letter to Lord Cecil, 20 December 1915, cited in Burgoyne, *Gertrude Bell*, 32.

8. Gary Troeller, "Ibn Saud and Sharif Hussein: A Comparison in Importance in the Early Years of the First World War," *Historical Journal* 14 (September 1971): 633. Cited in Stephen E. Tabachnick, ed., *The T. E. Lawrence Puzzle* (Athens, Ga.: University of Georgia Press, 1984), 39n.

9. Wingate to Clayton, 15 February 1916, PRO, F.O. 882/8, IS/16/2.

10. Clayton to Wingate, 28 January 1916, PRO, F.O. 882/12, IND/16/1.

11. Crew to Hardinge, 12 November 1914, Archives of India, quoted in Busch, *Britain, India and the Arabs*, 62.

12. Wingate to Hogarth, 12 August 1917, SAD W.P. 146/1.

13. Cox to Arab Bureau, 27 July 1917, PRO, F.O. 882/8, IS/17/8.

14. Cornwallis to Wilson, 21 September 1917, PRO, F.O. 882/8, IS/17/13.

15. Cornwallis to Symes, 3 October 1917, PRO, F.O. 882/8, IS/17/17.

16. Arab Bureau to Wingate, 29 October 1916, SAD W.P. 141/1.

17. Wilson note (undated), PRO, F.O. 686/37.

18. Cornwallis to Clayton, 28 November 1917, SAD C.P. 470/7.

19. Hogarth note, 31 December 1917, PRO, F.O. 882/8, IS/17/34.

20. Ibid.

21. Residency to F.O., 23 December 1917, PRO, F.O. 882/8, IS/17/32.

22. Hogarth to Wingate, 19 January 1918, Philby Papers, box 15, F5.

23. Philby to Mr. Allen from Oxford, 19 September 1960, ibid.

24. H.St.J.B. Philby, *Arabia of the Wahhabis* (London: Constable, 1928), 343.

25. Viceroy tel. no. 1062S, 2 September 1917, PRO, F.O. 882/9, IS/18/55.

26. Cornwallis to Residency, 5 September 1918, PRO, F.O. 882/9, IS/18/57.

27. F.O. to Residency, 21 October 1918, PRO, F.O. 882/9, IS/18/98.

28. Arab Bureau to Bassett, 7 January 1918, PRO, F.O. 882/9, IS/18/2.

29. Bassett to Arab Bureau (communicating a message from Hogarth to Wingate), 10 January 1918, PRO, F.O. 882/9, IS/18/9; Cox to F.O., 12 January 1918, PRO, F.O. 882/9, IS/18/8.

30. Bassett to Cornwallis, 12 January 1918, PRO, F.O. 882/9, IS/18/9.

31. Hogarth report to Wingate, 15 January 1918, ibid.

32. Meeting Report, 21 January 1918, PRO, F.O. 882/9, IS/18/11.

33. Arab Bureau to Political Department, Baghdad, 11 February 1918, PRO, F.O. 882/9, IS/18/13.

34. Hogarth report, "Position and Prospects of King Hussein," *Arab Bulletin Supplementary Papers*, no. 2, 1 March 1918, PRO, F.O. 882/13, KH/18/6.

35. Hogarth note on Philby draft, 2 July 1918, PRO, F.O. 882/8, IR/18/4.

36. Philby note to Hogarth, 11 July 1918, PRO, F.O. 882/8, IR/18/9.

37. Residency to F.O., 12 August 1918, PRO, F.O. 882/9, IS/18/35.

38. Symes note to Cornwallis, 15 August 1918, PRO, F.O. 882/9, IS/18/37.

39. Cornwallis to Residency, 23 August 1918, PRO, F.O. 882/9 IS.

40. Clayton enclosure in Cornwallis-Residency letters, 15 August 1918, PRO, F.O. 882/9, IS/18/46.

41. Philby note to Hogarth, 11 July 1918, PRO, F.O. 882/8, IR/18/9.

42. Political Department, Baghdad, to Cairo Arab Bureau, 18 August 1918, PRO, F.O. 882/9, IS/18/51.

43. Cornwallis to Residency, 31 August 1918, ibid.

44. Bassett to Arab Bureau, 11 September 1918, PRO, F.O. 882/9, IS/18/65.

45. Cornwallis to Residency, 13 September 1918, PRO, F.O. 882/9, IS/18/71.

46. Clayton memo, 17 September 1918, SAD W.P. 149/8.
47. A. T. Wilson to Balfour, 15 September 1918, ibid.
48. A. T. Wilson to Wingate, 16 October 1918, PRO, F.O. 882/9, IS/18/91.
49. Political Department, Baghdad, to Residency, 16 October 1918, PRO, F.O. 686/16.
50. A/Director, Arab Bureau to Residency, 15 October 1918, PRO, F.O. 882/9, IS/18/87.
51. Wingate to Balfour, 3 October 1918, PRO, F.O. 371/339, F2240.
52. Mackintosh to Wilson, 2 January 1919, PRO, F.O. 141/738/3894.
53. Garland note, "Lieut. Col. A. T. Wilson and the Khurma Crisis," 2 August 1919, PRO, F.O. 686/18.
54. Wingate to F.O., 17 February 1919, PRO, F.O. 686/17.
55. Garland, "Note on the Khurma Dispute," 14 June 1918, PRO, F.O. 882/21, IS/19/27.
56. Ibid.
57. Ibid.
58. A/Director, Arab Bureau to Clayton, 7 July 1919, PRO, F.O. 882/21, IS/19/36.
59. Jacob to Residency, 11 July 1919, PRO, F.O. 882/22, KH/19/18.
60. A/Director, Arab Bureau to Clayton, 7 July 1919, PRO, F.O. 882/21, IS/19/36.
61. Kidston minute, 1 January 1919, PRO, F.O. 371/3390, F2240.

Chapter 7

1. Wingate note, 26 August 1915, PRO, F.O. 882/13, MIS/15/9^.
2. Clayton note, 8 December 1915, PRO, F.O. 882/2, AP/15/13.
3. Kedourie, *Anglo-Arab Labyrinth*, 124.
4. Clayton to Wingate, 17 January 1916, SAD W.P. 136/11.
5. Clayton to Wingate, 28 January 1916, ibid.
6. Clayton memo to GHQ, 11 October 1915, PRO, F.O. 882/13.
7. Westrate, "Imperialists All"; Fromkin, *A Peace to End All Peace*, 469–70.
8. Hardinge to McMahon (undated), SAD W.P. 135/6.
9. Clayton to Jacob, 24 February 1916, PRO, F.O. 141/523, F950.
10. Storrs to Clayton, 6 March 1916, PRO, F.O. 141/587, F545; Clayton to Storrs, 7 March 1916, ibid.
11. Arabian Report, 12 March 1916, I.O.L., L/P&S/10/586/F785.
12. *Arab Bulletin*, no. 41.
13. Hogarth "Note on the Arab Question," 16 April 1916, PRO, F.O. 882/2, AP/16/2.
14. David G. Hogarth, *The Nearer East* (New York: D. Appleton and Co., 1902), 282.
15. *Arab Bulletin*, no. 77, 27 January 1918.
16. Hogarth text on "The Arab Situation," 1920, Hogarth Papers, F5.
17. George Lloyd to Pierce Joyce, Akaba Papers of Pierce Joyce, M/27.
18. Hogarth to a meeting of the Central Asian Society, *Journal of the C.A.S.* 10 (9 November 1922).
19. Text on "The Arab Situation," 1920, Hogarth Papers, F5.
20. Ibid.
21. Hogarth from Oxford to G. Bell, 11 April 1920, Philby Papers, Box 15, F5.
22. Clayton memo "The Future Political Status of Egypt," 22 July 1917, SAD C.P. 470/7.

23. Clayton to Sykes, 20 September 1917, Sledmere Papers of Sir Mark Sykes, DR 588.25, DT 82.97.

24. *Arab Bulletin*, no. 9.

25. 26 March 1917, Hogarth Papers, F2.

26. "Mesopotamian Mystery," *Times*, 27 December 1921.

27. Ibid.

28. "A Defence of the Arab Bureau," *Times*, 10 January 1922.

29. Uriel Dann, "Lawrence of 'Arabia': One More Appraisal," *Middle East Studies* 15 (May 1979): 158–59.

30. *Times*, 27 December 1921.

31. Wingate to McMahon, 1 December 1915, PRO, F.O. 141/587, F545.

32. Morghani memo, 6 May 1915, PRO, F.O. 882/5.

33. Storrs note on the Khalifate, 2 May 1915, PRO, F.O. 141/587, F787.

34. Arab Bureau "Notes on the Hussein-McMahon Correspondence," 24 April 1917, PRO, F.O. 882/12, KH/17/15.

35. Dawn, *Ottomanism to Arabism*, 45.

36. Ibid., 81–82.

37. Lt. H. Pirie-Gordon and Lt. H. C. Lukach, "Report on the Moslem Khalifate," 29 March 1915, PRO, F.O. 141/587, F545.

38. Hogarth report, I.O.L., L/P&S/10/586/F705.

39. W. Ormsby-Gore "Note on the Arabian Situation," 10 December 1916, PRO, F.O. 882/6.

40. Wilson to Cornwallis, 31 July 1917, PRO, F.O. 141/825, F1198.

41. See Kedourie, *Anglo-Arab Labyrinth*, 144–50.

42. Philby note to Hogarth, 11 July 1918, PRO, F.O. 882/8, IR/18/9.

43. Arab Bureau to Residency, 7 September 1919, PRO, F.O. 141/587, F787.

44. *Times*, 10 January 1922.

45. Sykes minute, 14 October 1918, PRO, F.O. 371/3384, F747.

Chapter 8

1. Clayton to Wingate, 6 December 1915, SAD W.P. 135/7.

2. Clayton to Parker, 10 December 1915, PRO, F.O. 882/2, AP/15/14.

3. Wingate to Clayton, 11 May 1916, SAD C.P. 470/2.

4. Wingate to Clayton, 20 January 1916, SAD C.P. 470/1.

5. Hogarth "Note on Sykes-Picot Agreement" to Capt. W. R. Hall (Naval Intelligence), 3 May 1916, PRO, F.O. 882/16, SP/16/12.

6. Hogarth note on interview with Fuad al-Khatib, 14 February 1917, PRO, F.O. 882/6, HR6/17/12.

7. Clayton note on second meeting, 8 December 1918, PRO, F.O. 882/3, AP/15/13.

8. Hogarth "Note on Sykes-Picot Agreement" to Capt. W. R. Hall (Naval Intelligence), 3 May 1916, PRO, F.O. 882/16, SP/16/12.

9. Clayton to Wilson, 18 April 1917, PRO, F.O. 882/12, KH/17/12.

10. Lecture text, Hogarth Papers, DS 42.1.

11. Sykes memo, 2 February 1917, PRO, F.O. 882/16, SP/17/1.

12. Hogarth to Clayton, 14 August 1918, Hogarth Papers, F3.

13. Hogarth, from the Residency, ibid., F4.

14. T. E. Lawrence, *Seven Pillars*, 58.

15. Hogarth note, 19 February 1917, PRO, F.O. 882/16, SP/17/3.

16. Comments by G. Lloyd on Sykes memo to Picot, 6 June 1916, PRO, F.O. 882/3, AP/17/7.

17. Clayton to Wilson, 28 April 1917, PRO, F.O. 882/12, KH/17/16.

18. Wingate's telegram no. 496, Cairo, 7 May 1917, repeating Sykes's telegram from Jeddah of 6 May 1917, PRO, F.O. 371/3054, 93334/86256. Cited in Kedourie, *Anglo-Arab Labyrinth*, 164.

19. Service historique de l'armee, Paris Section d'outremer, papers of the military mission to the Hejaz, 17 N. 498, Bremond's telegram to DeFrance no. 1440, Jeddah, 7 May 1917. From Kedourie, *Anglo-Arab Labyrinth*, 164.

20. Ibid.

21. Wilson to Clayton, 21 May 1917, SAD W.P. 145/6.

22. Arnold Talbot Wilson, *Mesopotamia*, 237–38.

23. Clayton to Symes (GHQ Cairo), 27 May 1917, SAD W.P. 145/7.

24. Arbur Cairo to Arbur Baghdad, no. 975, 16 July 1917, PRO, F.O. 882/18, TU/17/5, 71.

25. Clayton memo, June 1917, PRO, F.O. 882/6, HRG/17/52.

26. Hogarth "Note on Sykes-Picot Agreement," 9 July 1917, PRO, F.O. 882/3, AP/17/16.

27. Hogarth to Clayton, 11 July 1917, Hogarth Papers, F2.

28. Hogarth to Clayton, 20 July 1917, ibid.

29. Clayton to Sykes, 22 July 1917, PRO, F.O. 882/16, SP/17/39.

30. Clayton to Sykes, 30 July 1917, PRO, F.O. 882/3, AP/17/17.

31. Kedourie, *England and the Middle East*, 71.

32. Ibid., 86.

33. Monroe, *Britain's Moment*, 43.

34. Clayton to Sykes, 15 December 1917, SAD C.P. 470/8.

35. Clayton to G. Bell, 8 December 1917, SAD C.P. 470/8.

36. Clayton to Lawrence, 20 September 1917, SAD C.P. G/S 513/1.

37. Westrate, "Imperialists All," 228; Fromkin, *A Peace to End All Peace*, 194.

38. Clayton to Sykes, 18 October 1917, Sledmere Papers of Sir Mark Sykes, DS 244.4, DR 588.4.

39. G. Bell, "Report on Northern Arabia," 1917, PRO, F.O. 882/17, TR/17/1.

40. Ormsby-Gore note, 13 January 1918, PRO, F.O. 371/2281, F207.

41. T. E. Lawrence, "Syrian Cross-Currents," *Arab Bureau Supplementary Papers*, PRO, F.O. 882/14, MIS/18/2.

42. *Arab Bulletin*, no. 44.

43. Ibid.

44. *Arab Bulletin*, no. 32.

45. *Arab Bulletin*, no. 77.

46. Walrond to Clayton, 17 July 1918, PRO, F.O. 882/17, SY/18/12.

47. Walrond note "The Committee of Arab Brotherhood," July 1918, PRO, F.O. 882/17, SY/18/15.

48. Walrond, "Note on the Arab Movement," July 1918, PRO, F.O. 882/14, PA/18/11.

49. Hogarth interview with Dr. Faris Nimr, Arab Bureau Report, 12 June 1918, PRO, F.O. 141/654.

50. Symes note, 13 June 1918, ibid.

51. Paul C. Helmreich, *From Paris to Sevres: The Partition of the Ottoman Empire at the Peace Conference of 1919–1920* (Columbus: Ohio State University Press, 1974), 8.

52. Hogarth reply to the Syrians in Egypt, 25 June 1918, PRO, F.O. 371/3381, F146.
53. Antonius, *Arab Awakening*, 271–72.
54. Rose, "Britain in the Middle East," 303–4.
55. Clayton to Sykes, 4 April 1918, PRO, F.O. 371/3391, F4079, no. 76678.
56. Wingate to Sykes, 25 June 1918, PRO, F.O. 371/3381, F146.
57. A. L. Tibawi, *A Modern History of Syria* (London: St. Martin's Press, 1969), 268.
58. Hogarth memo on the Arab Question, 9 August 1918, PRO, F.O. 371/3381, F146.
59. Clayton to Wilson, 6 May 1918, PRO, F.O. 882/3, AP/18/2.
60. Hogarth draft of Anglo-French Declaration, PRO, F.O. 371/3381, F146.
61. Hogarth to Lord Robt. Cecil, 18 August 1918, ibid.
62. Hogarth draft, ibid.
63. Hogarth to Lord Robt. Cecil, 18 August 1918, ibid.
64. Memo by George Lloyd (undated), ibid.
65. Ibid.
66. Clayton letter, 8 September 1918, PRO, F.O. 371/3384, 18332/747, cited in Kedourie, *Anglo-Arab Labyrinth*, 199–200.
67. Mack, *Prince of Our Disorder*, 167.
68. Arab Bureau Note, April 1919, PRO, F.O. 882/24, SY/19/4.
69. E. L. Woodward and Rohan Butler, eds., *Documents on British Foreign Policy, 1919–1939*, 1st ser., vol. 4 (London: His Majesty's Stationery Office, 1952), nos. 184, 185, 225.
70. Clayton memo, 11 March 1919, SAD C.P. G/S 513/1.
71. Ibid.
72. G. Bell report to Paris Peace Conference, "Syria in October," November 1919, PRO, F.O. 882/24, SY/19/10.
73. Hogarth to Clayton, 30 March 1919, Hogarth Papers, F4.
74. Hogarth to Clayton from British delegation, Paris, 19 March 1919, ibid.
75. The King-Crane Commission, so called after its two members, Dr. Henry C. King and Charles R. Crane, was formerly the American section of an Inter-Allied Commission on mandates in Turkey. The British and French governments first agreed to send representatives of their own but subsequently changed their minds, and the "American section" visited the Levant on its own in the summer of 1919. See Kedourie, *Anglo-Arab Labyrinth*, 234.
76. Hogarth to Clayton from British delegation, Paris, 19 March 1919, Hogarth Papers, F4.
77. Clayton to Lord Curzon, 2 June 1919, no. 181, Woodward and Butler, *Documents on British Foreign Policy*, 263.

Chapter 9

1. Israel Cohen, *The Zionist Movement*, rev. ed. (New York: Zionist Organization of America, 1946), 52, cited in Tuchman, *Bible and Sword*, 216.
2. *Manchester Guardian*, 22 November 1915, cited in Sanders, *High Walls*, 291.
3. A. H. Hourani, *A Vision of History: Near Eastern and Other Essays* (Beirut: Khayats, 1961), 93–94.
4. Neville Mandel, *The Arabs and Zionism before World War I* (Los Angeles and Berkeley: University of California Press, 1976), 231.
5. Sachar, *Emergence of the Middle East*, 221.

6. W. Ormsby-Gore note on Jerusalem, 26 December 1916, PRO, F.O. 882/13, PA/16/2.

7. W. Ormsby-Gore to Sykes, 8 May 1917, Sledmere Papers of Sir Mark Sykes, box 2.

8. Clayton to Sykes, 20 August 1917, ibid.

9. Clayton to Sykes, 15 December 1917, Sledmere Papers of Sir Mark Sykes, DR 588.25, DS 149.

10. Hurewitz, *Diplomacy*, 26.

11. Clayton to Sykes, December 1917, SAD W.P. 147/6.

12. For a cogent discussion of these, see Elie Kedourie, *Arabic Political Memoirs* (London: Frank Cass, 1974), 248.

13. *Arab Bulletin*, no. 83.

14. Hogarth report, January 1918, PRO, F.O. 371/3411, F61891.

15. Clayton to F.O., 18 March 1918, PRO, F.O. 371/3391, F4079.

16. Clayton memo, 18 March 1918, SAD C.P. G/S 513/1.

17. Clayton to G. Bell, 17 June 1918, ibid.

18. Clayton to Clive Wigram, 17 June 1918, ibid.

19. Clayton to Bell, ibid.

20. Clayton to Symes, 13 April 1918, SAD W.P. 148/10.

21. Hogarth appendix to Palestine letter, 2 April 1918, PRO, F.O. 882/14, PA/18/5.

22. Akaba Papers of Pierce Joyce, I/O-18.

23. Clayton to F.O., 18 March 1918, PRO, F.O. 371/3391, F4079.

24. Cornwallis to Symes, 20 April 1918, SAD W.P. 148/8.

25. Hogarth report "The Syrian Political Situation Since 1800," 25 May 1918, PRO, F.O. 882/17, SY/18/10.

26. Hogarth Papers, F3.

27. Ormsby-Gore minute, August 1918, PRO, F.O. 371/3381, F146.

28. Hogarth's response to the above, August 1918, ibid.

29. Osmond Walrond, "Note on the Arab Movement," July 1918, PRO, F.O. 882/14, PA/18/11.

30. Clayton note, 12 March 1919, SAD C.P. G/S 513/1.

31. Hogarth to Clayton from British delegation, Paris, 30 March 1919, Hogarth Papers, F4.

32. *Times* obit., 4 June 1956.

33. Graves to Deakin from Jerusalem, 15 March 1922, Graves Papers, Archives of the *Times*.

34. Ibid.

35. Ibid.

36. Ibid.

37. Basil Liddell-Hart, *Colonel Lawrence: The Man behind the Legend* (New York: Dodd, Meade and Co., 1934), 628.

Chapter 10

1. Arab Bureau Report, January 1917, SAD W.P. 145/1.

2. From Cairo, 4 March 1918, Hogarth Papers, F3.

3. From Cairo, 12 May 1917, Hogarth Papers, F3.

4. Clayton secret note, 8 September 1918, PRO, F.O. 371/3411, F161891.

5. From Cairo, 5 April 1918, Hogarth Papers, F3.
6. Hogarth to Wingate, 9 July 1918, SAD W.P. 149/2.
7. Hogarth memo on the Arab Question, 9 August 1918, PRO, F.O. 371/3381, F146.
8. Hogarth to Clayton, 14 August 1918, Hogarth Papers, F3.
9. Wilson to Arab Bureau, 28 March 1917, PRO, F.O. 686/47.
10. Wingate telegram, 18 June 1917, PRO, F.O. 371/3048, F22841.
11. Wilson to Arab Bureau, 21 October 1917, PRO, F.O. 686/48.
12. Arab Bureau to Davenport, 24 April 1918, PRO, F.O. 686/49.
13. Wilson to Arab Bureau, 21 October 1917, PRO, F.O. 686/48.
14. Ibid.
15. G. Bell letter, 29 September 1919, Burgoyne, *Gertrude Bell*, 113.
16. Report by Lt. Comdr. H. Pirie-Gordon and Capt. C.A.G. Mackintosh, January 1918, I.O.L., L/P&S/10/576/F4744, pt. 2.
17. Report by Lt. Col. H. F. Jacob "A Plea for a Moslem Bureau," *Arab Bureau Supplementary Papers*, no. 6, ibid.
18. Ibid.
19. Ibid.
20. Allenby to W.O. Secretary, 17 May 1919, ibid.
21. Ibid.
22. Rennell-Rodd to Hardinge, 23 March 1920, PRO, F.O. 371/5196, F800.
23. McMahon to Grey, 25 January 1916, PRO, F.O. 371/2771, F18845.
24. Wingate to Hardinge, 25 January 1918, SAD W.P. 148/3.
25. War Office Draft, "Proposed Intelligence Service for the Middle East," I.O.L., L/P&S/10/576/F4744, pt. 2.
26. Shuckburgh minute, 25 August 1919, ibid.
27. Political Department, Baghdad, to Simla, 18 August 1919, ibid.
28. Hirtzel minute, 26 August 1919, ibid.
29. Young minute, 15 December 1919, PRO, F.O. 371/4208, F17610, no. 179006.
30. Curzon to Secretary of Army Council, 15 September 1919, I.O.L., L/P&S/10/576/F4744, no. 116302.
31. Secret War Office Report, " 'Arbur'; The Intelligence Service of the Near and Middle East," by Gen. Wm. Thwaites, 6 August 1920, PRO, F.O. 371/5196, KC/B/809.
32. Young minute, 3 March 1920, PRO, F.O. 371/5196, F800, E1619.
33. *Times*, 16 August 1920.
34. John Marlowe, *Late Victorian: The Life of Sir Arnold Talbot Wilson* (London: Cresset Press, 1967), 249.

Conclusion

1. T. E. Lawrence, "The War of the Departments," *Daily Express*, 29 May 1920.
2. Kedourie, *Anglo-Arab Labyrinth*, 201.
3. Presland, *Deedes Bey*, 246.

BIBLIOGRAPHY

Manuscript Collections

Great Britain. Public Record Office. Foreign Office Records. Material relating to this subject are generally confined to four files:

> FO/141—Papers of the British administration in Egypt.
> FO/371—A large volume of general Foreign Office correspondence and minutiae relating to the Near and Middle East.
> FO/686—Papers of the Jeddah Agency, 1916–20.
> FO/882—Arab Bureau papers: Reports and correspondence, 1916–20.

India Office Library, Political and Secret Department. Citations:

> L/P&S/10/576 File 4744/1915, parts 1 & 2—The war: Arab Bureau at Cairo: Intelligence service for the Middle East.
> L/P&S/10/586 File 705/1916, parts 1 & 2—Arab revolt: Mark Sykes's (Arabian) report, etc.
> L/P&S/10/645 File 110/1917—Arabia: printed correspondence.

L/P&S/10/683 File 2006/1917—Arabia: Arab confederacy.
Sudan Archive. School of Oriental Studies, University of Durham, Durham, England.
  Citations:
    SAD/W.P.—Private and official correspondence of Sir F. Reginald Wingate during
        his tenure as governor-general of the Sudan and as high commissioner
        of Egypt.
    SAD/C.P.—Private and official correspondence of Gilbert F. Clayton, 1916–18.
    Bell Correspondence—A small collection of letters between Gertrude Bell and Sir
        Valentine Chirol.

Private Papers

Archives of the *Times*.
  Graves Papers, a box of private correspondence of Philip Perceval Graves, 1919–35.
British Museum.
  Wilson Papers, private correspondence of Arnold Talbot Wilson, 1919–20.
Imperial War Museum, London.
  Material relating to the activities of T. E. Lawrence during World War I.
King's College, London.
  Akaba Papers of Pierce Joyce, miscellaneous papers on the Arabian war.
  Young Papers, assorted papers of Hubert Young.
Library of St. Antony's College, Oxford. Middle East Papers Collection.
  Allenby Papers, a small collection of private letters, 1918–19.
  Deedes Papers, a small assortment of wartime correspondence written by Wyndham
      Deedes, 1916–18.
  Hogarth Papers, private letters from David G. Hogarth to his family, along with
      miscellaneous notes.
  Philby Papers, a very large compendium of reports and correspondence relating to the
      Middle East.
  Sledmere Papers of Sir Mark Sykes, an assortment of reports, essays, and letters
      relating to the Middle East.
Parker Papers, personal diary of Alfred Chevallier Parker, 1916.
  I am greatly indebted to Mrs. Anne Edgerley of Saxmundham, England, for access.

Printed but Unpublished Sources

The *Arab Bulletin*—publication of the Arab Bureau circulated within the government.
    Access gained through the courtesy of Houghton Library, Harvard University.
Linabury, George. "British-Sa'udi Arab Relations 1902–1927: A Revisionist Interpreta-
    tion." Ph.D. diss., Columbia University, 1973.
Rose, Linda Carol. "Britain in the Middle East, 1914–1918: Design or Accident?" Ph.D.
    diss., Columbia University, 1969.

Westrate, Bruce. "Imperialists All: The Arab Bureau and the Evolution of British Policy in the Middle East, 1916–1920." Ph.D. diss., University of Michigan, 1982.

Reference Works

Palmer, Helen M., and E. T. Williams, eds. *Dictionary of National Biography, 1951–1960*. Oxford: Oxford University Press, 1971.
Who Was Who. Vol. 2, *1916–1928*. London: Adam and Charles Black, 1929.
Wickham Legg, L. G., and E. T. Williams, eds. *Dictionary of National Biography, 1941–1950*. Oxford: Oxford University Press, 1959.
Woodward, E. L., and Rohan Butler, eds. *Documents on British Foreign Policy, 1919–1939*. 1st ser., vol. 4. London: His Majesty's Stationery Office, 1952.

Books

Adelson, Roger. *Mark Sykes: Portrait of an Amateur*. London: Jonathan Cape, 1975.
Aldington, Richard. *Lawrence of Arabia: A Biographical Enquiry*. Chicago: Henry Regnery, 1955.
Aldridge, James. *Cairo*. Boston: Little, Brown, 1969.
Amajani, Yahya, and Thomas M. Ricks. *The Middle East: Past and Present*. Englewood Cliffs, N.J.: Prentice-Hall, 1970.
Amery, Leopold S. *My Political Life*. Vol. 2, *War and Peace, 1914–1929*. London: Hutchinson, 1953.
Antonius, George. *The Arab Awakening*. New York: J. B. Lippincott, 1939.
Armstrong, H. C. *Lord of Arabia, Ibn Sa'ud: An Intimate Study of a King*. Beirut: Khayats, 1966.
Barker, A. J. *The War against Russia*. New York: Holt, Rinehart and Winston, 1970.
Bell, Gertrude Lothian. *Amurath to Amurath*. London: William Heinemann, 1911.
———. *The Arab War*. London: Golden Cockeral Press, 1940.
———. *The Desert and the Sown*. London: Heinemann, 1907.
Bell, Lady Francis. *The Letters of Gertrude Bell*. 2 vols. New York: Boni and Liveright, 1927.
Benoist-Mechin, Jacques. *Lawrence D'Arabie, ou le Reve Fracasse*. Lausanne: Editions Clairfontaine, 1961.
Bray, Norman N. E. *Paladin of Arabia*. London: Unicorn Press, 1936.
———. *Shifting Sands*. London: Unicorn Press, 1934.
Bremond, Gen. Edouard. *Le Hedjaz dans la Guerre Mondiale*. Paris: Payat, 1931.
Buchan, John. *Memory Hold-the-Door*. London: Adder and Stoughton, 1940.
Bullard, Reader. *Britain and the Middle East*. London: Hutchinson, 1951.
Burgoyne, Elizabeth. *Gertrude Bell: From Her Personal Papers, 1914–1916*. London: Alfred A. Knopf, 1961.
Chambers, Richard L., and William R. Polk, eds. *Modernization in the Middle East*. Chicago: University of Chicago Press, 1968.

Charmley, John. *Lord Lloyd and the Decline of the British Empire*. New York: St. Martin's Press, 1987.

Clayton, Sir Gilbert Falkingham. *An Arabian Diary*. Edited by Robert O. Collins. Berkeley and Los Angeles: University of California Press, 1969.

Cornwallis, Sir Kinahan. Introduction to *The Arab War*. London: Golden Cockerel Press, 1940.

Darwin, John. *Britain, Egypt and the Middle East: Imperial Policy in the Aftermath of War, 1918–1922*. New York: St. Martin's Press, 1981.

Dawn, C. Ernest. *From Ottomanism to Arabism: Essays on the Origins of Arab Nationalism*. Urbana, Ill.: University of Illinois Press, 1973.

Falls, Cyril, and A. F. Becke, eds. *Military Operations in Egypt and Palestine*. London: His Majesty's Stationery Office, 1930.

Fisher, Sydney N. *The Middle East: A History*. New York: Alfred A. Knopf, 1959.

Flecker, James E. *Some Letters from Abroad*. London: Heinemann, 1930.

Forbes-Adam, Colin. *The Life of Lord Lloyd*. London: Macmillan, 1948.

Fromkin, David. *A Peace to End All Peace: Creating the Modern Middle East, 1914–1922*. New York: Henry Holt, 1989.

Gardner, Brian. *Allenby of Arabia*. New York: Coward-McCann, 1965.

Garnett, David, ed. *The Letters of T. E. Lawrence*. London: Jonathan Cape, 1938.

Glubb, John Bagot. *Britain and the Arabs*. London: Hodder and Stoughton, 1959.

Goldschmidt, Arthur, Jr. *A Concise History of the Middle East*. Boulder, Colo.: Westview Press, 1979.

Gooch, G. P., and H. V. Temperley, eds. *British Documents on the Origin of the War, 1889–1914*. London: His Majesty's Stationery Office, 1928.

Gottlieb, W. W. *Studies in Secret Diplomacy*. London: George Allen and Unwin, 1957.

Graves, Philip. *Briton and Turk*. London: Hutchinson, 1924.

———. *The Life of Sir Percy Cox*. London: Hutchinson, 1941.

Graves, Robert. *Lawrence and the Arabs*. London: Jonathan Cape, 1935.

———. *Storm Centres of the Middle East*. London: Hutchinson, 1933.

Great Britain. Admiralty Naval Intelligence Division. *Western Arabia and the Red Sea*. Oxford: Oxford University Press, 1946.

Hankey, Lord. *The Supreme Command, 1914–1918*. London: George Allen and Unwin, 1961.

Hardinge, Lord Charles. *Old Diplomacy*. London: John Murray, 1947.

Helmreich, Paul C. *From Paris to Sevres: The Partition of the Ottoman Empire at the Peace Conference of 1919–1920*. Columbus: Ohio State University Press, 1974.

Hinsley, F. H., ed. *British Foreign Policy under Sir Edward Grey*. Cambridge: Cambridge University Press, 1977.

Hogarth, David. G. *A History of Arabia*. Oxford: Clarendon Press, 1922.

———. *The Nearer East*. New York: D. Appleton and Co., 1902.

———. *Penetration of Arabia*. New York: Frederick A. Stokes, 1904.

Hollingworth, Clare. *The Arabs and the West*. London: Methuen, 1952.

Hourani, A. H. *Emergence of the Modern Middle East*. Los Angeles and Berkeley: University of California Press, 1981.

———. *Great Britain and the Arab World*. London: John Murray, 1946.

———. *Syria and Lebanon*. London: Oxford University Press, 1946.

———. *A Vision of History: Near Eastern and Other Essays*. Beirut: Khayats, 1961.

Howard, Harry N. *The King-Crane Commission*. Beirut: Khayats, 1963.

Howarth, David. *The Desert King: Ibn Sa'ud and His Arabia*. New York: McGraw-Hill, 1964.

Hurewitz, J. C. *Diplomacy in the Near and Middle East: A Documentary Record*. 2 vols. Princeton: Princeton University Press, 1956.

Kedourie, Elie. *Arabic Political Memoirs*. London: Frank Cass, 1974.
————. *The Chatham House Version and Other Middle-Eastern Studies*. New York: Praeger, 1974.
————. *England and the Middle East: The Destruction of the Ottoman Empire, 1914–1921*. London: Bowes and Bowes, 1956.
————. *In the Anglo-Arab Labyrinth*. Cambridge: Cambridge University Press, 1976.
Kent, Marion. *The Great Powers and the End of the Ottoman Empire*. London: George Allen and Unwin, 1984.
Khalidi, Rashid Ismail. *British Policy towards Syria and Palestine, 1906–1914*. Published for Middle East Centre, St. Anthony's College, Oxford. London: Ithaca Press, 1980.
Kinross, Lord. *The Ottoman Centuries*. New York: William Morrow, 1977.
Kirkbride, Sir Alec. *An Awakening*. London: University Press of Arabia, 1971.
————. *A Crackle of Thorns*. London: John Murray, 1956.
Klieman, Aaron S. *Foundations of British Policy in the Arab World: The Cairo Conference of 1921*. Baltimore: Johns Hopkins Press, 1970.
Knightley, Phillip. *The First Casualty*. New York: Harcourt Brace Jovanovich, 1975.
————, and Colin Simpson. *The Secret Lives of Lawrence of Arabia*. London: Thomas Nelson and Sons, 1969.
Lawrence, A. W., ed. *T. E. Lawrence to His Friends*. London: Jonathan Cape, 1937.
Lawrence, T. E. *Evolution of a Revolt*. London: The Pennsylvania State University Press, 1968.
————. *Secret Despatches from Arabia*. London: Golden Cockerel Press, 1940.
————. *Seven Pillars of Wisdom*. Garden City, N.Y.: Doubleday, 1935.
Leslie, Shane. *Mark Sykes: His Life and Letters*. London: Cassell, 1923.
Lewis, Bernard. *The Emergence of Modern Turkey*. London: Oxford University Press, 1962.
————. *The Muslim Discovery of Europe*. New York: W. W. Norton, 1982.
Liddell-Hart, Basil. *Colonel Lawrence: The Man behind the Legend*. New York: Dodd, Meade and Co., 1934.
————. *"T. E. Lawrence": In Arabia and After*. London: Jonathan Cape, 1934.
Lloyd, George Ambrose. *The British Case*. London: Eyre and Spottiswoode, 1939.
Lloyd, George (Lord). *Egypt since Cromer*. New York: Howard Fertig, 1969.
Longrigg, Stephen H. *The Middle East: A Social Geography*. London: Gerald Duckworth, 1963.
Mack, John E. *A Prince of Our Disorder: The Life of T. E. Lawrence*. Boston: Little, Brown, 1976.
Magnus, Philip. *Gladstone: A Biography*. New York: E. P. Dutton, 1964.
Main, Ernest. *Iraq from Mandate to Independence*. London: George Allen and Unwin, 1935.
Mandel, Neville. *The Arabs and Zionism before World War I*. Los Angeles and Berkeley: University of California Press, 1976.
Mansfield, Peter. *The British in Egypt*. New York: Holt, Rinehart and Winston, 1971.
————. *The Ottoman Empire and Its Successors*. New York: St. Martin's Press, 1973.
Marlowe, John. *Arab Nationalism and British Imperialism*. New York: Praeger, 1961.
————. *A History of Modern Egypt and Anglo-Egyptian Relations, 1800–1953*. Hamden, Conn.: Archon Books, 1965.
————. *Late Victorian: The Life of Sir Arnold Talbot Wilson*. London: Cresset Press, 1967.
————. *The Persian Gulf in the Twentieth Century*. New York: Praeger, 1962.
Meinertzhagen, Col. Richard. *Middle East Diary, 1917–1956*. London: Cresset Press, 1959.
Moberley, Frederick James, comp. *The Official History of the Campaign in Mesopotamia*. 4 vols. London: His Majesty's Stationery Office, 1923–27.

Monroe, Elizabeth. *Britain's Moment in the Middle East, 1914–1956*. Baltimore: Johns Hopkins Press, 1956.

————. *Philby of Arabia*. London: Pitman Publishing, 1973.

Morris, James. *Farewell the Trumpets*. London: Harvest, 1978.

————. *The Hashemite Kings*. New York: Pantheon, 1959.

Mousa, Suleiman. *T. E. Lawrence: An Arab View*. London: Oxford University Press, 1966.

Nasir, Sari J. *The Arabs and the English*. London: Longman Group, 1976.

Nevakivi, Jukka. *Britain, France and the Arab Middle East, 1914–1920*. University of London: The Athlone Press, 1969.

Philby, H.St.J.B. *Arabia of the Wahhabis*. London: Constable, 1928.

Pirie-Gordon, C.H.C., ed. *A Brief Record of the Advance of the Egyptian Expeditionary Force: July 1917 to October 1918*. London: His Majesty's Stationery Office, 1919.

Presland, John [pseud.]. *Deedes Bey: A Study of Sir Wyndham Deedes, 1883–1923*. London: Macmillan, 1942.

Robinson, Ronald, and John Gallagher. *Africa and the Victorians*. London: St. Martin's Press, 1961.

Rodd, James Rennell. *Social and Diplomatic Memories*. 3d ser., 1902–19. London: Edward Arnold, 1925.

Sachar, Howard M. *The Emergence of the Middle East, 1914–1925*. New York: Alfred A. Knopf, 1969.

Samuel, Viscount Herbert. *Grooves of Change*. New York: Bobbs-Merrill, 1946.

Sanders, Ronald. *The High Walls of Jerusalem*. New York: Holt, Rinehart and Winston, 1983.

Al-Sayyid, Afaf Lufti. *Egypt and Cromer: A Study in Anglo-Egyptian Relations*. New York: Praeger, 1968.

Smith, Wilfred Cantwell. *Islam in Modern History*. New York: New American Library, 1957.

Stewart, Desmond. *T. E. Lawrence*. New York: Harper and Row, 1977.

Stirling, Lt. Col. W. F. *Safety Last*. London: Hollis and Carter, 1963.

Storrs, Sir Ronald. *The Memoirs of Sir Ronald Storrs*. New York: G. P. Putnam's Sons, 1937.

Tabachnick, Stephen E., ed. *The T. E. Lawrence Puzzle*. Athens, Ga.: University of Georgia Press, 1984.

Thomas, Lowell. *With Lawrence in Arabia*. New York: The Century Co., 1924.

Thornton, A. P. *The Imperial Idea and Its Enemies*. New York: Doubleday, 1959.

Tibawi, A. L. *A Modern History of Syria*. London: St. Martin's Press, 1969.

Tuchman, Barbara. *Bible and Sword*. New York: Funk and Wagnalls, 1956.

Vansittart, Lord. *The Mist Procession: The Autobiography of Lord Vansittart*. London: Hutchinson, 1958.

Warner, Philip. *Kitchener: The Man behind the Legend*. New York: Atheneum, 1986.

Wavell, Sir Archibald. *Allenby: A Study in Greatness*. New York: Oxford University Press, 1941.

Wilson, Sir Arnold Talbot. *Mesopotamia: A Clash of Loyalties*. 2 vols. London: Oxford University Press, 1931.

Wilson, Jeremy. *Lawrence of Arabia: The Authorized Biography of T. E. Lawrence*. New York: Atheneum, 1990.

Wingate, Sir Ronald. *Wingate of the Sudan*. London: John Murray, 1955.

Winstone, H.V.F. *Gertrude Bell*. London: Jonathan Cape, 1978.

————. *The Illicit Adventure*. London: Jonathan Cape, 1982.

Winterton, Earl. *Fifty Tumultuous Years*. London: Hutchinson, 1955.

————. *Orders of the Day*. London: Cassell, 1953.

Young, Hubert. *The Independent Arab*. London: John Murray, 1933.

Zeine, Zeine N. *The Emergence of Arab Nationalism*. Beirut: Khayats, 1966.
————. *The Struggle for Arab Independence*. Beirut: Khayats, 1960.

Articles

Dann, Uriel. "Lawrence of 'Arabia': One More Appraisal." *Middle East Studies* 15 (May 1979): 154–62.
Fletcher, C.L.R. "Memoir of D. G. Hogarth." *Geographical Journal* 71 (April 1928): 321–44.
Hogarth, David G. "Mecca's Revolt against the Turk." *Century Magazine* 100 (1920): 403–9.
————. "Present Discontents in the Near and Middle East." *Quarterly Review* 234, no. 464 (October 1920): 411–23.
————. "Wahabism and British Interests." *Journal of the Royal Institute of International Affairs* 4 (March 1925): 70–79.
————. "War and Discovery in Arabia." *Geographical Journal* 55 (June 1920): 422–39.
Kedourie, Elie. "Cairo and Khartoum on the Arab Question." *Historical Journal* 7 (1964): 280–97.
Mousa, Suleiman. " 'A Matter of Principle': King Hussein of the Hijaz and the Arabs of Palestine." *International Journal of Middle East Studies* 9 (1978): 183–94.
Ormsby-Gore, William. "Great Britain, Mesopotamia and the Arabs." *The Nineteenth Century and After* 88 (August 1920): 226–38.
Vickery, Lt. Col. C. E. "Arabia and the Hedjaz." *Journal of the Central Asiatic Society* 10 (1923): 63–65.
Winterton, Lord. "Arabian Nights and Days." *Blackwood's Magazine* 207, May–June 1920, 585–608, 750–68.

INDEX

Page numbers in italics refer to illustrations

Printed in the United Kingdom
by Lightning Source UK Ltd.
123199UK00001B/211/A